When Baseball
Went White

When Baseball Went White

Reconstruction, Reconciliation, and Dreams of a National Pastime

RYAN A. SWANSON

University of Nebraska Press | Lincoln

Library of Congress Cataloging-in-Publication Data

Swanson, Ryan A.
When baseball went white: reconstruction, reconciliation, and dreams of a national pastime / Ryan A. Swanson.
pages   cm
Includes bibliographical references and index
ISBN 978-0-8032-3521-2 (hardback: alk. paper)
ISBN 978-1-4962-1953-4 (paperback: alk. paper)
ISBN 978-0-8032-5518-0 (epub)
ISBN 978-0-8032-5519-7 (mobi)
ISBN 978-0-8032-5517-3 (pdf) 1. Baseball—United States—History—19th century. 2. Racism in sports—United States. 3. Discrimination in sports—United States. 4. African American baseball players—United States—Social conditions. 5. United States—Race relations. I. Title.
G863.A1S955 2014
796.35709034—dc23   2013046027

Set in Minion Pro by Renni Johnson.
Designed by A. Shahan.

CONTENTS

ILLUSTRATIONS

INTRODUCTION

To say, as many historians have, that baseball's racial segregation resulted from a "gentlemen's agreement" is roughly the equivalent of asserting that the Civil War stemmed from a difference of opinion.[1] There is truth in both statements, but not nearly enough nuance to satisfy even the most recreational of inquisitors. This study attempts to find a better, more precise answer to baseball's segregation question. Baseball boomed in the United States in the 1860s and '70s, becoming a "perfect mania" among the soldiers returning home from the Civil War.[2] Black and white men flocked to urban ball fields. But even as Reconstruction legislators debated how to guide four million former slaves along the path to citizenship, segregation emerged quickly in baseball. White baseball leaders barred black baseball players from joining white leagues and clubs and from owning baseball property. Due to this discrimination, black men created separate baseball communities of their own. By the time the National League (NL) organized in 1876 (as Reconstruction ended), baseball had become an overwhelmingly segregated sport.

How did this happen? Neither historians nor the legion of journalists and baseball writers who have penned, quite literally, hundreds of thousands of pages about the game have fully addressed this question. Instead, the issue of baseball's segregation has been mostly passed over. "Nothing is ever said or written about drawing the color line in the [National] League," *Sporting Life* unapologetically observed in 1895. "It appears to be generally understood that none but whites shall make up the League teams, and so it goes."[3] This statement, while written more than a century ago, is surprisingly germane today. It neatly summarizes the historiography of baseball's segregation. Whereas much has been written on Jackie Robinson and the process of baseball's racial *de*segregation, not nearly enough attention has been paid to an obvious but oft-overlooked question: how did baseball develop to the point where it needed Jackie Robinson in the first place?[4] This study focuses on the "mechanics of baseball's segregation." The cities of Philadelphia, Richmond, and Washington DC anchor the analysis, allowing for the investigation of the North and South, both state and federal concerns, and black and white constituencies.

The fanatical desire by white baseball leaders to foster a "national game" was the preeminent force behind baseball's segregation. Northern baseball leaders worked tirelessly to spread baseball's popularity south of the Mason-Dixon line. White newspapermen and baseball writers spoke passionately about how baseball could heal and empower all Americans.[5] This desire to form a national baseball constituency (in a geographical sense) was not new during Reconstruction. At a convention in 1857, baseball leaders had boldly declared: "Base ball is about becoming a great national institution."[6] As the pursuit of nationalization and sectional "reconciliation" became the modus operandi, however, the fear of introducing political acrimony into the white baseball community became paramount. And therein David Blight's contention that "the practice of reconciliation" compromised racial progress is proved accurate again and again in baseball communities, only sooner.[7] White baseball players pursued civil rights—damning reconciliation almost immediately after the Civil War.

Henry Chadwick, the self-proclaimed "father of baseball," spoke repeatedly in "reconciliationist" terms, such as when he stated in 1866, "Our national game is intended to be national in every sense of the word."[8] He also clarified the racial complexion of this national game, as in his *Base Ball Manual, for 1871*: "Both games [baseball and cricket] rest, first, upon the desire of the Anglo-Saxon (we do not say Caucasian, or Aryan, because we like to be exact) to arm himself with a stick and drive a small round body with it; and, secondly, upon the desire of any other Anglo-Saxon who happens to be in the way to stop this body, to deprive the other of his stick, and 'bat' himself."[9] These two beliefs about baseball—that it was to be national and dominated by white men— were intertwined. Newspapermen encouraged reunion and warned against possible fractures that might hinder baseball's development.

White ballplayers were to avoid "undue partisanship" (read: issues of racial policy) so that "the great American game" might flourish. "This is the spirit," Washington's *Chronicle* wrote of baseball's great quest for apolitical behavior, "that should animate every organization, for without it dissentions may arise, and hard feelings originate therefrom, to the detriment and disfavor of the game."[10] Thus, ironically, in the name of creating a "national pastime," baseball excluded black ballplayers.

In addition to sectional reconciliation, the removal of political radicals from positions of leadership within the white baseball community, violence against black players, and the unequal partitioning of baseball land made baseball an increasingly white game. So too did the trend of linking baseball with Confederate-memorializing causes. Similarly, the emergence of the open professionalization in the 1870s solidified many segregationist trends. Equally as important, the success of black ball clubs, even amid hostile circumstances (*Memphis Public Ledger*: "The colored base ball brigade is one of the greatest nuisances about the suburbs of the city. Enough lazy, thieving niggers swing a base-ball bat to raise a thousand bales of cotton, if they would"), also influenced emerging baseball norms.[11]

Baseball historians have mostly passed over Reconstruction-era "baseballists." And those studies that have looked at Reconstruction baseball have focused primarily on the action on the field, rather than the broader context of baseball.[12] But the task of understanding the Reconstruction-era baseball segregation is important because it informs us about the process of segregating society at large and about the failure of political Reconstruction. Baseball here should contribute to discussions led by the likes of C. Vann Woodward and Eric Foner.[13] To be clear, this is a Reconstruction history—even though there are more bats and ball than legislators and political speeches. The entire nation, not just the former Confederacy, faced new postwar realities. Certainly, the national legislation of Reconstruction cannot be ignored. The Civil Rights Acts of 1866 and 1875; the passage of the Thirteenth, Fourteenth, and Fifteenth Amendments; and the work of the Freedmen's Bureau (active in Washington DC and throughout the South) all contributed to erecting a legal basis for racial equality. But despite these measures, segregation—both de facto and de jure—overwhelmed the national political and legal initiatives set forth by politicians.[14]

Baseball is a perfect conduit for the study of race relations during Reconstruction. As Elliott Gorn explains in his work on prizefighting, sports can provide unique insights into a culture: "Most workers did not spend their free time reading the *Rights of Man*, toasting Tom Paine, and struggling to resist oppression. . . . [Instead] look closely at [workers'] folklore and recreations, their pastimes and sports, for it has been in leisure more than in politics or labor that many men and women have found their deepest sense of meaning and wholeness."[15] I concur. Studying black and white baseball offers vital social and cultural context to the political history of Reconstruction. Although it has been warned that "history without politics descends to mere literature," history focused too narrowly on politics and politicians misses the mark as well.[16] By examining baseball communities in America's major cities, oft-peripheral abstractions will be presented in a more tangible fashion. The panic of 1873, for example, led to many baseball teams folding. Baseball also reveals how land was important to African Americans living in cities, just as it was in the countryside. Although not looking for the "40 Acres and Mule" promised by General William T. Sherman's Special Order No. 15, baseball clubs jostled for control of public space. Not surprisingly, black clubs rarely came out ahead in this struggle.[17]

Baseball clubs carved out space to play the game in the midst of office buildings and factories. Some teams played in beautiful public parks; others made do with rough, trash-hewn vacant lots. The field standards were not high. Still, the best—that is, flattest, driest, and most centrally located—parcels of space often teemed with baseball activity. Baseball's most supportive newspaper, the *New York Clipper*, rejoiced in the chaotic activity at baseball hot spots: "The way the balls fly in every direction is enough to remind a veteran of the army of the time when he found himself like the 'six hundred' in the Crimea, who had 'balls to the right of them, balls to the left of them.'"[18]

Competition for baseball grounds intensified when it became clear that there was money to be made charging admission to games. A baseball "enclosure" movement resulted. The battle for baseball space in Washington DC took place literally on the president's doorstep. The "White Lot," located between the Washington Canal (which today is Constitution Avenue) and the White House, played host to the District's biggest games of the 1860s and '70s. Presidents occasionally ambled down from the executive mansion to take in the action and invited visiting teams into the White House.[19] The sharing of baseball space, however, rarely lasted. In each city the dominant teams eventually took control of the best baseball space. Tellingly, when the Athletic Club of Philadelphia planned to open its new grounds in 1871, the *New York Clipper* reported: "A substantial board fence, ten feet high is to be erected, and other improvements made, so that the grounds shall be the finest in the country."[20] The description of the fence, and then everything else, accurately depicted the focus on controlling baseball space.

Both black and white ballplayers played roles in shaping how baseball's segregated environment emerged and functioned. Many white clubs did what they could to keep black clubs from using the best fields and joining leagues. Black players, however, were hardly waiting idly for invitations to join white teams. In fact, very little evidence exists to suggest that black ballplayers during the Reconstruction period yearned for positions on white clubs, and certainly not at the expense of their black-led and black-populated clubs. Equality rather than social proximity was the goal. Charles Douglass, the son of Frederick Douglass, for one, knew what it was to work with white men (in the Freedmen's Bureau and the Treasury Department), but he invested in playing baseball among black men—first with the Washington Mutual Base Ball Club (BBC) and then the Alert.[21]

White baseball players had professional opportunities that their black counterparts did not. "It is estimated that professional ball tossers get paid larger salaries than three-fourths of the ministers of the Gospel of the United States," the *Washington Sunday Herald* reported in October 1873. This was not a criticism. Ministers made less for good reason: "Religion is not the national game you know," the *Sunday Herald* explained.[22] Baseball's popularity following the Civil War crossed state lines, class barriers, and racial divides. The game grew up in urban environments, and the nation's biggest cities—New York City, Philadelphia, and Boston—were early leaders in the game. The nation's most populous city, New York City, and the still-independent Brooklyn, led the way. The New York Knickerbocker Base Ball Club had organized in 1845.[23] The Brooklyn Eckfords, the Brooklyn Atlantics, and the New York Mutuals each claimed, at one time or another during baseball's early years, to be the nation's "champion" club.

Ballplayers became regional celebrities in Reconstruction-era America. "Callow sportsmen worship them reverently, enthusiasts abase themselves before their spike boots, and at rural hostelries say 'that's them!' and compete with each other for the honor of carrying their bats."[24] Baseball developed quickly following the Civil War. The *New York Times* in 1869 estimated more than 1,000 baseball clubs were active in the United States and that more than two hundred thousand fans attended games annually. *Wilkes' Spirit of the Times* reported higher numbers, counting 2,000 organized clubs by 1867. Newspaper tallies make clear that dozens of clubs organized and played in each Philadelphia, Richmond, and Washington every year during the Reconstruction era. Philadelphia almost certainly had the most clubs of the three cities, nearly equaling New York City in terms of sheer numbers if not in the quality of its clubs. Baseball clubs varied significantly in their approach to and proficiency in baseball. The "Shoo-Fly" and "Don't Bodder Me" nines of the Census Bureau, for example, took an obviously lighthearted approach to the game, while the Washington Nationals, Philadelphia Athletics, and Richmond Pastime each pursued baseball excellence far more seriously.[25]

Baseball games attracted large and enthusiastic audiences. Crowds as large as forty thousand gathered to watch games between the clubs of Philadelphia and New York. Matches attracting more than a thousand fans occurred regularly in the 1860s. "It was a sight to behold the crowd," wrote one reporter, "as they stood waiting their turns to deposit their quarters previous to taking seats to see the grand base ball performances of the day."[26] In addition to the throngs of fans that assembled for games, the baseball men themselves loved to convene. In 1866, the first full year after the Civil War ended, 202 clubs—representing seventeen states and the District of Columbia—sent delegates to the convention of the National Association of Base Ball Players (NABBP). Baseball's organizing bodies—the NABBP beginning in 1857, then, in 1871, the National Association of Professional Base Ball Players (NAPBBP)—had annual conventions and played a significant role in determining the game's rules and customs.[27]

Newspapers also helped grow the game. Competition for baseball readers was fierce at times, leading to dissension among the baseball presses. The *Philadelphia Sunday Mercury*, for example, derided its crosstown baseball rival, the *City Item*, calling it a "weak, wishy-washy sheet."[28] This pattern generally played out in each city. One or two papers, whether as a market strategy or simply due to their editors' preference, became known as *the* baseball paper for the city. To supplement the coverage of the city presses, three major sporting dailies arose: the *New York Clipper* (1853–1924), *Wilkes' Spirit of the Times* (1861–77), and the *Ball Players' Chronicle* (1867–68). The *Ball Players' Chronicle* described the need for such sports-specific papers due to the fact that city dailies often became distracted with other issues: "The sudden absence of the base ball reports in the daily papers is no indication of a sudden close of the season, as about this time of year election topics absorb all the space the dailies have to spare to local topics, and the moral exercise of base ball is crowded out of the columns."[29] The sporting presses gave the baseball community the exposure it needed to transcend its early New York City base. The papers printed letters, answered baseball questions, announced rule changes, published schedules, and reported scores.[30]

Additionally, the press shaped the game's values and traditions. Henry Chadwick in particular took on a leading role in shaping baseball into a gentlemen's game. Chadwick wrote widely about baseball, mostly for the *New York Clipper*, and in books and pamphlets on the game's rules and results. Chadwick's 1868 guide, *The Game of Baseball: How to Learn It, How to Play It, and How to Teach It*, outlined the game's rules ("If the ball he hits should be caught by any one of the fielders before touching the ground—or 'on the fly,' as it is called—he is out") and urged players to engage in fair play and uphold orderliness at all times.[31] Chadwick sanctimoniously promoted baseball as the nation's most noble and "manly" pastime.[32]

One of the baseball community's strictest demarcation lines involved gender. Women in the 1860s and '70s had few roles in "official baseball"—they could not join baseball leagues and rarely competed in the admission-charging games covered by newspapers. Although women's college baseball games would become more common in the late nineteenth century and girls undoubtedly played at neighborhood sandlots, women's roles in the burgeoning game were usually confined to being spectators. Women's attendance was thought to keep the crowds orderly and bring respectability to the game, distinguishing it from unrestrained male pursuits such as boxing.[33]

In terms of the game on the field, modern baseball fans would recognize the nineteenth-century game as baseball. The game then, as now, revolved around one man throwing a ball and another attempting to hit it. But there were many rule debates. Two rule changes in particular—the adoption of the "fly game" and the codification of pitching standards—shaped the development of Reconstruction-era baseball. The debate over the "fly game" versus the "bound rule" dominated the National Association of Base Ball Players' convention of 1864. At issue was whether a fielder had to catch the ball "on the fly" to record an out or if it was acceptable to allow the ball to bounce first. The fly game, perceived as "manlier" and as rewarding "creditable risks," won out.[34]

The rule changes regarding the delivery of the ball to the batter also significantly shaped baseball's development. Ballplayers *pitched* because they were forbidden to throw. Rules gradually shifted from the pitcher having to release the ball from below the level of his waist to, by the late 1860s, below the level of his shoulder.[35] Even in 1868 when Chadwick published his baseball missive, however, the pitcher-batter relationship was not one of outright confrontation.[36] "When the batsman takes his position at home base, the umpire asks him where he wants a ball, and the batsman responds by saying, 'knee high,' or 'waist high,' or by naming the character of the ball he wants, and the pitcher is required by the rules to delver the batsman a ball within the legitimate reach of his bat and as near the place indicated as he can."[37] Pitchers changed speeds and mixed up their deliveries as much as possible, but the batters' advantage resulted in scores that often reached triple digits—an 1866 score of Richmond 76, Spotswood 102 not being overly atypical.[38]

Baseball's rules fit the times. Placing restrictions on pitchers, for the purpose of giving the batter a chance to hit the ball, meant to ensure fair competition. The ideas of amateurism, fairness, order, and respectability remained entrenched in late-nineteenth-century baseball culture. Throughout the rule changes of the 1860s and '70s, baseball ethos continued to include an emphasis on bringing together gentlemen for dignified competition. "The efforts of gentlemen to elevate the national game to something like dignity and refinement, are fast being realized," wrote one baseball reporter in 1869.[39]

This quest for respectability did not, it should be noted, immediately demand racial exclusion. Black baseball clubs existed as a part of the broad baseball community, albeit often on the periphery. One of the first reported games of baseball involving black men occurred in New York City in 1859. The Henson and Unknown Clubs, both of Jamaica, Long Island, engaged in a 54–43 battle. The *Brooklyn Eagle* reported on another black contest in 1862, this time between the Unknown and Monitor Clubs, and applied the respectability scale to the participants: "The dusky contestants enjoyed the game hugely, and to us a common phrase, they 'did the thing genteelly.'"[40] Deciding just how integrated baseball clubs and leagues should be, of course, became a central issue in the post–Civil War baseball world.

Although no major baseball cities will go untouched, this study uses Philadelphia, Richmond, and Washington DC as its mooring points. There are several practical reasons for these choices. First, the mid-Atlantic region had the most concentrated population of African Americans in the United States during the second half of the nineteenth century.[41] Second, the region was home to many of the nation's finest baseball clubs—black and white. Third, within the roughly two hundred miles that separated Philadelphia from Richmond, both the complexities and the overarching patterns of the Reconstruction era surfaced. Philadelphia demonstrated that those states above the Mason-Dixon line could hardly avoid the post–Civil War readjustment period. Richmond faced the Freedmen's Bureau and former slaves. Washington DC became engulfed in the politics of the federal Reconstruction process.

Philadelphians entered the Reconstruction era with a detachment that the residents of Richmond and Washington must have envied. A return to prewar normalcy seemed possible, as Philadelphia neither had suffered the war damage experienced by Richmond nor was it saddled with Washington's duties to administer Reconstruction or the teeming slave refugee camp that existed in the nation's capital. Philadelphia was the United States' second-largest city, possessing a seemingly sizable black population, 22,147 in 1870, the largest of any urban area in the North. Black Philadelphians, however, made up only 4 percent of the more than 670,000 residents of the city. White Philadelphians before and after the Civil War had bitter debates over the issues of race relations and civil rights. The city's tradition of strong pro-Southern sentiments and its legacy of abolition activism created conflict.[42]

During Reconstruction the city's divided loyalties continued to couple opportunity with opposition for black Philadelphians. The characterization of Philadelphia as "Up South," denoting the city's virulent strain of racism even though it was physically removed from the South, rang true. Because nearly 100,000 Philadelphians had served in the Union army, the city celebrated the military defeat of the South. What remained less cohesive, however, was the city's collective support for rebuilding the South, providing for the former slaves, and granting equal rights to the black residents of Philadelphia after the war had ended.[43] "Brotherly love" in Philadelphia, it often seemed, extended only as far as one's definition of whiteness.

Richmond, of course, faced trials following the Civil War that neither Philadelphia nor Washington DC had to confront. Retreating Confederates had burned the city in the final days of the war, crippling Richmond's banking and business sector. Most industries, including the city's vital tobacco factories and iron plants, did not return to their prewar production rates even by 1870. An economy that had been humming before the war sputtered badly after it, as one local daily lamented:

> In no branch of business in this city has the effect of the war been more sadly felt than in the manufacture of tobacco. Before the war our streets resounded with the cheerful songs of the negroes, as with willing hands they manipulated this great staple of Virginia in the factories which line every street of our beautiful city, but now the song is hushed, the factories are in ruins, many of the former proprietors are in their graves, many ruined by the disastrous fire of the 3rd of April and the negroes that once worked so merrily, being thrown out of work by the destruction of the factories, spend their time in idleness.[44]

The "negroes with willing hands" had been, of course, slaves, and the fires of April 3, 1865, had been set by retreating Confederates, but the reality remained that Richmond faced dire economic challenges during the Reconstruction era.

In nearly every aspect of Richmond's reconstruction, questions of race and manifestations of racism made progress difficult. How would blacks and whites work together, live together, and play together? What barriers would maintain white domination with slavery now gone? These questions resonated constantly in Richmond and other Southern cities. In addition to the legacy of slavery, Richmond's demographics made its race question more pressing to whites than in either Philadelphia or Washington. The 1870 census reported that blacks in Richmond (23,180) made up nearly half of the city's total 51,038 residents.[45]

Washington DC had strong connections to both the North and the South. The District sat between two slave states and just across the Potomac River from Confederate general Robert E. Lee's home. Southern transplants dominated Washington's citizenry. The presence of the federal government, though, defined the city in many ways. The District changed rapidly during Reconstruction. By 1870 the city's black population had increased nearly fourfold since 1860, from 11,131 to 43,404. In 1870 African Americans composed 33 percent of the population, compared to only 15 percent a decade earlier.[46]

Because it fell under the jurisdiction of the U.S. Congress, Washington DC functioned as a testing ground for Reconstruction and race policy. District slaves, for example, had received their emancipation in April 1862, six months before Lincoln's Emancipation Proclamation enacted the same freedom in the rebellious South.[47] African Americans in Washington and Georgetown received the right to vote in 1866, earlier than in many other places in the United States. The Freedmen's Bureau also had a postwar presence in the city. The city gained a measure of independent governance in 1867 and then lost it in 1870, returning to the status of a federally controlled territory.[48] Reflecting the position of their city, the baseball teams of Washington DC never quite fit with either their Northern or their Southern counterparts.

In these three cities, and in the broader constituencies that they represent, baseball served as a barometer of the Reconstruction process. Baseball teams never escaped the realities of their times when they took to the ball fields. Rather, baseball players played as they lived, amid a complicated and rapidly evolving post–Civil War society. For the historian there is great opportunity in analyzing America's "national pastime." The segregated world that baseball created in the 1860s and '70s mirrored, and helps explain, the segregated norms that would emerge subsequently outside the lines of the country's baseball diamonds. Unfortunately, as the "national pastime" went, on racial matters at least, so too went the nation.

PROMINENT PLAYERS AND CLUBS

Philadelphia

Raymond Burr—Member of the Pythian Base Ball Club, African American, Pythian Club representative at the 1867 Pennsylvania Association of Amateur Base Ball Players (PAABBP) convention

Octavius Catto—Member and officer of the Pythian Base Ball Club, African American, Union army veteran, instructor at Banneker Institute, political organizer

Thomas Fitzgerald—Cofounder of the Athletic Base Ball Club (president, 1861–66), Republican Party political organizer, owner and editor of the *City Item*, playwright, president of the National Association of Base Ball Players in 1863

Hicks Hayhurst—Member and president of the Athletic Base Ball Club, president of the PAABBP (1867)

SIGNIFICANT CLUBS

Athletic Base Ball Club
City Item Base Ball Club
Excelsior Base Ball Club (African American)
Keystone Base Ball Club
L'Overture Base Ball Club (African American)
Olympic Base Ball Club
Philadelphia Base Ball Club
Pythian Base Ball Club (African American)

Richmond

Alexander Babcock—"Father of Richmond baseball," deserted the Union army for the Confederacy during the Civil War, established the Richmond Base Ball Club, established the Pastime Base Ball Club, owner of an ice delivery business

Henry Boschen—Founder of the Pacific Base Ball Club, led baseball revival in Richmond in 1875, owner of a Richmond shoe factory

Edward Cohen—Banker, first president of the Richmond Base Ball Club, president of Richmond's Kesher Shel Barzel lodge, a "pioneer of Richmond Jewry," delegate at the Virginia Association of Base Ball Players in 1866

SIGNIFICANT CLUBS

Old Dominion Base Ball Club
Pacific Base Ball Club
Pastime Base Ball Club
Reindeer Base Ball Club (African American)
Richmond Base Ball Club
Robert E. Lee Base Ball Club
Southern Base Ball Club
Union Base Ball Club (composed of federal officers)

Washington DC

Charles Douglass—Son of Frederick Douglass, African American, served in the Union army, member of the Alert Base Ball Club, member of the Mutual Base Ball Club, federal government employee

Arthur Gorman—U.S. senator (Maryland), president of the NABBP (1867), personal friend of President Andrew Johnson, member and officer of the National Base Ball Club

Nicholas Young—Federal government employee, member of the Olympic Base Ball Club, officer in the NAABBP, NAPBBP, and National League

SIGNIFICANT CLUBS

Alert Base Ball Club (African American)
Capital Base Ball Club
Creighton Base Ball Club
Jefferson Base Ball Club
Mutual Base Ball Club (African American)
National Base Ball Club
Olympic Base Ball Club
Potomac Base Ball Club

When Baseball Went White

PART 1

The War's Over, 1865–67

Chapter 1

Washington DC

A Game to Be Governed

Like many young veterans, Nicholas Young did not go home after the Civil War. Young wanted something more or maybe just something different than his hometown, Albany, New York, could offer. So he migrated to Washington DC in pursuit of a government career. On his first day in his new city, Young stumbled upon a baseball game, on the grounds of the White House, featuring two of the nation's best teams. Thousands of fans watched the action. Young was hooked. Young stayed in the capital city for three decades thereafter. And while Nicholas Young went to the District for a civil service career, it was his pastime outside the office—and indeed outside—that earned him a place in history. Young entered the city as a devoted but small-time cricket player; he left, some thirty years later, as the president of baseball's National League.[1]

Alongside Nicholas Young, Arthur Gorman helped shape Washington DC's white baseball community and the broader organization of baseball. Gorman, like Young, played adequately, but made his real contributions to the game by organizing players, clubs, and leagues. Gorman in particularly played a leading role in encouraging white Southerners to join the burgeoning baseball community. Gorman also played ball while climbing the political ladder. He became a U.S. senator representing Maryland in 1881. A lifelong Democrat, Gorman led segregation efforts both in baseball and in the U.S. Congress. Together Gorman and Young laid the foundation for baseball to become a highly organized, and racially exclusive, professional sport.

On the spectrum of racial tolerance among its white population, Washington DC existed about halfway between Philadelphia and Richmond. Black ballplayers in Washington, including the son of Frederick Douglass, had greater opportunities than those in Richmond, but fewer than those in Philadelphia—or in New York City or Chicago. During the post–Civil War baseball boom, the game became popular with respectable white men, many of whom worked for the federal government. As the game became increasingly profitable (through gate admission fees and club membership dues), Northern baseball leaders acted to protect the game from controversial and unsavory elements that might tarnish the game. Northern leaders also pursued sectional reconciliation, hoping to expand the game's popularity in the former Confederacy.

Growing Washington DC Baseball

Nicholas Young got his start in sport as a cricketer in upstate New York. He learned the "imperial game" from English immigrants, weavers who worked in Albany factories.[2] Americans copied their foreign-born coworkers and took up the game, and, according to Young in his late-life memoir, "in a very few years we had become, by constant practice, so proficient that we could beat them [the English] at their own game."[3] It was through cricket that Young met two men who would go on to shape the early years of baseball in America—George and Harry Wright.[4] Young rose through the cricket ranks to become an "all-star," chosen to represent New York State in a game against the players of New York City in 1860.

Shortly after Young's all-star appearance, Lincoln won the White House and the Civil War began. Soldiering stopped Young from finding a game of cricket for almost two years. Then, in the winter of 1862–63, Young and some like-minded friends used a lull in the fighting to get together a game. Young's unit, composed of New York men, challenged a Philadelphia unit to a cricket match. The result was a spectacle that nearly equaled the famous wartime baseball game in Salisbury, North Carolina. The Salisbury game, immortalized by Otto Boetticher's idyllic illustration, had involved Union soldiers playing a baseball game in a Confederate prison while hundreds of prisoners and Confederate guards watched.[5] According to Young, his cricket match garnered the participation or attention of every man but one from his company. The New Yorkers prevailed. It was the beginning of the end of Young's cricket career.

Young's Civil War baseball experience supports Harold Seymour's general theory regarding the war's effect on baseball. The war neither completely made nor acutely hindered the growth of the game.[6] In Young's case he learned the rules of baseball, while still maintaining his ties to cricket. Scarcity of cricket competition, however, ultimately compelled Young and his fellow cricketers to accept baseball challenges. In April 1863 Young's group of cricketers took part in a match of the "New York Game." It was, according Young's memory, "the first game that I ever played or witnessed that was governed by a regular code of rules."[7] The war itself splintered Young's band of cricket players. Young's division met Confederate charges on the Gettysburg battlefield in July 1863. When the three-day bloodbath had ended, only Young and two others of his fifteen to twenty "cricket boys" had survived. Young watched throughout the remainder of the war as enemy bullets cut down his cricket teammates. "In nearly every great battle up to the close of the war," Young recalled, "at least one or two more would have their wickets knocked down, or be thrown out before reaching base."[8]

Young arrived in Washington DC in August 1865. Within hours of setting foot in the District, Young found his way to the White Lot—the hub of the city's baseball activity. It was an auspicious address. Located on White House grounds, the White Lot's proximity to the president resulted in "first-fan" visits and gave Washington baseball an air of importance. Games had taken place at the White Lot since before the Civil War began. During the 1860s and '70s Presidents Andrew Johnson and Ulysses S. Grant both visited the grounds and met with ballplayers. Many clubs used the prominent baseball space. When the government business day ended, hundreds of ballplayers descended upon the president's lawn for an afternoon game.[9]

On the day of his arrival in the District, August 28, 1865, Young picked up on the baseball buzz permeating the city. The game had become "a perfect mania," according to Washington's *Daily National Intelligencer*.[10] The Washington Nationals were set to face the Philadelphia Athletics. Young joined more than ten thousand spectators watching Thomas Fitzgerald's famous Athletics take on the hometown Nationals. Although the outcome was never in doubt (the Athletics scored eighty-seven runs, including twenty-three home runs, to the Nationals' twelve), big-time baseball captivated Washington DC and Young.[11]

Not one to sit by passively and watch, Young wasted little time getting involved in Washington's sporting community. On the same day as the Athletics-Nationals game, Young attended the founding meeting of a new cricket club. Young clearly saw himself as more than a sports participant; he wanted a role in organizing his pastimes. So Young introduced himself simply "as an American and a cricketer" and joined up immediately. After a few matches, however, the club turned its attention to baseball. There were not enough cricket teams in the region to sustain regular play. During the following season, Young accepted an invitation to become a founding member of the Olympic Base Ball Club of Washington DC. From this point forward, Young spent an increasing amount of time dedicated to baseball. Young's rise to baseball leadership coincided with Washington DC's golden baseball days. Washington DC during the 1860s briefly challenged New York and Philadelphia for baseball supremacy. Remembering this period after the fact, the *New York Sun* concluded that "Washington did more for baseball when it was needed than any city in the United States."[12]

"No More Swapping Buttons"

The Washington DC Young came to was a city awash in sectional animosity and racial tension. Thus, as he worked to shape baseball's policies toward the South and black ballplayers, Young acted amid a community grappling with precisely the same issues. Washington DC had been denied its long-awaited postwar celebration. President Abraham Lincoln's assassination plunged the city into mournful chaos, overshadowing even the peace achieved at Appomattox on Palm Sunday 1865.[13] Andrew Johnson, a Southern Democrat and former slaveholder turned pragmatic unionist, assumed the presidency of the United States upon Lincoln's death. Little more than a month later, on May 29, 1865, Johnson announced his hasty "Proclamation of Amnesty and Pardon" plan. Johnson's plan, which allowed for easy pardons for most Southerners, created more confusion and controversy.[14]

The citizens of Washington DC were stridently divided on many issues of race and Reconstruction. The white citizenry, however, exhibited almost no division on the issue of black suffrage. A referendum on black suffrage in the District in 1865 garnered 7,303 votes against and only 36 in favor.[15] Washington's city council led the fight against the

U.S. Congress's attempt to institute universal suffrage in the District on the grounds that white men were undoubtedly the superior race and thus endowed with the responsibility of leadership. The city council's official statement on the issue had few ambiguities and suggested that the District was years away from black suffrage: "The white man, being the superior race, must . . . rule the black. . . . It took Briton a thousand years to emerge from his only half-civilized condition . . . to qualify him for the exercise of this right, how long would it reasonably take the black man, who but two hundred years ago was brought from Africa."[16]

As a former soldier Nicholas Young understood that replacing sectionalism with reunion, whether in the nation's capital or elsewhere, or even in baseball, would be difficult. Young recalled in his memoir the confusion and bitterness that came with Lincoln's death occurring so closely after Appomattox. "The war was over and the Blue and Gray mingled together in a very friendly fashion, trading buttons, etc. until we received the news of the assassination of our great and good President, Abraham Lincoln. While the Union soldiers didn't feel that the Confederate soldiers were, in any way, responsible for the tragic death of the President, they drew the line quick and there was no more swapping of buttons."[17] Lincoln's death coincided with the beginning of the baseball season in the mid-Atlantic region. The ground had thawed, and even with Lincoln's death shrouding the capital for months, baseball clubs took to the fields. The National Base Ball Club of Washington DC broke the mourning period by traveling to Fort Meigs, Maryland, to play a match against a club composed of members of the 133rd Regiment of New York Volunteers. In front of a vast concourse of spectators, the Nationals triumphed, 26–19.[18] That the game went on even during the mourning period probably surprised no one. Baseball and politics had already coexisted in DC for nearly a decade; recreation had juxtaposed serious debates in the District since the capital's founding. During the Reconstruction era, politicians and government bureaucrats often became ballplayers, putting aside their official duties for at least a few hours each week. Recreation, of course, never completely trumped the concerns and tensions of the day, but games did provide many with a needed social outlet.

The federal government employees who played baseball were firmly indoctrinated in organizational methods. They understood hierarchies and management and directive policy. Thus, when they took to baseball, they also organized the game in a bureaucratic fashion. Fun and recreation, it seemed, had to be regulated. The Nationals and Olympics led the way in DC in establishing club constitutions, fund-raising policies, and executive leadership structures. Baseball in this way served as a suitable recreational outlet for government men. It was "manly," but refined enough to fit accepted standards of decorum and the scheduling demands of a federal government job. It was respectable, but not too exclusive. The game required some financial resources, but was not prohibitively expensive. In short, baseball embodied the respectability and relative accessibility of federal employment.[19]

Newspapers utilized baseball to explain Washington DC society and politics. There were no sportswriters yet; a single reporter might be responsible for submitting stories on baseball, politics, and crime. In this context baseball became a favorite metaphor for describing broader events. Henry Chadwick, using "Old Chalk" as his *Brooklyn Morning Programme* pen name, for example, used baseball to describe Andrew Johnson's impeachment trial and the partisanship surrounding Washington DC. Impeachment was a ball game between Andrew Johnson of the National Club and Thaddeus Stevens of the Constitution Club. Mostly siding with Johnson, the account poked fun at the politics of the U.S. Congress:

Andy Johnson, who had a fight with Stevens, the pitcher of the nine, not long since and the quarrel has not been made up yet. Johnson, it appears, wanted to play certain points in the game . . . but Stevens wouldn't pitch as Johnson wanted him to and as the rest of the nine joined Thad. Stevens against Johnson, who is the occupant of the first base in the National nine, of course the game had to be postponed. Finally Johnson tried to organize a new nine for the club, and then the row began. Johnson began by placing Larry Thomas in as catch in place of Ed. Stanton. . . . The rest of the nine then took part with Stevens, and putting Stanton in the nine again, said they had found a man to take Johnson's place, and boldly announced that they were ready to "Wade" in and "fight it out on that line if it took all the summer." . . . They charged him [Johnson] with selling the games of the club, and of putting men out purposely on his own side in match games. How the mess will end I can't tell.[20]

Perhaps the baseball analogy made too little of a political situation that threatened the very foundations of U.S. democracy, but the analysis made clear how deeply entrenched baseball had become in society after only a few years of widespread play.

Many federal government offices fielded their own teams. This created a unique wrinkle in white Washington's baseball community, an aspect of baseball enthusiasm that neither New York City nor Philadelphia exhibited. Announcements for government games (the "Redemptive Division of the Treasury Department" versus the "Third Auditors Club," for example) filled Washington's papers during the 1860s and '70s. Fun and frivolity ruled this stratum of baseball activity. The Government Printing Office named its club the "Typos' Base Ball Club."[21] The Record and Pension Division of the Surgeon General's Office decided to form two clubs, dividing its baseball men into those married and those single for scrimmages.[22] Lighthearted as the games usually were, the government baseball contests contributed to the entrenchment of the game in Washington's respectable white communities.

Washington DC's white baseball clubs exhibited many of the intermittent traits of racial exclusivity that could be found in federal government offices.[23] A steadily evolving but still patchwork system of exclusion affected both baseball and the federal government workforce. Charles Douglass and his baseball teams, the Washington Mutuals and Alerts, were caught in this confusing system. Black ballplayers suffered the most, but Washington's racism was convulsive and unpredictable. Irish ballplayers faced their share of discrimination, too, in baseball and in federal government hiring practices. "Notice to first basemen— The National Club of Washington are looking for a first baseman about here. . . . Terms—First-rate position in the Treasury Department: must work in the Dept. until three o'clock, and then practice at base ball until dark. *No Irish need apply*."[24] Irish ballplayers, despite the *Chronicle*'s jab and others like it, did crack white baseball rosters, however. In this way, the inclusiveness of whiteness was revealed. Irish residents of DC often faced discrimination, but—unlike black ballplayers—they did not suffer complete exclusion.

Charles Douglass's Cause

Black baseball players in Washington DC navigated a racial purgatory of sorts. The District was a place where race relations remained in flux and where the reverberations of slavery seemed to bump up frequently against ideas of racial progress. Black baseball in Washington took its place among a variety of everyday black-white struggles. Inherent in the quest of black baseball clubs to find success (borne out in prestige, financial stability, land use, and games against white clubs) were ideas about autonomy, equality, and opportunity—the same considerations driving many black Washingtonians to build schools and fight for equal access to federal jobs. Charles Douglass, son of the famous Frederick Douglass, led Washington's first generation of black ballplayers. He countered the leadership of Young and Gorman. Douglass was not a prodigal son; he took to the ball field not out of rebelliousness or indifference to his father's cause, but rather as his own means of fighting for it.

Over the course of the five years following the Civil War, Charles Douglass helped organize the Alert and Mutual Base Ball Clubs of Washington DC. He played for the clubs, too. He did so while working for the federal government and raising a family. Taking cues from his father, Douglass never suggested that the integration of baseball at all costs was his goal. Instead, Douglass focused his attention on building successful and respected black-led clubs. Generally speaking, only when black clubs were denied access to public spaces or refused recognition by national associations did black baseball leaders shift their focus to open resistance. Land usage and organizational inclusion were often the lines drawn in the sand.

Black baseball, in Washington DC and often elsewhere, exhibited the blend of operational pragmatism and a steely commitment to equality advocated by Frederick Douglass. When he had been asked for his definition of social equality, Douglass made clear that the point was to improve the lot of black Americans: "What is social equality? Is it to walk the streets with others, to ride in the cars, to drink the same water? If these constitute social equality, than I am for it. . . . But if it be understood that we are endeavoring to force our white neighbors to invite us in their drawing-rooms, to allow us to marry their sons and daughters—if this is social equality then I contend that it is wrong."[25] In Charles Douglass's baseball world, then, social equality seemed to support the creation of strong black-led clubs that then fought for equal access to baseball grounds and the opportunity to compete at baseball's highest levels. There is no evidence of black ballplayers clamoring to join white baseball clubs.

The population surge that Washington DC experienced during Reconstruction dramatically altered the racial composition of the city and made the tasks of Young, Gorman, and Douglass all the more complex. In a special census taken in 1867, DC's population was tallied at 126,990, with 88,327 white and 38,663 black residents. The population in 1860, by comparison, had been 75,080, with 60,764 white and a total of 14,316 black residents (11,131 free blacks and 3,185 slaves). Thus, in a period of seven years, the white population had increased by a robust 45 percent. But the black population, which would continue to grow with the estimated 33,000 blacks who came to Washington during and after the war, had increased by nearly 170 percent. The District's population was a far more racially diverse one than baseball's cities to the north. The total black populations in those northern cities—Boston (3,496), Brooklyn (4,944), Chicago (3,691), and New York (13,079), for example—were minute, creating a minority population that was more invisible than threatening.[26] Thus, in uncovering the story of segregation, it is vital to remember that the racial situation varied significantly region by region and city by city.

The District of Columbia had long possessed a unique racial makeup. The city contained slaves before the Civil War, but never in great numbers and always in the midst of a large free-black population. This large presence of free blacks distinguished DC from Southern cities. Within slave states, only the cities of St. Louis and Baltimore had more free blacks than slaves at the beginning of the Civil War, as Washington DC did.[27] One must look back to 1830 to find a census listing more slaves than free blacks in the District. Thus, in 1862, when the federal government abolished slavery in Washington DC, only 3,000 slaves remained to be freed. Still, the region was hardly a safe haven for blacks, before or after the Civil War. The District enacted a series of black codes (before they were called that) in the early nineteenth century, which limited the social freedom of free blacks.[28]

Because of Washington DC's unique demographics and the dominant presence of the federal government, Charles Douglass and his black teammates and neighbors experienced the daily tumult of Reconstruction in a unique way. Congress reigned over the District of Columbia, with starts and stops, just as it did over the South during Reconstruction. In 1865 Washington DC fell almost completely under the jurisdiction of the U.S. Congress. The House Committee on the District controlled Washington's near-every function. DC, however, had a brief "cup of coffee" as an autonomous government. Members of a "civil rights association," including Charles Douglass's Social Equality Republican Club, collected twenty-five hundred signatures in support of universal suffrage. And between 1867 and 1870, the District enjoyed a period of "home rule," during which blacks voted and succeeded in electing the racially progressive Sales J. Bowen as mayor. This period was fleeting, though. In 1871 the passage of the Territorial Bill put Congress back in control. The bill also rescinded from citizens (black and white) the right to vote on most issues.[29]

Charles Douglass fit the general profile of a Washington DC ballplayer. Like most baseballists, Douglass hailed from the North (having spent his formative years in Rochester, New York) and made his living as a government employee, working as a clerk in the Freedmen's Bureau and later for the Treasury Department. He had served in the Union army during the Civil War and, like Nicholas Young and countless others, sought new opportunities in the nation's capital during the Reconstruction era. Throughout the 1860s and '70s, Douglass labored diligently if ingloriously for the burgeoning federal government, trying to provide his family with a home and a modicum of stability. Unlike most young black men in the immediate postslavery years, Charles Douglass had little chance of surpassing or even equaling the accomplishments of his famous father.[30]

Letters of appeal and called-in favors from Frederick Douglass made finding a job considerably easier for Charles than for most black men. Still, as his father organized, cajoled, and argued in pursuit of equal rights for blacks in America, Charles struggled to find his own path.[31] Baseball became his outlet, his opportunity to lead black men and to improve, if subtly, the plight of black Americans in the nation's capital. While his father attended a handful of games as his schedule permitted, baseball seemed to resonate with the younger black man more forcefully than those at or beyond middle age. The influx of young black men to the capital created a ripe environment for the growth of sports clubs, which the Alert and Mutual Clubs seized upon.[32] These baseball organizations fit in with the myriad of other fraternal organizations that gave black men forums for camaraderie and political activism.

Charles Douglass had been anointed at birth to play a role in the ongoing struggle for black rights in America. He was named after Charles Remond, one of Frederick Douglass's closest compatriots in the antislavery crusade of the 1840s.[33] Living up to the legacy and expectations of his father was no small task. Charles did not find glory in the Civil War. Although he was a member of the famous, all-black Massachusetts Fifty-Fourth Regiment, Douglass spent most of his military career seriously ill. Douglass stayed behind when the Fifty-Fourth made its legendary assault on Fort Wagner in South Carolina. Had he gone, of course, there might not have been a baseball story to tell. More than half of the soldiers in the black regiment were killed or injured during the assault. With his father pulling strings in the background, Charles was eventually transferred to another, less active, black unit and then honorably discharged.[34] Charles's older brother Lewis Douglass became the family's war hero, not only because he actually fought, but also by becoming the first sergeant major of the Fifty-Fourth Massachusetts.

In the regular letters that went back and forth between Charles and his father, it became clear that the younger Douglass—like many young black men fighting for survival in the postslavery economy—had financial problems. Jobs were scarce and fleeting, and wages rarely met living expenses. In many cases black men could not collect payment even for work they had already performed.[35] The District's Freedmen's Bureau office could address only a handful of the dozens of complaints it saw daily. On various occasions Charles requested money from his father in order to help with paying off debts or building a house. His salary as a federal employee, one hundred dollars per month when he started at the Freedmen's Bureau, provided some stability, but hardly wealth.[36]

Douglass joined the Alert Base Ball Club of Washington DC after the war ended and, like Young and Gorman, almost immediately took on a leadership position. His motivations for selecting baseball in particular are unclear. One might hypothesize that Douglass found that he could escape the shadow of his famous father and his financial worries on the ball field. Or perhaps after he sat out the Civil War fight, baseball's emphasis on manliness was appealing. Regardless, Douglass committed significant time to his new club. Unlike the National Base Ball Club, however, Douglass's Alert Club left behind no constitution or other formative documents. Thus, historians are forced to pick up the story in July 1867 when the Alerts entered the national black baseball scene as a fully organized and ready-for-competition club. The Alerts would clumsily arrange their public debut by inviting themselves to Philadelphia for a match against the Pythians on July 5, 1867.

The White Lot

Geographical proximity to power, in nineteenth-century Washington DC as today, was a designation of significance. While still regarded by many in the 1860s as a muddy swamp, Washington DC was growing up according to Pierre L'Enfant's master plan.[37] Proximity to the White House and the U.S. Capitol denoted importance. L'Enfant also included what is today known as the National Mall in his plan. Public spaces were interspersed with privately owned buildings and government offices. This sensible division of land made inner-city baseball possible.[38]

Because many baseball games took place on late weekday afternoons, the White Lot's proximity to government buildings made it especially desirable. "As soon as the hour for closing business in the departments arrived, there was a general march for the ballgrounds," noted one District newspaper.[39] It is also plausible to assume that the White Lot's proximity to the White House registered as important with Washington's baseball organizers for nonlogistical reasons. Washington's baseball men were political men. Led by Nicholas Young (a successful civil servant) and Arthur Gorman (a future senator), the cadre of successful white men who played baseball in their free time likely appreciated the significance of playing in the shadow of the White House.

According to the *New York Clipper*'s 1866 season preview, Washington's White Lot teemed with baseball activity. The National and Union Clubs shared a clubhouse and field on one side of the grounds. The Potomac and Jefferson Clubs controlled a field on the side of the acreage farthest opposite the National-Union field. In the center of the grounds, the city's amateur and "new clubs" practiced and played. The

1. White Lot. *Frank Leslie's Illustrated Newspaper*, December 12, 1874. Library of Congress, LC-USZ62-108154.

city's Washington and American Cricket Clubs also used the center of the grounds to keep alive the "imperial game" in the city. If this activity was not enough, a half-dozen junior ball clubs used "all the spare ground on the margin" for their games.

The shared field bustled with baseball activity. It was a truly public space. Baseballs and baseball players crisscrossed the grounds. "What a crowd of ball players there are on the field every day. In fact the way the balls fly in every direction is enough to remind a veteran of the army of the time when he found himself like the 'six hundred' in the Crimea, who had 'balls to the right of the them, balls to the left of them.'"[40] Those who have visited a Major League ballpark or the White House can appreciate the historical uniqueness of this situation. Baseball clubs today do not share well; neither does the president enjoy constant company in his yard.[41] But in 1866 the arrangement made sense. The White Lot allowed numerous clubs access to a first-rate and geographically convenient field. It was a situation that would not last long. Indeed, the changing relationship of the baseball community with the White Lot reveals much about the evolution of the game and its players in the District.[42]

A National Convention on Reconciliation

Like Nicholas Young, Arthur Gorman personified Washington DC's mix of government and baseball. When the Civil War ended, Gorman was twenty-six years old and already had thirteen years in politics under his belt.[43] Gorman had become a House of Representatives page at age thirteen, before transferring to the same role in the Senate. There he struck up a friendship with Senator Stephen Douglas of Illinois, serving as his personal secretary during the famous Lincoln-Douglas debates of 1858, and Andrew Johnson from Tennessee.[44] By 1865 Gorman served as the postmaster of the Senate, a position he gained with the support of then vice president Johnson. Gorman had managed to befriend the reticent Johnson. The two became close enough that Gorman visited Johnson in Tennessee during the war while Johnson served as military governor. The two men maintained ties as Johnson took over the Lincoln White House. The relationship proved beneficial to Gorman, the Washington Nationals, and baseball in general.[45]

At the close of the Civil War, Gorman's National Base Ball Club reigned nearly unchallenged as the District's premier club. The club had formed in November 1859. The club's constitution set the standards: no more than forty members, fees of fifty cents at initiation and twenty-five cents per month, and "field exercises" on at least the first Monday of every month. The club elected officers (a president, vice president, secretary, and treasurer), but submitted most decisions to the voting membership. The number necessary to constitute a quorum for transacting business was, of course, nine.[46]

Gorman had been a part of the National organization since its inception. He had also helped organize early baseball in Baltimore. Gorman's primary contribution to DC baseball came as an organizer; his play on the field drew little attention, positive or otherwise. When he did make the playing nine, Gorman often played catcher—a brutal position. Without gloves or a mask, catchers faced the decision of whether to stand near enough to the plate to make a play when needed or far enough back to avoid serious injury from a tipped ball.[47] By 1863 Gorman had assumed the presidency of the Nationals. It was Gorman who organized the Nationals-Athletics meeting that created such an impression the day Young had happened upon it. Gorman was, according to the *Clipper*, one of the "prime movers of everything calculated to advance the interest or extend the popularity of baseball."[48] This cause—advancing the national game—appeared repeatedly in the *Clipper* and other dailies interested in sports. Regulating and organizing the game, baseball advocates argued, should precipitate the expansion of baseball's popularity.

Gorman's political ties paid off repeatedly for the Nationals. Due to Gorman's friendship with President Johnson, the Nationals received permission to build a small storage facility on the White Lot, establishing a private foothold on the otherwise public space. With the political upheaval of the period, however, Gorman got caught in the fray at times as well. He lost his position in the Senate post office when Johnson fell out of favor. But Johnson quickly arranged for Gorman to take an internal revenue collector position in Maryland's Fifth District, sending a handwritten note on Gorman's application stating that "special attention is called to this case." The career move took Gorman away from the day-to-day leadership of the Nationals, but it prepared him to take on a more significant leadership role in baseball.[49]

At the close of the 1866 season, Arthur Gorman traveled from Washington to join delegates representing 202 ball clubs at the tenth annual meeting of the National Association of Base Ball Players. The meeting took place in New York City, as it always had. Tension was evident from the start. The bitterness and divisions from the Civil War, not surprisingly, had not dissipated. Baseball in the South, as will be discussed in subsequent chapters, seemed to function mostly as a method of highlighting emerging Lost Cause sentimentality. The numbers of baseball players in the South lagged significantly behind those in the North. In this light, conventioneers took pains to welcome delegates from below the Mason-Dixon line—five from Maryland, ten from the District of Columbia, two from Tennessee, and one each from Kentucky, Virginia, and West Virginia.[50] *Beadle's Dime Base Ball Player*, *The Book of American Pastimes*, the *Brooklyn Eagle*, and the *New York Clipper* all, in the weeks following the convention, noted the reception given to Southern teams. "The applause which greeted the responses from the Southern clubs afforded ample proof of the truly conservative feeling which prevailed at the Convention."[51] "Conservative" in this case had little to do with issues involving fiscal policy or social behavior or temperance. Rather, "conservative" in baseball communities concerned ongoing Reconstruction decisions and racial policies. More specifically, conservative baseball men rejected aggressive civil rights reform.

Henry Ellard, writing forty years later about his father's role in early baseball development, elaborated further on the pivotal 1866 convention: "The bitter sectional feeling between the North and the South was quite strong at this time. It had been difficult to subdue the antagonism which had been engendered by the war . . . and it is pleasant to note that the applause and cheers were never stronger than when the name of one of the Southern delegates was proposed as a candidate for the presidency of the Association."[52] Arthur Gorman was that "Southern" delegate nominated for the association's presidency.

Gorman's conservative, Southern credentials did not necessarily fit neatly into the Civil War–era paradigm. Gorman hailed from Maryland and had spent most of his life in Washington DC. But opinions on race and the changes being proposed by Reconstruction politicians were the gauge here, not strict geography. Gorman's close relationship with Andrew Johnson and his support for Stephen Douglas made him a Southerner, at least in the baseball world.[53]

Gorman won the election for the National Association of Base Ball Players presidency. He became the first non–New Yorker to hold the post. In ascending to the leadership post, Gorman was baseball's first "affirmative action" hire. The *New York Clipper* had led the push for Gorman before the 1866 convention even began. According to the *Clipper*, Gorman had the potential to increase the popularity of baseball in the South. The *New York Clipper* consistently referred to Washington as a Southern baseball town and the Nationals as the "champions of the South."[54]

The Gorman nomination attempted to navigate the confusing waters of postwar sectionalism. In many ways the National Club itself did not fit with either the North or the South. Many self-identified Southerners, even those residing in Washington, wanted nothing to do with the club. A letter to the editor addressed to the *Union* in July 1866 made this hostility clear:

Your reports in referring to the reception accorded this Club, alludes to them as "Southerners," and as the "Champion Club of the South." . . . [T]here is not a single member of the National Club who has any claim to the *proud title of "Southerner"*; on the contrary, nearly every one of them having come from the North during the late *Abolition war*, and the majority of them having served in *that army of mercenaries which invaded the South*. . . . I am unwilling that they should be awarded any honors, or receive any encomiums under color of their supposed or assumed Southern character. . . . Allow me to add that the Potomac Base Ball Club of this city [DC] is the only organization of the kind in the vicinity that can really claim the *honor (!)* of being called a "Southern" club, or of *representing Southern sentiment.*[55]

"Representing Southern sentiment" rested at the heart of baseball's version of sectionalism. Labeled the champions of the South by the Northern press, the Nationals were summarily booed in Louisville as invaders from the North.[56] The *Ball Players' Chronicle* explained this booing matter-of-factly: "The latitude of the home of the Nationals was too far north to elicit the impartial award of approbation which a club from some more Southern locality would have received."[57] The explanation was nonsensical in literal terms; Washington DC and Louisville sat at nearly the same latitude, and Kentucky had been a key border state during the war. Still, Washington DC managed to draw criticism from the North for its Southern tendencies and from the South for its Northern allegiances. Washington DC in the baseball community, like in Reconstruction politics, was understood as both a solution and a problem.

Although Gorman's "Southernness" did not satisfy everyone, there is no doubt that his selection as president of the National Association of Base Ball Players was a reconciliationist move. Sectional tension, understandably still lingering only a couple of years after the end of a war that had claimed more than a half-million lives, stood in the way of baseball's expansion. And expansion had been a reverberating priority, almost an irrationally intense pursuit actually, in the white baseball community for years. Many baseball leaders, including Henry Chadwick, were fixated on the idea that baseball must be national in scope. Chadwick, he of "father of baseball" fame, spoke repeatedly in "reconciliationist" terms. "Our national game is intended to be national in every sense of the word," Chadwick preached in October 1866, shortly before Gorman's selection as president.[58] The 1866 *Base Ball Player's Book of Reference* made a similar pledge to facilitate the national growth of baseball. "We have to state that, whether Base Ball be regarded as a desirable means of physical exercise, and exciting game for the masses, a recreation for the refined classes of the community, or an out-door sport devoid of every objectionable attribute the most fastidious moralist could charge it with possessing, it is equally to be commended to the patronage of every reputable citizen, North, East, South, and West as the most suitable game for the national out-door sport of the American people."[59] Additionally, the *New York Clipper* and other pro-baseball newspapers articulated several schemes for "popularizing our national game" shortly after the Civil War ended.[60]

Arthur Gorman won the presidency of the NABBP because white baseball leaders in the North believed that Gorman would appeal to white Southern ballplayers. His selection meant that reconciliation would happen on Southern terms.[61] Gorman hailed from slave country and had a well-chronicled connection to Andrew Johnson. Many Southerners (as will be demonstrated subsequently) viewed President Johnson as the South's protector. Gorman also had the prerequisite experience organizing baseball clubs. Thus, the *Ball Player's Chronicle*, as the 1867 season got under way and Gorman's leadership tenure began, considered Gorman's ascension to have been a necessary and pragmatic step. "The culminating point in the effort made to show the base ball world that sectional prejudices did not rule the fraternity of the North," the *Chronicle* recapped, "was the election of Mr. Gorman as President of the National Association for 1867."[62] With such a preemptory stand made to encourage sectional reconciliation, the mechanics of segregation were lubricated. The white baseball community had made its first official act toward reconciliation, and consequently its first step away from supporting black baseball clubs' inclusion in the National Association.

Chapter 2

Richmond

Make It a Southern Game

Baseball took a bit longer to take hold fully in Richmond, Virginia, and in most Southern cities, than in Northern cities. The 1865 season came and went with only a smattering of games in former Confederate states. In 1866, however, baseball flourished. And it was at the end of the 1866 baseball season, a season highlighted by dozens of games in the former Confederate capital, that the Richmond Base Ball Club ignited a baseball scandal. The scandal demonstrated that desires for a "national game," supported by efforts such as the selection of Arthur Gorman as president of the NABBP, would face competing priorities in the South. The scandal also made clear that racial policies would be a preeminent matter in the growth of a national baseball community.

The Richmond Club started the controversy by rather audaciously breaking baseball's rules of decorum and refusing an invitation to play a match game against Richmond's Union Base Ball Club. At about the same time, the leadership of the Richmond Club also indicated that it had no plans to join the National Association of Base Ball Players, nor did they expect that other Southern clubs would submit themselves to such a national organizing body. The simple reason given by the Richmond Club's secretary for both these rejections: "we are Southerners."[1] The gauntlet had been thrown down.

Thus, while Washingtonians Arthur Gorman and Nicholas Young focused on nationalizing baseball, white baseball leaders in the South worked toward very different ends. Certainly, the environment for baseball activity in states like Virginia and South Carolina differed greatly from that in the North. Confederate soldiers returned home defeated, to a South that had been broken by the fighting. Scarcity of food and shelter reigned as the most immediate of concerns. But still, even in such circumstances, the men of the South quickly began to form social organizations—perhaps hoping to replace camaraderie and community provided by their bygone military units. Southerners as a whole looked for means by which to reestablish everyday life and move beyond the tragedies wrought by the Civil War. Baseball clubs served these purposes.

That men in cities such as Richmond, Virginia, found time for baseball in the 1860s at all still seems surprising. The *Richmond Times* reported on "Base Ball" in 1866 alongside its coverage of Reconstruction policies, a draining outbreak of cholera, the Freedmen's Bureau's ration policies, and the rebuilding of burned sections of the city. In the article "Base Ball," the *Times* explained in October 1866, "This exciting game and health-inspiring game that has been much in vogue in the North for many years has become very popular here."[2] Baseball blossomed in Richmond and other Southern cities—Atlanta, Charleston, Chattanooga, Louisville, Nashville, New Orleans, and Savannah especially—both because and in spite of the destruction wrought by the Civil War. Baseball leaders such as Richmond's Alexander Babcock took a Northern game and made it fit in Southern society. Not surprisingly, questions regarding race and sectionalism played prominently in this formative process.

Richmond's white baseball leaders had even less to say about race than their counterparts in Philadelphia or Washington, or Chicago, New York City, or Boston. To be precise, most white ballplayers in the South said nothing about race as it pertained to baseball. The leading white Richmond clubs never banned black participation. Similarly, Richmond's white newspapers almost never commented (negatively or otherwise) on the activities of black baseball clubs. Instead, racial exclusion was an unstated but universal principle of Southern baseball right from the start. Thus, analyzing the mechanics of segregation in Richmond, and thereby the South, is a different task. It involves interpreting circumspect language and symbolic actions more than observing legal developments or even overt conflicts.

The *Richmond Times* and *Richmond Daily Dispatch* reported enthusiastically on baseball in 1866 especially. Juxtaposing these baseball reports, both papers also regularly published stories that painted former slaves as lazy, dishonest, and unintelligent. Calls for extreme segregation ("Have we not pointed out the advantages of emigration to Liberia, a country where they can get plenty of yam, plantain and rum?") persisted.[3] On the prospect of baseball serving as a means to reconnect the North and South, virtually no evidence exists to suggest that Richmond men wanted to use the game to forge new bonds with the men who had, only months before, stood across from them on the battlefields of the Civil War. In fact, as the National Association was electing Arthur Gorman as an olive branch of sorts, Southern teams reveled in the "Lost Cause" skirmishes that quickly defined the postwar period. Richmond's white baseball players made their priorities known by the causes they supported.[4] When the city's ballplayers raised money for charitable causes (a typical endeavor for sportsmen of the nineteenth century), their funds went to support the building of statues honoring Robert E. Lee and Thomas "Stonewall" Jackson or to give fallen Confederates proper burials in Richmond's bucolic Hollywood Cemetery.[5] Even the names of Richmond's baseball clubs—the Secesh, Dixie, and Robert E. Lee, among others—honored the Confederacy and highlighted Richmond's stubborn resistance to Reconstruction. In short, although baseball was mostly new to the city, the men of Richmond played baseball, and indeed used baseball, on their own terms.

Very Different Fields of Play

As the baseball season began in 1866, Richmond still existed as a shattered shell of its former self. The physical damage done to the Confederate capital had, ironically, occurred with only a few fighting days remaining in the Civil War. And Richmond's own citizens and military protectors had done most of the damage. Richmonders torched their city so that the Union army would find nothing of use when it marched into the capital in April 1865. Cornelius H. Carlton, a young Confederate soldier from Richmond, had witnessed his friends and neighbors destroying their own city, scribbling in his diary as he sat on the opposite banks of the James River: "April 3rd—What a terrible morning—Richmond burning; gunboats burning and their magazines exploding, magazines along the fortifications exploding; Oh what a *terrible* morning."[6] The fires destroyed a thousand buildings in Richmond's downtown business district, burning nearly all of Richmond's major banks and grocers, as well as the offices and equipment of several of Richmond's newspapers.[7] By the time crews had extinguished the blazes, the bridges spanning the James River no longer provided safe passage.

Richmonders did not suffer alone. Atlanta, Charleston, Columbia, and Savannah, among others, each faced significant wartime destruction. Interestingly enough, these heavily damaged cities, along with New Orleans, became the bastions of postwar baseball in the South. This connection between urban destruction and Southern baseball should not be missed. Baseball in the South did not seem to flourish in cities that most closely mirrored Northern urban areas. Rather, baseball's major cities in the South were, because of the war's toll and racial demographics, the most different from New York or Boston. Journalists traveled through the South reporting on the devastation. Of Atlanta Sidney Andrews wrote, "The ruin is not so massive and impressive as that of Columbia and Charleston, but as far as it extends it is more complete."[8] Many assessors judged Charleston to have suffered most. An English observer concluded, "Never had a completer ruin fallen upon any city than fell upon Charleston."[9] Nevertheless, baseball quickly rose up from the ashes.

In light of the difficulties experienced by Richmonders and Southerners during Reconstruction, the *Richmond Times*, on more than one occasion, pondered why and how baseball became so popular. Foremost, the paper concluded that Richmond's young men needed a forum for socializing and a means to exhibit postwar independence. The men had also acquired, according to the *Times*, the habit of socializing: "The experiences of four years' of army life have rendered the young men of the South wonderfully gregarious. To move, live, and have their being in large bodies, seems to be somewhat essential to them. Now that they can no longer claim the fond associations of Company 'A' or 'B,' they still demonstrate their love for society of each other by establishing organizations for the accomplishments of other objects. The societies of war were no sooner dissolved than associations of a peaceful character were formed."[10] The *Times* claimed that the "wonderfully gregarious" men of Richmond had formed more baseball clubs, per capita, than any other city in the country.[11] It was a dubious claim, but a telling one nonetheless.

Studying Reconstruction baseball in Richmond reveals anew how the struggle to organize a postslavery racial paradigm played out in

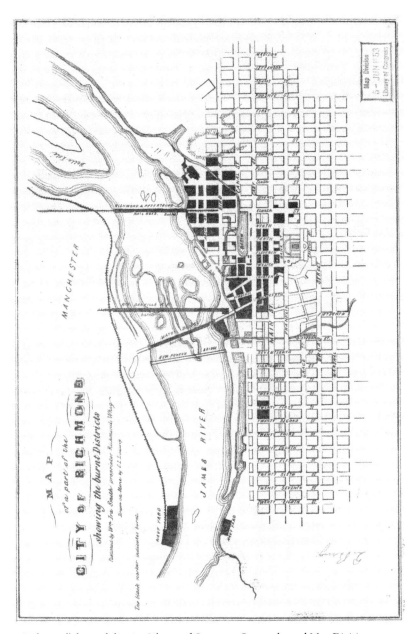

2. Richmond's burned district. Library of Congress, Geography and Map Division.

the South. Although some baseball activity had existed in Richmond and other large Southern cities before the outbreak of the Civil War, Southern baseball really began after Appomattox. White Richmonders in the 1860s and '70s used baseball as a means of parsing out the new realities that confronted them following their military defeat. Baseball became, at times, a way to fight back, albeit in a gentlemanly fashion. To many Southern whites, there were no unimportant battles or insignificant activities (including baseball) when it came to prohibiting race mixing. The war ended slavery and nullified secession; everything else remained up for debate. These sentiments come through clearly in the newspapers of Richmond and the actions of its citizens. The *Richmond Daily Dispatch*, for example, understood the Reconstruction struggle to be nothing less than a continual "War of the Races" that whites could not afford to lose. "Laws and bayonets and sordid fanaticism all combined," the *Dispatch* resolved, "cannot force the highest of the five races . . . to live in peace with the lowest of that five upon terms of equality."[12]

Yet only one hundred miles to the north in Washington DC—home to Douglass, Gorman, and Young—Reconstruction politicians tried to do exactly what the *Daily Dispatch* declared impossible. Reconstruction politicians attempted, with varying levels of enthusiasm and effectiveness, to promote racial equality for Richmond and the rest of the South. During the first years of Reconstruction, the Republican Congress passed significant legislation, including the Civil Rights Act of 1866, and crafted the Fourteenth and Fifteenth Amendments.[13] But outside of Congress, the two sides—those committed to racial separation and those who supported racial integration—understood the parameters of the contest differently. White segregationists, including those who played baseball, had a simple and cohesive policy regarding segregation: whites and blacks should *never* come together as equals. This maxim was the guiding principle for Richmond baseball. On the other side, proponents of racial progress spent much of their time trying to decide where to focus integration efforts and determining those activities in society where segregation was either permissible or inevitable. This difference in cohesiveness and clarity between the two sides' understanding of the struggle created a decided advantage for those white Americans, and baseball players, who supported racial segregation.

Alexander Babcock, Father of Richmond Baseball

Alexander G. Babcock established the Richmond Base Ball Club in July 1866, bringing organized baseball to the city.[14] Edward Cohen, a commodities broker at Richmond's Merchants and Mercantile Bank, served as the club's first president. Cohen, a "pioneer of Richmond Jewry," also served as the president of Richmond's Kesher Shel Barzel lodge (a national Jewish fraternal order).[15] Cohen's selection to lead the new baseball club demonstrated that whiteness, not religion or ethnicity, was the fundamental criterion of entry to organized baseball in Richmond. J. S. Riley and J. V. Bidgood, bookstore owners, assumed the roles of treasurer and secretary, and Babcock took on a club-director position for Richmond's first significant baseball club.[16]

In light of the fact that the club's initial meetings took place at the Bidgood and Riley Bookstore, and given Richmond's rising obstinacy to Northern influence, one cannot help but wonder if the club quite literally formed with *The Lost Cause* close at hand. Edward A. Pollard, the wartime editor of the *Richmond Examiner*, published his massive *The Lost Cause* in 1866. In a matter-of-fact style, Pollard laid out for his fellow white Richmonders and Southerners a story of gallant Confederate armies competing against the insurmountable resources and thuggish tendencies of the Union army. Pollard had inaugurated the debate over the Civil War's history, but in the closing pages of the seven-hundred-page work he also gave marching orders to white Southerners: "The war has not swallowed up everything. . . . [T]he war properly decided only what was put to issue: the restoration of the Union and the excision of slavery. . . . [T]he war did not decide negro equality; it did not decide negro suffrage; it did not decide States Rights. . . . And these things which the war did not decide, the Southern people will still cling to, still claim, and still assert in them their rights and views."[17] Pollard wanted Southerners to protect their way of life; the white baseball clubs in Richmond and other Southern cities led this call to arms in the sporting world.

The Richmond Club held its first match on July 12, 1866. It was a scrimmage really, involving only the players of the Richmond Club, but the *Dispatch* still covered the gathering. The game took place in the western quadrant of the city, on land just across the street from

Elba Park and north of the city's vast Hollywood Cemetery. Proximity to Hollywood mattered. If Washington DC oriented itself around the White House and the U.S. Capitol, Richmond focused on Hollywood Cemetery. The cemetery was a point of pride in the slowly recovering city and an indication of city priorities. One visitor passing through Richmond only days before the Richmond Club's match noted the juxtaposition of the manicured cemetery and the carnage of the city's burned district. The "luxuriant growth . . . and above all, the graves of our beloved and glorious Confederate dead, make Hollywood the most charming spot within my knowledge," the traveler asserted. The business district, on the other hand, was nothing more than "ghastly piles of rubbish, brick and mortar, standing walls, and gaping cellars with yawning chasms."[18] It was altogether fitting that the Richmond Club hosted its inaugural gathering between the shrine to the Confederate dead and the dark reminder of the Union victory.

The Richmond Base Ball Club's first interclub match came a month later and was an exercise in memorializing a Confederate hero. On August 4, 1866, Babcock and his teammates met the Ashby Club, also of Richmond. The Ashby Club, Richmond's press noted, played in "honor of the illustrious deceased Southern Cavalier" General Turner Ashby. The game that resulted was a four-and-a-half-hour grind, decided 43–34 in favor of the Ashby Club. The *Richmond Times* determined the event's importance by evaluating the crowd assembled: "A goodly number of ladies were present on the above auspicious occasion, and, by their smiles, encouraged their favorite." On actual baseball matters the Richmond press was a bit lost (the *Times* reported that one team scored forty-three *innings* to the other's thirty-four), but still baseball fever had arrived.[19]

Alexander Babcock was Richmond's Nicholas Young, organizing baseball clubs and matches and generally overseeing the infrastructure of a growing game. In a rare mix Babcock had both a baseball pedigree (predating the Civil War) and a stalwart Confederate résumé. Babcock did not hail from Richmond, however, or even from the South. Rather, Babcock had made his antebellum home in New York City. Babcock had played for the reputable Brooklyn Atlantics. When the Civil War came Babcock joined the Union army and served in Company D of New York's Seventy-First State Militia. In this post and on this side, Babcock lasted only three months.[20] For reasons left unexplained, Babcock switched to the Confederacy and served as a captain in Richmond's Third Battalion for Local Defense in 1863 and 1864. Babcock then transferred from that unit to the Artillery Company of the Forty-Third Battalion, Virginia Cavalry, under the leadership of the daring John Mosby. With Mosby's men often referred to as "the Guerilla band," Babcock became the "Big Guerrilla."[21]

Babcock served Richmond and the Confederacy well during the war. Thus, it makes sense that he stayed in Richmond after the conflict ended. Babcock's war record benefited him greatly, in business and society. In 1866 the *Richmond Daily Dispatch*, for example, vouched for Babcock's character and urged Richmonders to purchase their ice from a Confederate hero: "Captain A. G. Babcock, well known to everybody who lived hereabouts during the memorable four years, having himself cooled down considerably since that time, proposes to keep the citizens of Richmond cool during the approaching hot term by supplying them with any quantity of pure, clear ice daily."[22] Babcock, like other veterans, retained his military title for life. He remained a "captain," and thus forever a Southern patriot. That a man with Captain Babcock's résumé controlled baseball in Richmond certainly mattered in terms of the trajectory of the game.

According to city council records and tax bills, Babcock struggled to make a profit as an ice dealer, even with his reputation and connections. Of course, after the war, most men, black and white, took on whatever work they could find. Unemployment plagued the city.[23] Baseball players as a rule were the fortunate minority who had great-enough financial resources to pursue recreation. By cross-referencing Richmond's annual city directory with baseball box scores, one learns that Richmond ballplayers held a wide variety of jobs, including banker, constable, salesman, carpenter, ice dealer, mechanic, laborer, shoe repairman, magistrate, policeman, news agent, hotel clerk, printer, tobacconist, stonecutter, "plate turner," iron puddler, gas inspector, "liquorsman," and bookkeeper.[24]

In a second act of blatant disloyalty (the first, of course, being his switch from the Union army to the Confederates), A. G. Babcock abandoned the Richmond Base Ball Club before the team finished its first full season. Babcock decided to start over in order to build up an even more competitive baseball club. He founded the Pastime Base Ball Club in late-September 1866 and assumed this club's presidency from the start. The Pastime recruited the city's best white players. Less than one week after organizing, the Pastime took the field for their first match, winning 135–33.[25]

Despite the difficulties of postwar Reconstruction, the summer of 1866 gave rise to hundreds of white men joining Alexander Babcock, the Richmond Base Ball Club, and the Pastime Club on the city's ball fields. Throughout the South as a whole, baseball participation increased rapidly during the 1866 season. The *Atlanta Daily Intelligencer* reported on more than fifty games during the late 1866 and early 1867 season. The *Savannah Daily News and Herald* boosted that the play of its clubs "could scarcely have been better" and that the Savannah boys would soon take "a ball or two" from their more experienced Northern counterparts.[26] Fans also began to turn out. The elite clubs of Savannah and Charleston in particular competed before thousands of paying spectators within a couple of short seasons after the Confederacy's death.[27]

The *Richmond Times* lavished its city's white baseball community with generous press coverage. Baseball had become, the paper surmised, the "modern requisite for a 'two horse town.'" Further classifying the activity, one editor described baseball as the city's newest sickness: "Cholera having disappeared [it had not subsided completely], and the chills, in a measure, abated, the baseball fever is the last mania with which our people have been afflicted."[28] During the 1866 season the *Richmond Times* and *Richmond Daily Dispatch* published more than 150 articles concerning baseball. Although tallying an exact count of the Richmond clubs is difficult due to the capricious nature of teams commencing and folding, one can conservatively conclude that at least thirty baseball clubs played in the city during the 1866 season. Still, no Richmond club played more than ten games during the 1866 season. Despite its late start, the Richmond Pastime compiled the city's best record, at 8–2.[29]

The Bonds of Baseball, the South, and Whiteness

Whereas Henry Chadwick, whose Virginia-raised wife might have offered him a dose of reality, preached that baseball would "be national in every sense of the word," Southern baseball players embraced the language and practices of sectionalism.[30] They commemorated the rebellion. Some examples of this Southern tendency were overt. In August 1866, for instance, the *Richmond Daily Dispatch* sternly warned a new club that had taken on the designation of "Keystone Club" to find a more fitting, more Virginian name. Other vestiges of sectionalism took a more nuanced approach. When it came to uniforms, the baseball men of the South did not forget what they had been wearing for the past four years. In the face of restriction by the U.S. Army against wearing one's Confederate uniform, the Richmond Pastime wore garb regularly described as including "Confederate grey pantaloons." This statement via wardrobe became common in Southern baseball. In Atlanta a "Grey Jacket Base Ball Club" formed also in 1866. Beyond dress the commemoration of Confederate leaders became a part of white Southern baseball. In Richmond the Ashby Club made clear that its play was meant to honor Turner Ashby, the "gallant Confederate raider, whose deeds of valor in time gone by so often struck terror to the hearts of the federal invaders."[31] Dozens of teams throughout the South played in honor of leading generals, especially Robert E. Lee and Thomas "Stonewall" Jackson.

Although uniforms, tributes, and descriptions might, on the surface, seem inconsequential, the semantics and visuals of the Southern game exposed the priorities of its white players. Racial exclusion came by inference and via a resolute commitment to maintaining Southern distinctiveness even while taking up a Northern game. Thus, Leon Litwack's thesis, that "the racial distinctions that characterized the immediate post-emancipation years were almost always understood rather than stated," rings true when considering the baseball realm of Richmond and the South.[32]

A more formal manifestation of Southern separatism also percolated in 1866. Richmond baseballers led the discussion about forming an organizing body, composed solely of Southern clubs, to challenge the National Association. The *Richmond Times* received dozens of letters during the 1860s from clubs spread across Virginia and the South, asking for rule clarifications and inquiring about the prospect of Southern clubs coming together at a convention. The *Times* printed one such letter in its October 3, 1866, edition: "As your paper seems to be the general champion of the baseball fraternity in Richmond

all of our baseball players here [Alexandria, Virginia] are beginning
to patronize it, and every evening we look with eager eyes over your
local column for information in regard to matches that have been and
are to be played, besides trying to get information about the 'Southern Baseball Convention' that we hear will meet before long."[33] In the
end the proposed Southern convention never occurred. But the idea
of not only rejecting the National Association but also joining with
like-minded Southern teams appealed to many Richmonders, Virginians, and Southerners. Of the dozens of clubs in Virginia, only one—
the Union Club of Richmond, not an accepted member of the city's
baseball community (as will be demonstrated)—saw fit to send a representative to the North-led National Association of Base Ball Players
convention in 1866.[34]

Richmond clubs did meet for a Virginia state baseball convention
in 1866. Edward Cohen presided, and Alexander Babcock represented
the interests of Richmond baseball at the gathering held in Richmond's
city hall. The men decided at the meeting that another meeting should
be called; this one would be a formal state convention set for 1867. Virginia men would organize and control their own baseball interests.
This represented the only palatable option. Cohen clarified his priorities for organizing: "The chief objects of such a Convention are, to
further the cause of base ball by giving it that influence and position to
which its bearing upon the health and morality of any community so
just entitles it, and to meet the objections and inconveniences which
Clubs in this state must have to attending the National Convention."[35]

Black Baseball?

While Richmond's newspapermen served the white baseball community by publishing letters and fostering organization, these same
papers never mentioned black baseball in the city. Never—at least not
until 1875. In light of this dearth of information about black baseball,
one might question whether black Richmonders played baseball at
all. Perhaps it was not segregation at work, but rather that black men
in Richmond, many of them former slaves, simply ignored the new
game. This scenario, though possible, is highly unlikely. Consider the
sources first. Until the *Richmond Planet* began circulation in 1879,
Richmond did not have a black newspaper. This left the *Richmond*

Daily Dispatch and *Richmond Times*, both well known for their racist reporting, to cover black games.

Further supporting a hypothesis that black baseball clubs organized in Richmond during Reconstruction are the numerous examples of such activity in other Southern cities. Perusing newspapers from 1865 to 1875, one learns of the activities of black baseball clubs in Atlanta, Baltimore, Chattanooga, Galveston, Little Rock, Memphis, Mobile, Montgomery, New Orleans, and St. Louis, among others. Black baseball in Georgia was popular enough within five years of the war's end that a Macon club organized a "colored championship" for the state in 1870. Teams from Atlanta, Griffin, and Milledgeville, among others, traveled to Macon for the competition. During the same week in Georgia, another "sable" tournament took place in Brunswick.[36] A complete lack of baseball activity would have rendered the black population of Richmond, some twenty thousand strong, radically different from its counterparts in cities from Boston to New Orleans.[37] Thus, although confirmation of black baseball activity in Richmond did not surface until 1875, analyzing the extenuating circumstances suggests that segregation simply forced black baseball clubs so far to the periphery of the baseball community that records are hard to come by.

There is an irony to consider when analyzing the development of Richmond baseball in 1866 and the mechanics of segregation set in motion at this time that should not be missed. That irony—that the firm segregation of the game began in earnest the same year as the passage of the Civil Rights Bill of 1866 and the Fourteenth Amendment— makes obvious the limitations of Reconstruction policies in post–Civil War America. The Civil Rights Bill had almost no connection or application to baseball. Indeed, while the bill, passed over the opposition of Gorman's friend President Johnson, guaranteed black Americans the right to "purchase, lease, sell, hold, and convey real and personal property," black baseball clubs in Richmond could barely set foot on the city's primary baseball grounds.[38]

Above all else Richmond baseball in 1866 brought together like-minded and like-hued players and spectators. Whiteness trumped religious and class barriers, varying levels of baseball proficiency, and neighborhood identities on the baseball field. Players usually joined clubs based upon a shared work association or neighborhood, but then enjoyed inclusion in the broader baseball community. The Westham Club represented Richmond's Sydney neighborhood. The Old Dominion and Stonewall Jr. Clubs drew their members from the Church Hill area of the city.[39] Each of these clubs joined the broader community and had no difficulty finding match opponents.

The most significant example of this race-based unity can be seen in the acceptance of Manchester's baseball clubs. Manchester had long existed as a stepchild to Richmond. The city sat on the opposite side of the James River from Richmond. Despite fueling Richmond's economy with its many business and manufacturing establishments, and despite the social connections between the two adjacent towns, Richmond would not officially absorb Manchester until early in the twentieth century. Residents of Manchester often chafed at the haughtiness of the Richmonders:

> The way in which Richmond and Manchester behave toward each other is quite singular. The former reminds me of a girl who, poorly raised, by a stroke of good fortune becomes the petted wife of some rich and stupid old bachelor. Thus suddenly improved in condition, she makes the most of it. She decks herself in all the extremes of fashionable folly, assumes lofty, flaunting airs, and hastens to forget the humility of her origins. Richmond is rich. . . . Richmond is large . . . Richmond is proud. . . . Richmond pities Manchester. . . . [T]here is a touch of arrogance and conscious superiority in the behavior of Richmond people toward us which it is my misfortune to despise.[40]

Despite this dynamic, respect and generosity usually characterized the relationships between the white ballplayers of Richmond and Manchester.

When the Alert Base Ball Club of Manchester formed in August 1866 (first as the Dixie Club), the *Richmond Times* described its members as "working men" and confirmed that the club was composed of "good material, and bids to become a first-class [club]."[41] Class could have been a divider here. The Manchester club's captain, James B. Fitzgerald, worked as a carpenter. Mostly bachelors and laborers, the Manchester players' schedules limited club activities to Saturday evenings. Practices and games occurred weekly during that period of brief respite. Still, the club enjoyed all the baseball pageantry common for the period. Within its first few months of existence, the Alert Club invited "ladies" to attend, unfurled a club flag, and coupled action on the field with addresses from distinguished citizens.[42]

Although almost always labeled as a team from Manchester, the Alerts were accepted. The Alert arranged games. Within weeks of organizing, the Alerts hosted the also new Pastime Club at Marks Park. The Pastime walloped the Alerts, 126–17, and the *Times* postulated (incorrectly) that the tally represented "the largest score made in the United States this season."[43] The men of Manchester, accustomed to decades of being slighted by Richmonders, took the field regularly against the best clubs Richmond had to offer. Whiteness bridged class divides and, in this case, the James River. The Southern game brought Fitzgerald the Irish carpenter and Cohen the Jewish stockbroker together.

The Exception to Whiteness

The singular exception to unity by whiteness in Richmond baseball involved a baseball club made up of Freedmen's Bureau agents. While the white baseball community in Richmond found a place in its midst for Jews, unskilled laborers, and residents of Manchester—all groups that experienced social discrimination in the city at times—those white men charged with protecting the rights of black men became social outcasts among Richmond's white baseball players. The Union Base Ball Club of Richmond discovered this reality as the busy 1866 season wound down.

Controversy surrounded the Union Base Ball Club during its two-year existence. Richmond newspaper reporters tried to pin down exactly what the Union Club members did when they were not playing baseball. The *Richmond Times* concluded somewhat hopefully that the Union ballplayers seemed to work as clerks, not as soldiers. "In relation to the status of the 'Union Club,'" the newspaper reported, "we are authorized to state that its members are not composed of army officers. Most of them are attached to Government departments in the capacity of clerks, etc."[44] The clerk occupation, of course, was a common one among baseball men. The *Daily Dispatch* also researched the Union Club, concluding that the "Union Club is entirely composed of

Federal officers." When considering the prospect of a match between the Union and Richmond Clubs, the *Dispatch* worried about the game being used "to make political capital." The paper also understood the reluctance of the Richmond Club to travel to the Union Grounds, which were "situated very near a Federal camp."[45]

That the Union Club received a less than a cordial welcoming to the Richmond baseball community probably did not come as a surprise to the club members themselves. The relationship between formerly Confederate Richmonders and the occupying federal force was a strained one. The issue of altering the city's racial norms worried many whites. The young diarist Carlton noted the presence of federal troops after the war and had no doubts about their motivations for descending upon Richmond: "We are now under military rule. Officers of the 'Freedmen's Bureau' are posted throughout this southern country to carry out the emancipation and 'protect' the negro."[46] Despite these tensions, or maybe in an attempt to minimize them, the federal soldiers organized a baseball team and tried to join in the city's competition.

The bonds of whiteness and the tradition of baseball hospitality were strong, but even they could not save the Union Base Ball Club from rejection in Richmond's Confederate-memorializing baseball community. After organizing, the Union Club conducted a few practices and then began looking for competition. This effort to become a part of Richmond's baseball community set off a controversy in Richmond and in broader baseball circles. It began innocuously. The Union Club wrote the Richmond Club in October 1866, requesting a match. The Union Club's J. F. Dooley, adhering to baseball protocol, penned the formal challenge: "Sir,—Having been authorized, I hereby challenge the Richmond Club to a match game of base-ball, single game, to be played at any time between the 5th and 20th of October, and according to the rules of the National Association. Please advise me of the action of the club as early as possible. Should the club think proper to decline the challenge, you will oblige me by stating plainly the reasons therefore."[47] The letter clearly tested the waters. One might argue, in fact, that the letter meant to pick a fight. In comparing Dooley's letter to the challenge letters that other baseball clubs sent back and forth regularly (many of which were published in newspapers), Dooley's request for an explanation of a refusal stands out as unusual. The Union Club probably anticipated a rejection and wanted documentation regarding their treatment by other Richmond clubs. Whether the reference to the National Association resulted from ignorance regarding Richmond's Southern-based baseball community or was meant to provoke a reaction is difficult to discern. Regardless, the letter did not sit well with the Richmond Club.

The task of replying to the Union Club's challenge fell to J. V. Bidgood, the bookseller and secretary of the Richmond Base Ball Club. Bidgood wasted little effort on diplomacy in his response to the Union Club's challenge. There would be no game. "Sir,—Your communication of the 21st instant is before me. I am instructed to state that the Richmond Base-Ball Club does not desire and will not play the Union Club a single game. We are not, nor do we expect to be, members of the National Base-Ball Convention. Our reason: we are Southerners. Hoping this may be satisfactory."[48] "We are Southerners" was reason enough for Richmond's premier (at least for the time being) baseball club to reject a potential match. Reunion and reconciliation, ideals of great concern to Chadwick and other national baseball leaders, did not sway the Richmond ballplayers.

News spread quickly of the Richmond Club's decidedly direct act of sectional agitation. The *New York Clipper*, baseball's most prominent voice, pounced first, suggesting that the slight would resonate far beyond Richmond. Baseball's future in the city, according to the *Clipper*'s Richmond correspondent, rested on defeating sectionalism. The *Clipper* correspondent had determined that "real" baseball had yet to come to Richmond precisely because Northern-based clubs had not visited the city: "We have had no matches of importance as yet, but soon expect to see some sport of this kind, if sectional prejudices will permit."[49] The Richmond Club did not act alone in refusing to play the Union Club. The *Clipper* reported that Richmond's Old Dominion Club had drawn a challenge from the Union Club as well, which it refused "for reasons which are apparent to all."[50]

Adding further context to the Union–Richmond Club controversy, during the 1866 season a particularly salacious racial scandal captured the city's attention. Miscegenation, with the federal government's tacit approval, had become the city's new panic.[51] In July 1866 Peter Cary, a member of Company G, Second Battalion, of the United States Army, stationed in Richmond, married Henrietta Johnson, a mulatto former slave. The *Richmond Times* gravely reported the perceived transgression as "the first case of miscegenation which has disgraced Richmond."[52] The fact that an occupying soldier would have the gall to marry a former slave solidified the worst suspicions of some Richmond residents, namely, that the federal government had designs on forcing radical racial integration.

The reaction of the national baseball press to the Union Club's rejection hinted at organized baseball's concern over reconciling with white Southerners. The *Clipper* demanded unity in baseball, but it did so amid a fog of geographic and cultural misunderstanding. And the *Clipper* failed to comprehend or chose to ignore the rather obvious fact that white Richmond *wanted* to remain separate and distinct, both in baseball and in most other activities. Thus, when the *New York Clipper* appealed to the Richmond Club for increased bisectional hospitality, most Richmond ballplayers paid no attention. Richmond ballplayers had no interest in the North-led baseball nation. Still, Chadwick and his fellow baseball leaders in New York pressed for reunion: "Until this example was set by the 'Richmond club,' nothing of a sectional character has emanated from a single club in the country; those North, as far as they have had opportunity to do so, manifesting a feeling quite the reverse. We trust to see the Richmond Club reverse their action by challenging the Union Club, if they are Southern *gentlemen*, and not of that class who bring discredit on the name of Southerners."[53] The Richmond Club, apparently unmoved by this argument, offered no response.

Only as frustration mounted over the Richmond Club's obstinacy did the *Clipper* and Northern baseball leaders begin to address the true issues at stake. Three weeks after reporting on the controversy, with the Richmond Club demonstrating no remorse for its stand, the *New York Clipper* issued a thinly veiled threat that exposed the undercurrent driving the conflict. The paper suggested that if playing the Union Club offended the Richmond Club so greatly, a different opponent could be rustled up. "A more suitable match," the *Clipper* seethed, "might be arranged by pitting one of our colored nines against the flower of the Richmond and Old Dominion Clubs, providing the 'boys in black' interpose no obstacles. What say the parties?"[54] With this verbal jab the *Clipper* cast off its typical gentlemanly tone and made clear the negotiating chips on the table. The *Clipper* understood the Richmond baseball community's commitment to racial segregation. The proposed mixed-race game was a mostly empty threat, but the threat played on Southern white ballplayers' greatest fears.

The Richmond Club's rejection of the Union Club made clear that baseball was a venue in the struggle over racial segregation. The *Philadelphia Inquirer*, a paper that only occasionally concerned itself with baseball, joined in the criticism of the Richmond Club. Unfortunately for the *Inquirer*, the paper mixed up some of the particulars. The Philadelphia paper somehow came to the conclusion that the Union Club actually made its home in Washington DC, not in Richmond. The *Philadelphia Inquirer* attempted to stir the pot further with its own report, connecting the politics of Reconstruction with the budding game of baseball in Richmond:

> Baseball and Reconstruction—Some things outside of theatre are as good as any comedy played inside. Among these "some things" we note this, which has recently transpired at Richmond, Virginia, and it's all about baseball. It seems there is a club in existence in Washington DC composed of government employees. This club, in its child-like innocence, challenged the "Richmond" club to play a match game, never dreaming but that the "glove" would be taken from the ground by the "cavalier." Judge, then, ye baseball men of the Atlantic and Athletic clubs, of the surprise which seized the challengers when they received the following laconic and highly chivalric billet down from the challenged party. Read it, and then, answer whether you are ready to place yourselves in a position to receive the same snubbing at the hands of "gentlemen" and "southerners."[55]

The *Inquirer* followed this harangue with a copy of the "We are southerners" letter. Interestingly enough, while the *Philadelphia Inquirer* made the mistake of calling the Union Club a DC team, it accidentally exposed another aspect of Richmond's simmering sectionalism. It mattered little that the Union Club resided in Richmond. Residence in the South did not make one a Southerner.

The Richmond Club's decision to protect its white Southern values by avoiding contact with Northerners did not decide the issue for all white clubs in the city, let alone in the South. Rather, the refusal to play was only one approach to making a point. The *Richmond Daily Dispatch*, for one, argued that Richmond clubs should use baseball to fight back and to demonstrate Southern superiority. A *Dispatch* editorial postulated: "We never before heard of the existence of the 'Union Club' (so called). . . . But we think the Richmond boys should have accepted the challenge." Then, throughout a rambling five-hundred-word editorial that followed, the paper pondered the political nature of the controversy and searched for the downside that might result from a Richmond–Union Club meeting. "We are not yet aware whether [the Union Club] is a political organization or not. . . . The only objection that we could possibly admit to such a course [the two clubs playing] may be found in the fact that the Union Club requested the Richmond to state their reasons for refusing to play; from which it may naturally be supposed that the 'loyal' Club desired to make political capital."[56] The editorial demonstrated a sense of distrust and near paranoia that pervaded Southern society even as postwar reunion was being advocated by many Northern ballplayers.

The *Dispatch* urged the Richmond Club to take the challenge in order to "exhibit another instance of southern prowess over northern boastfulness by beating the 'Union Club' badly," but also to be careful. Thus, while the *Dispatch*'s plan of action was the exact opposite of what the Richmond Club did, the goal—Southern distinctiveness—was the same. On a practical level, playing against Northern clubs (even those based in Richmond) provided an opportunity to improve the state of the game in the city. But despite the very public flap that had erupted over its harsh stand, the Richmond Club held fast in its refusal to play the Union Club. The two clubs never met.

While the Richmond Club took a principled stand that won it many fans in Richmond, other white baseball clubs proceeded differently. Not long after the Richmond Club's rejection, the Spotswood and Ashby Clubs accepted the Union Club's challenges. The fact that differences of opinion arose within Richmond's white baseball community, regarding the level of animosity appropriate over a baseball game, is revealing. The implementation of segregation was rarely neat and rarely pushed forward by unanimous consent. Thus, in Richmond's baseball community, two clubs refused to meet the Union Club on the field. Two other clubs decided that the baseball field was an altogether fitting place to meet such an adversary.

As for the ever-obstinate Richmond Base Ball Club, its gallant stand (at least in the eyes of many white Richmonders) did not save it from decline. In the very same issue of the *Richmond Daily Dispatch* that summarized the Richmond–Union Club controversy, the paper announced that Alexander Babcock had formed his new baseball team.[57] It took only a matter of weeks for Babcock's all-star Pastime Base Ball Club to quickly surpass the Richmond Club for city supremacy. Although one might postulate on the relationship between the Richmond Club's rejection of intersectional baseball and Babcock's departure from the club, Babcock did not explain how the two events overlapped.

The Union Club, for its part, did not give up hope of finding matches in Richmond during the fall of 1866. The Union Club met and defeated the Spotswood Club (70–21), the Ashby Club (51–26), and the Olympic Club (39–36) in quick succession.[58] Then Alexander Babcock's newly formed nine agreed to a match game with the Union men. The championship of Richmond was at stake.[59] The Pastime-Union match stretched across several days in early-October 1866. Although newspaper accounts did not clarify the reason, either rain or darkness forestalled the ballplayers from playing the final innings, with the score standing at a lopsided 51–14 in favor of the Pastime. The game resumed on October 8, 1866, and no great miracle occurred for the Unionists. The final tally favored the Pastime club 135–33. It was, the *Times* noted, a "glorious victory for the Pastime." The Union Club would not take the city's championship.[60] The Union Club quickly issued a challenge for a rematch, but to no avail. Playing and defeating the Union Club once seemed enough for the Pastime men; they issued no response to the Union Club's November request for a game.[61]

Thus, white Richmond's efforts to make and keep a Southern version of baseball had won out, at least temporarily, on the field. Overall, through a variety of messages and conduits, Richmond baseball leaders had made clear that very different objectives existed for ballplayers in the South. Reunion was not a priority; preserving racial separation was paramount.

Chapter 3

Philadelphia

Baseball's Boomtown

Philadelphia's baseball community dwarfed those of Washington DC and Richmond. Philadelphia had more ballplayers than its mid-Atlantic neighbors and, by all indications, better ones. The Philadelphia Athletic, Bachelor, Keystone, Olympic, Quaker City, and West Philadelphia Base Ball Clubs were the most prominent of the hundreds of clubs that organized and played in Philadelphia during the 1860s and '70s. The *New York Clipper* touted the Philadelphia Athletic Base Ball Club as among the very top baseball organizations in the country, equal to the Atlantic Club of Brooklyn, the Mutuals of New York City, and the Red Stocking Club of Cincinnati.[1] In terms of black baseball, the Philadelphia Pythians, led by Octavius Catto, enjoyed considerable success as well. The Pythians hosted visiting clubs and traveled north into New York for games and south to Baltimore and Washington DC. The club won 90 percent of its contests. The *Philadelphia Sunday Mercury*, a paper that sprinkled racial slurs throughout its pages regularly, and the *Philadelphia Press* provided regular coverage of the city's black baseball clubs. Generally speaking, the city's white baseball community, led by the powerful Athletics, allowed black clubs to use many of the area's best fields. Relations between white and black clubs were mostly amicable and open, if far from balanced.

Thus, when Philadelphia's *North American* commemorated fifty years of baseball in the city in 1907, there was much to celebrate. The city had a unique position in the baseball world. The Philadelphia baseball community had recovered quickly from the Civil War. In fact, Philadelphia teams began engaging in interstate matches again as early as 1863. To celebrate this baseball past, the *North American* published a

3. Philadelphia's baseball landscape. A. Athletic base ball grounds (1865–1870), B. Athletic base ball grounds (1871–1877), C. Pythian meeting rooms, D. Octavius Catto's residence, E. Al Reach's base ball store, F. Keystone base ball grounds, G. Banneker Institute, H. Location of 1871 election riots, I. Orion base ball grounds, J. City hall, K. Liberty Hall, L. Commonwealth base ball grounds, M. W. Philadelphia base ball grounds, shaded area: highest black population. *Genealogy of Philadelphia County Subdivisions*, 2nd ed. (Philadelphia: Department of Records, 1966), 72.

lengthy article on Philadelphia baseball written by Al Reach, a former Philadelphia Athletic and, by the beginning of the twentieth century, a sporting-goods tycoon. In the article the former second baseman made sure to mention that the players of his day had been equal or superior to those playing at the beginning of the twentieth century. "Men hit as hard, caught as well and threw as accurately and strongly thirty years ago as they do today," Reach assured readers.[2]

Reach also looked back winsomely on the "wonderful elasticity" and "matchless possibilities" of baseball during the Reconstruction era. In noting these characteristics, Reach boasted about baseball's malleability and recalled how the game had vacillated between different rules and customs in its earliest years. On the seemingly simple issue of balls and strikes alone, for example, Reach had witnessed several significant changes. "First three balls gave a man his base, then we got it up to seven, only to reduce it gradually to four. One season we played four strikes; another year a player was credited with a hit every time he got a base on balls; we abolished the base for a hit with pitched ball then returned to it; we made a rule imposing a strike for a man on every unsuccessful attempt to bunt, and finally reached the foul-strike rule, the most important of all modern baseball legislation."[3] Although Reach's concept of "elasticity" has some historical merit, Philadelphia baseball, and indeed baseball in New York, Boston, and Chicago as well, did not evidence this elasticity for long when it came to racial matters. Rather, during the Reconstruction era, white clubs rapidly separated themselves from black ones. Philadelphia's baseball milieu, especially regarding black participation, became increasingly less fluid and elastic.[4]

The Leading Men

Both the Athletics and the Pythians won the majority of their games and were "champions" in the haphazard, pre–National League sense of the designation.[5] But Philadelphia's baseball community clearly revolved around the Athletics. The *New York Clipper* regularly gushed over the Athletics' prowess on the field and the club's service as an ambassador of the game: "There is no better plan of popularizing our national game than of interchanging visits among the clubs of principal cities in the Union. The Philadelphians were among the first to carry out this excellent method of popularizing baseball. . . . [A]mong the most determined and successful tourists of the fraternity may be included the Athletic Club, of Philadelphia, the acknowledged champion organization of the Keystone State."[6] The *Sunday Mercury* set its baseball calendar by the activities of the Athletics: "The season of baseball may be said to have fairly commenced in this city. The Athletics took the field yesterday afternoon, and played their inaugural game."[7]

Neighborhood by neighborhood, baseball clubs formed throughout Philadelphia. The *Philadelphia Press* estimated that some three hundred clubs had formed in the city by 1866. Most new clubs prominently identified themselves as residents of a particular city ward. The "Stable Rangers," for example, claimed the Fifth Ward as their home base. The "Blue Dusters" (Eleventh), "Nothing Like It" (Fourth), "Silver Spring" (Third), "Monitor" (Seventeenth), "Evelyn" (Third), "Mohawk" (Sixth), "Ereon" (Fourth), "Carrol" (Twentieth), "Norma" (Eleventh), and "Buffalo" (Seventh) Base Ball Clubs all saw fit to include their city address as part of their organizational announcements.[8] As in Richmond and Washington DC, baseball united the white male population even as it increased neighborhood pride on a club-by-club basis.

The Athletic Base Ball Club had organized on May 31, 1859. The founders were members of a musical society in the city. Colonel Thomas Fitzgerald took the most active role in running the club. Fitzgerald was the prominent editor of a Philadelphia daily—the *City Item*.[9] A political and social leader in Philadelphia, Fitzgerald counted the Radical Republican Charles Sumner as an intimate friend, and he campaigned for Abraham Lincoln in both 1860 and 1864. Although the Republican Party dominated in Philadelphia during Reconstruction, Fitzgerald's radicalism was unusual for the city. Under the leadership of Fitzgerald, the Athletics moved quickly through the ball games of the era, beginning with townball and then dabbling in cricket, before reorganizing on April 7, 1860, as a baseball club. The club won its first game, versus the Mercantile Club of Philadelphia, 75–26. Consistent success followed. In 1862 the Athletics merged with the United Club to increase its numbers. In 1863, with the Civil War raging on the battlefields of their own state, the Athletics made their first baseball tour.[10]

Fitzgerald carefully guided the rise of the Athletics and cultivated the club's reputation. The club shortly came to rival the Atlantics of Brooklyn as baseball's preeminent club. The Athletics' leadership recruited players judiciously. Only "gentlemen of the highest respectability" filled the roster. According to the *Clipper*, many of the Athletics held "positions of honor and trust in mercantile, mechanical, and professional life."[11] The Athletic players enjoyed celebrity status in Philadelphia.

The members of the Athletic, always popular with our citizens, were warmly greeted yesterday afternoon as they came on the field. Urchins not yet in their teens were delighted as their favorites "tumbled out" to take positions in which they have won honorable celebrity. ~There goes old Birky," exclaimed one. "Yes, but there's Al Reach," sings out a Reachite; "and yonder," cries out another, "is Smithy." . . . "But look at McBride, ain't he pitching," say half a dozen voices, as Dick lets himself out and sends the ball whizzing with that peculiar twist which we have heard extolled, oft and oft again.[12]

The 1865 Philadelphia city directory listed only one of the club's players in its annual "who's who" of the city: Elias "Hicks" Hayhurst (occupation—gentleman).[13] In coming years, however, directories would identify the Athletic players as clerks, entrepreneurs, and telegraphers, and also as working in "liquors" and "shippen."[14] Mostly, the Athletic players focused on baseball as their vocations.

The Athletics began their 1865 season by commemorating the recently assassinated Abraham Lincoln. The club issued a heartfelt resolution on April 17, 1865: "Resolved, that the nation has met with a heart-rending calamity in the death, by an assassin of its kindly, wise, merciful, much-loved Chief, Abraham Lincoln. Resolved, that we deeply sympathize with the family of the deceased. Resolved, that we have entire confidence in the intrepidity and patriotism of Andrew Johnson. Resolved, that we tender our earnest sympathies to Honorable William H. Seward and Family."[15] The resolution revealed a few truths about the men of the Athletic Club. They were Unionists, and most supported the Republican Party. In the years between 1866 and 1892, in fact, a series of Republican politicians would lead the Athletic Club. Hicks Hayhurst, Colonel Thomas Fitzgerald's successor, was a Republican who served on Philadelphia's city council in the 1870s.[16] Republicanism in Philadelphia, however, did not necessarily indicate support for black rights. Although Athletic Club members through the years would demonstrate many personal acts of kindness toward their black counterparts in Philadelphia, they did not aggressively champion progressive racial causes.

In 1866 the members of the Philadelphia Athletic Club, numbering more than four hundred, reelected Thomas Fitzgerald to his fifth year as president of the club. The Athletics had flourished under his leadership (a fact that Fitzgerald's own newspaper, the *City Item*, unabashedly pointed out). The club had won dozens of games, improved their field and clubhouse, and padded their treasury. Gross receipts for the 1865 season topped $5,000. Also in 1866, the Pennsylvania Legislature passed a special motion allowing for the incorporation of the Athletic Base Ball Club.[17] Because of its early success, the Athletic Club, unlike most other baseball clubs, had the financial resources to capitalize on the late- and postwar baseball boom. At the club's annual meeting in 1866, the club treasurer reported the team's recent financial history: a profit of $317.94 during the 1864 season—a sizable sum given the uncertainty surrounding the war and the presidential election—and $307.18 in profit in 1865. The club patted itself on the back in the 1866 report, noting that its ball field at Columbia and Seventeenth had been thoroughly upgraded and that "no club did so much towards extending the popularity of base ball, or made such rapid progress towards gaining the highest pinnacle of fame, as the Athletics did."[18] On the field the Athletics won thirty-nine of their forty-one contests in 1866, including several wins against prominent clubs from New York City.[19]

Making Room for Octavius Catto and the Pythians

The successes of the Athletic club, led by Thomas Fitzgerald and later Hicks Hayhurst, begot exclusivity. The Athletic Club supported black baseball to an extent but, not surprisingly, focused primarily on protecting its own reputation and financial resources. Throughout baseball's northern cities, unwritten rules set limits on the extent to which white baseball leaders could support their black counterparts. No overt declarations of racism came from the Athletic Base Ball Club, but the post–Civil War baseball culture of Philadelphia still featured an uneasy commingling of black and white clubs.

Philadelphia was not Richmond or Savannah, but neither was it a safe haven for African Americans. In 1862 Frederick Douglass had condemned the wartime racial attitudes of white Philadelphians. "There is not perhaps anywhere to be found a city in which prejudice against color is more rampant that in Philadelphia. . . . It has its white schools and its colored schools, its white churches and its colored churches, its white Christianity and its colored Christianity . . . and the line is everywhere tightly drawn between them."[20] Philadelphia had a history of racial violence. Whites in the city had fought to stop blacks from voting in the 1830s. And if anything, the city became more racially restrictive as the Civil War approached. In 1854, for example, the State of Pennsylvania determined that all school districts with more than twenty black students must provide segregated educational facilities.[21]

As the Pythian Base Ball Club emerged in Philadelphia's robust baseball community, competing for resources with clubs such as the Athletics, it also joined a myriad of black fraternal organizations trying to navigate through the opportunities and prejudices that post–Civil War Philadelphia held for black men. A long history of black men organizing existed in the city. More than one hundred black benevolent organizations operated in Philadelphia, some established as early as 1823. The African Methodist Episcopal (AME) Church, headquartered in Philadelphia, dominated the city's religious scene.[22] Additionally, fraternal societies such as the colored Masons and Odd Fellows were scattered throughout the city. These organizations provided tangible services such as insurance, burial benefits, and credit assistance to the city's black population. When the Pennsylvania State Equal Rights League held its convention in 1866, eleven auxiliary chapters represented Philadelphia alone.[23] Thus, black baseball clubs joined a community of organizations available to black men during the Reconstruction era.

The Philadelphia Pythian Base Ball Club organized on June 6, 1866. The club joined the black Excelsior Base Ball Club, which began play a few months earlier.[24] During the 1860s the Pythians, Excelsior, L'Overture, Active, Gegan, and Liberty Clubs faced off against each other on Philadelphia's black baseball circuit. Other organizations, such as the Buffalo Base Ball Club, were probably composed of black players as well, but incomplete reporting makes verifying their race difficult.[25] Through these half-dozen clubs, black men had proportional representation in Philadelphia's baseball community. Black residents never made up more than 4 percent of Philadelphia's total population during the Reconstruction years.[26] Though strikingly small, Philadelphia's percentage of black residents tripled that of its rival northern and midwestern cities. In terms of demographics, black baseball players faced a much different environment in the North than in the South. Boston, Brooklyn, Chicago, and New York City (baseball's most important cities) all shared nearly identical racial complexions. Each city's black population represented between 1.2 percent and 1.3 percent of the total city population.[27] There were, obviously, very few black residents or ballplayers as compared to the overwhelming white majority. Thus, black baseball meant something different in these cities than in Baltimore, Richmond, or New Orleans, where upwards of half the population was black.

The Pythians had first called themselves the "Institute," due to the fact that most of their players either taught or worked at the Banneker Institute of the City of Philadelphia. Organized in 1854 and named for Benjamin Banneker—an eighteenth-century black mathematician and astronomer—the Banneker Institute brought together black men regularly for literature readings and debates. The organization's motto touted the transformative benefits of education: "When men are in the pursuit of useful knowledge the noblest attributes of their nature are called into requisition."[28] The organization had close ties to the Institute for Colored Youth (ICY), which had been started by Quakers in 1832. The baseball club, however, dropped the uninspired "Institute" moniker before ever playing a game. Because most of the ballplayers were also members of the local Colored Knights of Pythias chapter, the baseball club became known as the Pythians.[29]

After organizing and playing a handful of games in 1866, the Pythian Base Ball Club began interclub play in earnest during the 1867 season. The club opened with a contest against the L'Overture Club. The Pythians started hot and showed no mercy, running up a score of 62–7 versus their hapless hosts. Octavius Catto (second basemen and team captain) and Joe Cannon led the way, scoring eight runs each. The lopsided score was not uncommon during this era of batter-friendly rules.[30] In covering the Pythian-L'Overture game, the *Sunday Mercury* made no mention of race. The paper did not need to. Although both clubs had only recently joined the city's baseball fraternity, the L'Overture name, undoubtedly a tribute to François-Dominique Toussaint L'Overture, who led the successful Haitian revolution of 1801, made the complexion of the players obvious. The name also hinted at an aggressively independent spirit among the black ballplayers.

The Pythians moved on quickly to the next challenge. One week after humbling the L'Overture, the Pythians took the field against the "champion" Excelsiors. The Pythians romped to a 39–16 victory in a game, described rather blandly by the *Sunday Mercury* as "interesting and exciting," played on the grounds of the Quaker City Base Ball Club.[31] A. J. Jones, a seaman by trade, led the Pythian effort with flawless fielding at third base and five runs scored.[32] The *Mercury* again left race out of its reporting.

The *Sunday Mercury*'s writers assumed that its baseball-savvy readers already knew the race of the Pythian and Excelsior Clubs. The *Sunday Mercury* had a long record of racist reporting, one that often mixed with baseball news. An 1868 quote on blacks and baseball ("Why would negroes make better baseball players than white men? Because they are better at whitewashing, and in hot weather, they play a stronger game.") was representative of the paper's derogatory reporting.[33] That the Pythians in a matter of weeks had risen to the top of the pecking order among black baseball clubs in Philadelphia reflected the ambitions of its leadership, particularly Octavius Catto.

Octavius V. Catto helped lead the Pythians both on and off the baseball field. As the captain and a middle infielder, Catto functioned as a modern-day player-manager, setting the batting order and positioning players around the diamond. Catto was particularly well suited for his leadership role. He was educated, passionate, and well known in Philadelphia. Catto had enjoyed as privileged an upbringing as a black man could hope for in the nineteenth-century United States. Born free in 1839, Catto was the son of Reverend William T. Catto, a Presbyterian minister in Charleston, South Carolina. In Philadelphia especially, where the AME Church had begun and thrived during the Reconstruction era, Catto's credentials as a "preacher's kid" prepared him for leadership.[34]

William Catto moved his family from South Carolina to Philadelphia when Octavius was only five years old. Though hardly a bastion of racial equality, Philadelphia held more opportunities for free blacks than did the slave society of Charleston. Schools for blacks existed in Philadelphia. Octavius enrolled at the Institute for Colored Youth. There Catto studied under the guidance of Ebenezer D. Basset, who would later become the minister to Haiti in 1869.[35] While a student Catto read the classics of Western literature and learned the fundamentals of mathematics. He also became an accomplished cricket player.

After graduation Catto floundered a bit. Still a teenager, Catto probed the possibilities the United States offered an educated black man. Catto left Philadelphia for nearly six years. Curiously, Catto spent much of his wandering period in slave country, some of it in Richmond. The conditions he encountered below the Mason-Dixon line probably did not shock Catto. In Richmond, like Philadelphia, discrimination commingled with opportunity. The realities of urban slavery in Richmond allowed for some manifestations of black autonomy.[36] Though slavery was no small technicality, Catto might well have noticed the depressingly similar conditions of free blacks and slaves in U.S. cities. In both conditions black men could experience some independence, but count on discrimination.

In 1859, at the age of twenty, Catto returned to Philadelphia and to the Institute for Colored Youth. There he taught literature, math, and classical languages. It was a noble cause, teaching the next generation of black men, many of whom left Philadelphia to further black education in other cities.[37] The Civil War then interrupted Catto's teaching and cricket-playing days. Catto enlisted in the Union army's Philadelphia colored militia. He also rallied other black men to the cause. A pamphlet circulating in Philadelphia in 1863, signed by Catto, made clear the young teacher's militancy: "This is our golden moment. The government of the United States calls for every Able-Bodied Colored Man to enter the Army for three years of service. . . . Men of Color! All Races of Men—the Englishman, the Irishman, the Frenchman, the German, the American have been called to assert their claim to freedom and a manly character, by appeal to the sword. . . . Men of color to Arms! Now or Never!"[38] Catto had a respectable military career. He rose to the position of major and inspector of the all-black Fifth Brigade. Catto, however, had little chance of becoming a hero. He experienced neither the danger nor the excitement of the battlefield. He did not join the thousands of black soldiers who fought and died in support of the Union cause. Instead, Catto and most of his regiment of black Philadelphians remained encamped in the city's suburbs. There they waited anxiously for the call to action that never came.[39]

Philadelphia's colored regiments received no bounties for their service, as white regiments did. The black men earned just ten dollars per month and daily rations. Additionally, the mere presence of black men in uniform sparked insecurities among the white population, even in Philadelphia—a mecca of prewar abolitionism. This white paranoia caused humiliating slights for Catto and his men. "The Negro regiment drilled and camped outside of the city was forced to sneak in civilian's clothes to the train that was to carry them to the battle-field, lest they should be mobbed for fighting for their country," the *New National Era* reported.[40] Still, Catto made the best of the situation. Located in the Philadelphia suburbs, Catto acquired the military skill of passing free time. He became a baseball player.[41]

In an 1865 speech to the Union League Association, a prosuffrage organization of which Catto founded a Philadelphia chapter, Catto voiced his vision for the future: "It is the duty of every man, to the extent of his interest and means to provide for the immediate improvement of the four or five million of ignorant and previously dependent laborers, who will be thrown upon society by the reorganization of the Union. It is for the good of the nation that every element of its people, mingled as they are, shall have a true and intelligent conception of the allegiance due to the established powers."[42] A devout Christian, Catto coupled his baseball activity with service as the corresponding secretary of the Pennsylvania State Equal Rights League—a group determined to desegregate the streetcars in Philadelphia. Catto also belonged to the Colored Knights of Pythias, Republican Party, Fourth Ward Black Political Club, Franklin Institute, Philadelphia Library Company, and Union League. Catto tried to chip away at the racial barriers of academia. He joined the all-white Academy of Music, only to be singled out when he tried to attend a lecture.[43]

In addition to his credentials and activism, Octavius Catto's personal charisma gained him leadership opportunities. Catto was, to put it simply, well liked. News of his engagement, for example, brought heartfelt congratulations from well-wishers across the country. "It filled my heart," Bill H. Wormley wrote from South Carolina, "with joy unspeakable when I saw that some fair young lady had won the gallant heart of our most noble Catto."[44] Catto's wealth distinguished him from the majority of the city's black population. In a city where much of the black population fought off (or succumbed to) poverty on a daily basis, Catto achieved relative financial security. The Banneker Institute provided a relatively healthy and stable salary.[45]

Catto and the Pythians toed the line between pushing for equality and making the best of a bigoted environment. The Pythians tried to claim the city as their own. As the club's reputation grew, hosting visitors became an important part of the Pythians' mission. Philadelphia's press took notice of the club's rising fortunes. By July 1867 the *Sunday Mercury* trumpeted the Pythians' winning record: "As almost every reader of the *Mercury* knows, the Pythian Club, of this city, stands at the head of all colored organization here-abouts."[46] Members of the Alert Base Ball Club of Washington DC invited themselves to visit Philadelphia. Leaders from the two clubs set the Pythian-Alert match for July 6, 1867. Catto oversaw preparations himself, securing use of the city's best fields for the game and arranging suitable overnight accommodations for the visitors. A week before the match Catto boasted of his accomplishments to the Alert Club: "We have secured the grounds of the Athletic Base Ball Club and all conveniences (the best in the city) have been put at our disposal."[47] Catto also arranged for Hicks Hayhurst, a member of the Athletics, to serve as umpire for the match.

A look at the club's finances reveals that the Pythians had the financial wherewithal to rent a plot of land for a ball field, had such an opportunity presented itself. The club spent several hundred dollars in 1867 providing food and entertainment for visiting clubs. The prominent white clubs of the city—the Athletic and Olympic Clubs—leased grounds from the city (the Water Department in particular) at favorable rates. The Pythians, however, never received such an opportunity. The "champion" Pythians relied on fitting their schedule around the games of the city's white ball clubs. This scenario foreshadowed the problems teams in the Negro Leagues faced in the twentieth century, when black ball clubs usually played in Major League stadiums, often as victims of predatory rental rates, when white tenants took their road trips.[48]

There were enough fields to go around, but not all were open to black clubs. Within a four-mile radius of the Pythian meeting rooms, at least five ball fields existed to which the Pythians never gained access. Most prominently, the Keystone Base Ball Field, at Eleventh and Wharton, was located less than a half mile away from the Pythian headquarters; the Pythians rarely used it. The problem with the Keystone Field was that it was located on the south side of Bainbridge Avenue. The street served as an informal line of racial demarcation between Philadelphia's Irish and black populations. The Pythians played many of their games in Camden, New Jersey, across the Delaware River.[49]

The Alerts' visit to Philadelphia demonstrated that the Pythian Base Ball Club functioned as a conduit for African American connectedness. Indeed, the Pythians' entire organizational structure pointed to a broader role in the black community than simply fielding a baseball club. The Pythians used baseball as a means to bring together successful young black men. While the Pythian Club's "service" (baseball) was unique, the Pythians actually mirrored the organizational structures of the other black fraternal organizations in the city. Strong leadership, a clearly defined hierarchy, and meticulous record keeping allowed the Pythians to function efficiently. The Pythians' voluminous store of records (letters, receipts, box scores, and the like) makes it obvious that the club took baseball seriously and guarded its reputation closely. Record keeping ensured accountability. When, for example, treasurer Thomas Charnock bought a baseball, the club recorded the price ($1.20) and noted the date Mr. Charnock received his reimbursement. There would be no financial scandals. The club secretary also took special care to represent the club well and to build relationships with other organizations. Letters took on a formal, diplomatic tone: "The action of the Club requires me to perform the pleasant duty of tendering you this letter of acceptance with the suggestion that, if it should be consistent with your inclinations and arrangements, the game be played on Saturday, the 6th of July. Hoping that the suggestion may meet your approbation, I am very respectfully your obedient servant."[50] Most fraternal clubs of the period took similarly formal and diligent approaches to governing their affairs.

Decisions on whether to accept a match challenge, such as the one issued by the Alerts, came from the Pythian leadership. The Pythians annually elected a president, vice president, secretary, and treasurer, as well as a governing board. This hierarchy was also nearly universal in the fraternal world. During the 1867 season, the Pythians' first as a fully functioning club, the club chose James Purnell as president, Raymond J. Burr as vice president, Jacob C. White as secretary, and Thomas Charnock as treasurer. Jefferson Cavens, Henry B. Bascom, and Joel Selsey made up the governing board, and Octavius V. Catto served as the field captain.[51]

The officers of the Pythians—like Babcock, Fitzgerald, Gorman, and Young—were more socialites and social activists than baseball players. Men who had no business catching or throwing a ball in front of an audience joined up for social reasons and served the Pythian Club where their talents fit. The club's first president, James Purnell, for example, never took the ball field for the Pythians. His name, in fact, did not appear on any playing roster, despite the fact that the club fielded four "nines," in 1867 and 1868.[52] Instead, Purnell focused on administrative tasks. The Pythians and black baseball fit into Purnell's broader portfolio of activism. Even as he acted as the Pythian Base Ball Club president in 1867, Purnell also founded the Liberty Hall Association, an organization meant to encourage a "spirit of self-improvement" among "colored" Philadelphians.[53] Of the board members, only Jefferson Cavens played well and regularly. Cavens manned first base for the club's first nine and was among its leading batters and run scorers.[54]

Membership in the Pythian Club required sacrifice and commitment. The Pythians demanded service from their men, primarily through participation in one or more of the club's various committees. These committees met regularly and produced a plethora of thoroughly mundane reports. Committees formed to secure playing grounds and meeting rooms, to perform financial audits, as well as to take care of tasks such as selecting uniforms. The challenge from the Alert Club sprang the Pythians' Committee on Reception into action. After weeks of feverish preparation, the committee had doled out $78.26 to fund a lavish reception for the Alert Club. The Pythians also paid for the Alerts' boarding expenses—a measure not uncommon in the years immediately following the Civil War.[55] From a purely fiscal standpoint, it was an outlandish sum. By way of context, the Pythians paid the Banneker Institute $6.25 a month to rent a room, $5.50 for a dozen bats and a ball, and about $50.00 to outfit the entire club in uniforms.[56] But the reception expenditure demonstrated the Pythians' ascendant social priorities. For the Alert Club reception, the Pythian Committee on Reception dutifully filed a detailed expense report demonstrating exactly where the money had gone:

Provided board for them [Alert] at Mrs. Sebastian's. Escorted them from and to the Depot. Escorted them from and to the Base Ball Grounds. Provided entertainment on Friday and Saturday evenings. Provided silk badges with the name of the Club thereon.

THE BILL:

Ice cream, Raspberries and Plain Cream—11.75
Six pair spring chickens—6.75
1 Al a mode—6.00
30 lbs ham and 5 beef tongues—10.40
Dish Hire—4.38
Knives and Forks—2.70
1 box segars—3.00
1 Gal claret Wine
4 doz rasped rolls—4.20
Groceries—2.21
Oranges and Ice—1.00
Cheese pickles and Butter—1.65
Bar Fare—6.17
Mrs. Furmans services and rent of 2 rooms—9.25
Ribbon for badges—2.80
Printing—3.50
Total—$78.26[57]

The Pythians apparently counted the evening worth the cost in order to form bonds between Philadelphia and Washington DC's "best" black men. The Pythians demonstrated convincingly to their visitors that in Philadelphia, a black man could play on the city's best field (albeit with the white club's permission) and enjoy a luxurious banquet. The Pythians' hosting prowess paralleled the customs of elite white baseball clubs, many of which similarly placed great emphasis on the duty of social hosting.[58]

Unfortunately, the Alert-Pythian contest did not live up to the extravagant preparations. The clubs battled back and forth in a spirited contest for four innings before a summer thunderstorm sent the players and spectators scurrying for cover. With the game starting and stopping several times, the Pythians recorded the game as a 23–21 victory, while the *Mercury* and *Clipper* settled on a score of 21–18 in favor of the Alert Base Ball Club. The discrepancy arose due to the rain stoppages. After four complete innings the score stood 21–18 for the Alert. The Pythians led off the fifth inning with a flurry of hits and runs, but before the Alert could even get three outs rain stopped the game. Thus, the score reverted back to what it had been at the end of the fourth inning, giving the Alert Base Ball Club a disputed victory. Umpire Hayhurst had no choice but to cancel the game's remaining innings.[59]

Despite the abbreviated action on the field, the endeavor of bringing together the men of the Alert and Pythian Clubs had been significant for Philadelphia. The *Sunday Mercury* exhibited a hesitant enthusiasm for the event that mirrored the sentiments of many white Philadelphians. The paper in its reporting affectionately termed the Pythians "our fellows" and covered the game with the same attention prominent Athletic or Olympic contests received. But there was awkwardness in the *Mercury*'s fawning. After calling the Pythians "our fellows" in passing, for example, the editors of the paper felt it necessary to clarify for the readers that "by that we mean the Pythians." Such support could not, during the early years of Reconstruction in Philadelphia, be assumed.[60] The treatment of black men—whether as a members of baseball clubs or not—remained in flux.

Paternalism and Deference

The Pythian-Alert game would not have taken place at all had the Athletics refused the Pythians permission to use their field. Because the Pythians did not lease or own their own grounds, plans for matches such as the one with the Alerts could be undone at the last minute due to a scheduling change by the owners of the grounds. By all indications, the Pythians maintained excellent relations with the Athletic Base Ball Club. Indeed, they had to. The Pythians used the Athletic ballpark regularly, and Fitzgerald and Hayhurst served as umpires in Pythian contests on more than one occasion. Hayhurst's support in particular was crucial. At one time or another the president of the Athletics, president of the Pennsylvania Association of Base Ball Players, and member of Philadelphia's city council, Hayhurst had the respect of the city's baseball and political leaders alike. His relationship with the Pythians, and the limits of that relationship as demonstrated in the next chapter, went a long way toward determining the Pythians' place in Philadelphia baseball.[61] Beyond Hayhurst the Athletic players in general appreciated the efforts of their black counterparts. For the Alert game the best Athletics—Dick McBride, John Radcliff, John Sensenderfer, and Weston Fisler—all made it out to the field.

Although in a less tangible manner than the ballpark struggle, the white press also played a significant role in determining the Pythians' place in the baseball spectrum. At times the Pythian Club had its accomplishments belittled by paternalist reporting, Philadelphia's white press treated the Pythians and other black clubs with nearly equal parts paternalism, condescension, and genuine affection. The *Mercury*, for example, frequently emphasized the mentorship of white players to their black counterparts, a relationship that virtually no corroborating evidence exists to support. "The experts [Athletics] were present and by their advice kept the Pythians down to their work," the *Sunday Mercury* reported of the Alert-Pythian match, as if the Pythians might have lost interest without the Athletics' guidance.[62] Because the Athletics never consented to a match against the Pythians or even took the practice field with their black counterparts, the contention that the white ballplayers were the experts and the black ballplayers the novices was simply assumed rather than verified.

Not all white press reports on black baseball were negative. Press paternalism often looked, well, paternal. Exhibiting a vacillating opinion on racial equality, Philadelphia's newspapers often countered racist reporting by celebrating the accomplishments of black clubs. The *Sunday Mercury*, which once bemoaned the "ignorance, squalor, degradation, and brutal instincts of the African," also jealously protected the interests of local black clubs from out-of- town criticism and called for financial support for black clubs' tours.[63]

In 1867 the *Mercury* took up the causes of both the Excelsior and the Pythian Clubs. After the Excelsior nine visited New York City for a match, the New York papers criticized their behavior. "The New York Papers, as usual," the *Mercury* reported, "are in a muddle concerning the Excelsior (colored) Club, of this city, which last week, defeated a colored club belonging to that city. They apply the title of Champions to the Excelsiors, and then abuse and ridicule them, after the fashion of New York."[64] The *Mercury* pointed out indignantly that the Pythians, not the Excelsior, were the colored champions of Philadelphia. The paper had no doubt that the Pythian Club would represent its native city well, both on and off the field: "Should [the Pythians] ever conclude to visit New York, an opportunity will be afforded Philadelphia defamers to see a well behaved set of gentlemen."[65]

The key to the strange balance of integration and segregation in Philadelphia's baseball community seemed to rest on the "proper" behavior of the black clubs. The Pythians had to exhibit proper deference to their white counterparts in order to maintain harmonious relationships. Proper requests were to be followed with proper gratitude. Thus, glowing thank-you letters went out almost immediately after a game played at the Athletic facility or umpired by a member of the Athletics. Following the Alert contest, for example, the Pythians sent a letter meant to "impress the earnestness with which we all unite in thanking the members of your Organization." The letter concluded with a dose of Victorian flattery: "Permit me, My Dear Sir, to express on behalf of the Pythians an ardent desire that the Athletics may ever in the future, as they have always in the past sustain the well earned title of Champions of our national game."[66] Hicks Hayhurst received a similarly gushing note of appreciation for his service as umpire. These regular acts of deference were the price of using the best field in the city.

In short, race "rules" governing baseball fit the description of Philadelphia's "social intercourse," put forth by W. E. B. DuBois some thirty years later. The patterns of interaction between white and blacks had been established in the immediate postslavery years. As DuBois explained, unwritten rules governed relationships such as the one between the Pythians and Athletics. "If [a black man] meets a life long white friend on the street, he is in a dilemma," DuBois explained. "If he does not greet the friend he is put down as boorish and impolite; if he does greet the friend he is liable to be flatly snubbed. . . . White friends may call on him, but he is scarcely expected to call on them, save strictly for business matters."[67] The black-white relationship as evidenced through the relationship between the Pythian and Athletic Base Ball Clubs was neither hostile nor completely one-sided. Genuine affection and camaraderie existed, but proper order had to be respected. This order included a built-in level of dependency on the part of the Pythians due to the fact that white ball clubs controlled the baseball fields and white men dominated the city's press.

A Battle for Control of the Athletics

The racial climate of Philadelphia's baseball community changed dramatically in 1866 due to a leadership struggle within the Athletic Club. Because of the Athletics' prominence, the president of the club wielded significant influence in the broader baseball world. Thomas Fitzgerald, a founding member of the Athletics, had enjoyed this influential position from 1860 until 1866. Then, rather suddenly, the Athletics forced Colonel Fitzgerald to resign from his position as club president in 1866. Hicks Hayhurst, an Athletic Club board member and officer, eventually took over. Although the details surrounding the divorce are murky, one thing is certain: the move had little to do with the club's performance on the baseball field. The Athletics had risen steadily to the top of baseball's hierarchy, and Fitzgerald's credentials as a baseball man were above reproach. The *New York Clipper* had publicly lauded Fitzgerald and the *City Item* in 1865 as key figures in Philadelphia's shift from cricket to baseball and in making Philadelphia a leading baseball city. "The breaking out of the rebellion, however, drew off much of the material forming the principal cricket clubs, and then baseball began to come in to vogue, the influence of the Athletic Club and the efforts of Col. Fitzgerald of the *City Item*, Col. Moore and others being greatly beneficial in bringing the national game of ball of America prominently before the community as a recreation worthy of the heartiest encouragement."[68] In addition to his duties with the Athletics, Fitzgerald served as president of the National Association of Base Ball Players in 1863. In serving in this capacity, Fitzgerald called to order and facilitated the National Association's pivotal discussion on adopting the modern "fly game." When the famous Brooklyn Atlantics and New York Mutuals played games, Fitzgerald was often asked to umpire.[69]

Buffeting his service as a baseball leader, Thomas Fitzgerald had connections throughout Philadelphia society. He published and edited the *City Item*. Fitzgerald served on the executive board of the Philadelphia public schools. He was also a popular playwright, whose productions regularly packed Philadelphia's theaters. Fitzgerald's *Light at*

Last proved so popular at Philadelphia's Arch Street Theatre, in fact, that the Broadway theaters soon came calling. As an artist Fitzgerald espoused populism over elitist exclusion; he argued that arts were for the masses and that music should be included in the curriculum of Philadelphia's public high schools.[70] And in addition to publishing the *City Item* from 1846 well into the 1870s, Fitzgerald served as foreman of Philadelphia's grand jury and as the "superintendent of bonded warehouses" for Philadelphia's port authority.[71] Thus, Fitzgerald before, during, and after his ouster from the Athletics was well known and respected in Philadelphia—exactly the type of man that the burgeoning gentlemen's sport targeted for inclusion.

Fitzgerald's forced resignation came on the heels of the Athletics' membership reelecting Fitzgerald to the club's presidency in 1865 and 1866, without even a single dissenting vote. Shortly after his 1866 reelection, however, an incident or series of incidents, the exact nature of which is difficult to reconstruct, occurred that led to calls for Fitzgerald's ouster. As a part of the equation that led to Fitzgerald's dismissal, some members of the Athletics seemed to oppose the machine-politician manner in which Fitzgerald used his influence as the publisher of the *City Item* and as the president of the Athletics. Fitzgerald certainly knew how to trade favors; most men of his stature did.

In the months following Fitzgerald's ouster, details about the rift gradually seeped out through the press. Politics oozed beneath the surface of the conflict. Fitzgerald used the *City Item* to suggest that pettiness on the part of jealous club leaders caused the ouster. The *Sunday Mercury*, already a rival of the Republican-leaning *City Item*, became the mouthpiece of the Athletics. The *Sunday Mercury*'s Democratic allegiance had taken an acrimonious tone even during the Civil War, calling Lincoln "the elongated baboon at Washington. . . . The lank, lean, filthy-mouthed, slab-sided, six foot thing that disgraces the seat once honored by Washington."[72] The Athletics, through the *Mercury*, argued that Fitzgerald's behavior (left unspecified) forced the gentlemanly club no choice but to formally expel him, which was done shortly after Fitzgerald had resigned from the club's presidency.

The war of words that erupted in the Philadelphia newspapers reflected poorly on both parties. Fitzgerald fired the first shot on May 5, 1866, by printing the *Wilkes' Spirit of the Times* announcement on the Athletics' situation: "Col. Fitzgerald, publisher of the *City Item*, Philadelphia, and for a long time the efficient president of the Athletic Club, of that city, has, we regret to learn, resigned the latter position, to which he was lately re-elected without a dissenting voice."[73] Fitzgerald reprinted the same article in his next issue as well, making it clear that he had supporters in the baseball world. Fitzgerald then went on the offensive when he filed a complaint with the NABBP, reporting that the Athletics paid their players, a charge that may have been true and still held some moral weight in 1866. Next he charged the Athletics with degrading baseball's reputation by fielding a team with members who had been arrested for drunkenness.[74]

The *Sunday Mercury* shed any vestige of impartiality in response. Referring to Fitzgerald as "Fitzitem" or "Dead Beat" (often shortened to D. B.), the *Mercury* accused Fitzgerald of a history of "blackmailism and dead-beatism."[75] The *Sunday Mercury* offered the following as an account of why Fitzgerald had been relieved of his duties.

When he [Fitzgerald] visited New York in the spring, and sent a demand to Burton's Theatre, in that city, for *twelve free tickets and a private box,* the bearer of the refusal was told by the angry editor that when Mr. Burton came to Philadelphia he would give him *fits.* Mr. B. has visited Philadelphia, and he finds that "*Fits* means blackguardism." . . . [W]e have full and interesting particulars concerning the *modus operandi,* by which these things are "did" . . . together with the number of free carriage rides that the great D. B. indulged in and which the Board of Control are respectfully asked to verify. . . . The Athletic Club—composed of gentlemen—was ever the subject of attack while this fellow was their President. They were frequently made acquainted with his manner of doing things, and were made to blush more than once by knowledge of his contemptible meanness, as practiced upon those whom they recognized as friends.[76]

These charges, while filled with moral indignation, could not have been the entire story. If indeed Fitzgerald liked to be treated as a dignitary, requesting free tickets and taking complimentary carriage rides, he fit the norm among baseball's and society's leading gentlemen.

Only in the final line of the *Mercury*'s list of charges is there a hint at what might have been at the root of the fight—Fitzgerald's "meanness" toward the "friends" of the Athletic Club. The Athletic Club certainly had many friends and admirers. The club prided itself on being instrumental to the nationalization of baseball. The Athletics traveled throughout the Northeast especially, to both cities and rural hamlets, "with the view of extending the popularity of their favorite game."[77] Regarding Fitzgerald's alleged "meanness," the colonel's *City Item* certainly provided a ready vehicle. In the weeks before the Athletic-Fitzgerald rift became public, the *City Item* published a number of editorials that Southerners, whites committed to racial segregation, and political conservatives would have considered offensive (or, to put it more simply, "mean"). In February 1866 Fitzgerald denounced conservative Copperheads as traitors. In March he urged Philadelphians to support the Freedmen's Bureau in their quest to protect former slaves. In April, just weeks before splitting with the Athletics, Fitzgerald predicted the collapse of the Democratic Party. And a week later Fitzgerald argued for the passing of the Civil Rights Bill of 1866.[78]

Many members of the Philadelphia baseball community—a community led by the Athletics—professed either subtle or overt kinship with the South. The Athletic-championing *Sunday Mercury* expressed such fondness consistently. That the *Mercury*, which had called Lincoln a baboon and derided ideas of racial equality, lavishly supported the Athletics suggests that the majority of Athletic Club members had similarly conservative views on matters of race and Reconstruction. Fitzgerald, in contrast, had no sympathy for those who sympathized with the South during the war or agreed with its values following the fight. Fitzgerald had a long record as a partisan political organizer and as a proponent for black equality. During the war he spoke at dozens of "grand rallies for the Union." Fitzgerald also denounced those organizations that expressed sympathy for the wartime South in his *City Item*, demeaning the Philadelphia Keystone Club, for example, as a "pro-slavery, rebel-pitying, Union-moaning, Government hating, broken-hearted, mutual admiration society of the false Democrats of Philadelphia."[79] In light of Fitzgerald's personal ledger of baseball and societal credentials and the Athletics' consistent success on the field and financially, it is plausible to assume that the Athletics ousted Colonel

Fitzgerald at least in part for his radical views on race relations. It was Fitzgerald's views on race in particular that distinguished him from his ball-playing brethren in Philadelphia more than any other issue.

Fitzgerald had no problem defending himself. Considered by Charles Sumner to be one of the finest orators and debaters in the nation, Fitzgerald poked fun and jabbed at his former team. He had the *City Item* at his disposal. Fitzgerald dashed off several letters to the *Sunday Mercury*, calling for the A's to recognize their mistakes. To the Athletic Club, he wrote: "Repent of your folly, and return to the arms of the one who has ever considered you in the light of a loving parent, and who weeps as he signs himself, Fitzitem."[80] In the midst of this verbal back-and-forth, multiple fractures become evident. It was a case of Fitzgerald versus the Athletic Club, the *City Item* versus the *Sunday Mercury*, and a social radical versus an increasingly conservative white baseball community.

The Thomas Fitzgerald–Athletic Club power struggle most likely centered on Fitzgerald's commitment to aggressive race reform and the Athletic Club's concern over not alienating the city's pro-South citizens. Fitzgerald's *City Item* prided itself on challenging inequality. The paper promoted universal suffrage: "There is one certain remedy for this danger [Union sympathizers losing political power], and that is found in universal suffrage—a measure which has become essential to the preservation of the rights of loyal white and black men."[81] Whereas the passage of the Fifteenth Amendment in 1869 would decide the issue, Philadelphia in 1866 was still fiercely divided on the topic. More broadly, Fitzgerald's motto for the *City Item*, that the paper be "constantly aggressive in all that relates to the equality of Man before the Law and ever striving to break down barriers of Prejudice and Caste," undoubtedly unnerved much of Philadelphia's conservative population.[82]

After the Civil War ended the *City Item* had also defended blacks on the all-important labor question. "We are continually informed that the negro will not work unless he is obliged to," Fitzgerald mused. "Does it ever occur to these captious critics that in this respect a Sambo shows himself to be 'a man and a brother,' that in this respect, if in no other, he resembles the white man?"[83] The Athletics' mouthpiece, the *Sunday Mercury*, in contrast, pushed for the colonization of the United

States' black population as late as 1874. "It might not be right or kind, or even possible to compel the whole black population of this country to emigrate; but if they would go willingly, it would be a blessed thing for them, as well as for the whites."[84] Politically, the Sunday Mercury, like most papers, did not straddle the partisan fence. The paper championed Pennsylvania Democrats for unmasking "the Federal and State miscegenationists." The paper also had had no patience for the Radicals, calling Thaddeus Stevens, for example, the "son of Lucifer and brother of Beelzebub."[85] Fitzgerald's friend Charles Sumner elicited similar reactions.

In early-September 1866 the Athletics released an official resolution explaining why Fitzgerald had been expelled from the club. The explanation came after a summer of squabbling back and forth between the two parties. The resolution still left much unexplained. The Athletic Club, though, expressed its distaste for the volleys that Fitzgerald had launched, via the City Item, at the Athletic Club after his removal as president. But regarding Fitzgerald's original sins, the Athletic Club rather opaquely resolved that it had been Fitzgerald's ignorance of "the decencies of social intercourse, the privacy of business relations and the sanctity of domestic life" that led the club to split ways with its founder.[86]

As 1866 drew to a close the Sunday Mercury continued to pound away at Fitzgerald. In additional to slandering Fitzgerald and the City Item generally, the Mercury posited specifically that Fitzgerald lost out on his leadership position because of his associations. To be a Sumner or Lincoln man in Philadelphia raised eyebrows. Additionally, Fitzgerald's ties to John W. Forney (nicknamed "the dead duck" by Andrew Johnson after publicly criticizing the president) drew particular contempt. Losing any sense of decorum, the Mercury lashed out at Fitzgerald, labeling him "the most obsequious 'dorg' that ever licked the great Dead Duck's boots."[87] Forney, for his part, had served in a variety of civil service and appointed posts in the Lincoln administration. He was, to many, a respected power broker. As secretary of the Senate, Forney would go on to lead the charge for Johnson's impeachment. The Sunday Mercury, undoubtedly voicing the opinions of many Athletics and Philadelphians, felt association with a man such as Forney made Fitzgerald unfit for his esteemed position with the A's.

The struggle to oust Thomas Fitzgerald from the Athletic Club embodied elements of the broader Reconstruction-era struggle in Philadelphia. Fitzgerald's stance on race relations was his most controversial view and his most potent liability in the racially conservative baseball community. It probably cost him. The level of fervency behind one's support for racial progress could not surpass certain unstated ceilings without drawing a considerable backlash. It might have been acceptable for Fitzgerald to editorialize that blacks should have some civil rights in the South, for example. But to tout universal suffrage in the years immediately following the Civil War, for Philadelphia as well as the South, crossed an important divide. In what turned out to be a win for those white baseball leaders opposed to black participation, Fitzgerald likely lost his position of authority in baseball because of his commitment to racial equality.

Historians have appreciated Thomas Fitzgerald for his role in growing the game of baseball and for his efforts to foster integrated baseball play (to be discussed subsequently).[88] He has been cited as the leader of the ascendant Athletic Base Ball Club during the Civil War era. Some histories even suggest that Fitzgerald might have been part of the Olympic Town Ball Club (Philadelphia's oldest baseball club) and helped facilitate the Athletics' trip through Europe in 1874.[89] What has been overlooked, though, is how Fitzgerald's removal as president of the Athletic Base Ball Club in 1866 fit into a broader pattern of events. The Civil War ended. Baseball boomed. Many baseball leaders like Henry Chadwick sought to nationalize the game. Southern baseball clubs, however, as evidenced by the "we are Southerners" letter, resisted these efforts. Arthur Gorman won the presidency of the National Association of Base Ball Players precisely because it was thought that his conservative credentials would heal sectional divides that plagued baseball's growth. And then Thomas Fitzgerald—a successful baseball organizer, a civic leader, a baseball-friendly voice in the press—was removed. That a radical like Fitzgerald was ousted from one of baseball's most prominent leadership posts in 1866 cannot be counted a coincidence. The white leadership of the game sought a conservative path; Fitzgerald did not fit. Thus, Colonel Fitzgerald, who might have been Branch Rickey some eighty years before the actual trailblazer, found himself knocked out of white baseball's upper echelon.

PART 2

Sorting Out New
Divisions, 1867–69

Chapter 4

Philadelphia

Setting Precedent

On October 16, 1867, Raymond J. Burr, vice president of the Philadelphia Pythians, found himself inside a stately Harrisburg courthouse petitioning for baseball's integration. His was the only black face in the chambers. Thomas Fitzgerald, due to his removal from the Athletic Base Ball Club during the prior season, did not attend the assembly. Burr had journeyed to the state capital from Philadelphia to make his case before members of the Pennsylvania Association of Amateur Base Ball Players (PAABBP) that the Pythians—one of the nation's most prominent black baseball clubs—should be granted full membership in the organization. The Pythians had recently completed their remarkably successful 1867 season, one filled with victories over nearly all comers and trumpeted by laudatory headlines in Philadelphia's *Sunday Mercury* and *Inquirer* newspapers. The club followed proper protocol and traveled to the convention to apply for inclusion into the state baseball association.[1]

By attending the meeting Burr took part in an early baseball tradition. Baseball players in the 1860s and '70s congregated nearly as much as they played. Local, statewide, and national conventions brought ballplayers together frequently. The game's rules were still negotiable, and league affiliations had yet to take hold; thus, there was much to talk about.[2] The gatherings mimicked the political motions of Reconstruction and of most fraternal organizations: the assembled ballplayers elected officers, committees debated proposals, and delegates lobbied for their causes. The proceedings generally featured more rambling speeches than definitive decisions. At the PAABBP convention of 1867, however, Raymond Burr's mere presence determined that the gathering would produce more than backslapping and self-congratulatory motions. By presenting the formal membership application of the Pythians, Burr forced Pennsylvania's white baseball community to make a statement regarding the burgeoning game's policy on race.

Investing in Black Baseball

The backstory to Burr's visit to Harrisburg in October began during the summer of 1867. The Pythians played well and often. The July visit of the Washington DC–based Alert Club marked the beginning of the Pythians' successful, but expensive, season. As demonstrated, the club spent heavily to host and play the best black clubs the Northeast had to offer. The Mutual BBC of Washington DC followed on the heels of the Alerts' visit to Philadelphia. Mutual secretary George D. Johnson made first contact with the Pythians in early-April 1867 to express his admiration for the Pythian Club. "The Mutual Base Ball Club of Washington DC. . . has instructed me to address you a friendly note, congratulatory of the high position you, as an organization have attained in our National Game," Johnson wrote.[3] The Pythians' Henry Bascom responded with a formal challenge. Hosting again proved to be a costly endeavor for the Pythians, with the reception bill totaling $58.16. But the visit was a success for both clubs. The match received a bevy of press coverage, led by that of the *Sunday Mercury*. The Pythian Club, the paper had crowed in anticipation of the match, "stands at the head of all colored organizations."[4] The *New York Clipper* also reported on the game, providing its baseball-obsessed readers with the final score and statistics for the contest.[5] Even the *Philadelphia Inquirer*, rarely attuned to baseball action, reported on the matchup, encouraging fans to attend the "interesting and exciting game."[6]

As for the contest itself, a large crowd (probably several thousand) swarmed the Athletics' grounds. Members of the Athletic Club, Dick McBride and Wes Fisler among them, again came out to see the Pythians play ball. After nine intense innings, the score stood at 44–43, with the Mutual having toppled the hometown club. The *Mercury* again, though, took up the Pythians' case and objected to the loss. The umpire had overstepped his bounds, the paper argued, by haphazardly calling strikes and balls in an effort to speed up the game. No rule at this time compelled the umpire to make such calls. But on this day the umpire, a "Mr. Moore" of the Athletics, must have had other business to which to attend. Rather than the players deciding the outcome, a called strike ended the game with a Pythian stranded on third base. Even more strangely, Mr. Moore, whom the *Mercury* derided as "nervously incompetent," refused the Mutuals' motion to change pitchers. In this game, on this day, one pitcher would have to do. And thus, under these strange circumstances, the Pythians suffered their first (and only, it would turn out) official loss of the 1867 season.[7]

After tangling with Washington DC's two ball clubs, the Pythians rested for the remainder of July. Perhaps the all-consuming and expensive visits of the Alert and Mutual Clubs required a vacation of sorts. Or maybe the stifling July weather caused the pause in the schedule. Because teams in the 1860s simply scheduled one match at a time, this midseason break did not disturb any prearranged matches. After a couple of weeks, the Pythians reemerged. The Alert and Mutual Base Ball Clubs insisted that the Pythians travel to Washington DC for a visit.

Although the hosting club took care of lodging and feeding visiting clubs, the Pythians still bore some significant expenses when it traveled. The train passage had to be secured. Uniforms needed mending, and the equipment had to be in good order. Such expenses went beyond the Pythians' normal operating fund. The Pythians sent out fund-raising letters to all their members and supporters. A typical letter went to C. C. Berry, a new member of the club. The letter told Berry of the club's plans and requested that the member go beyond his normal support to make the trip a reality: "Knowing your interest in our organization, I can not but feel that our appeal to you will meet with a hearty and liberal response." The final ploy came by way of a scribbled reminder on the back of the letter: "Notify C. C. Berry of his election as an active member. Entrance fee $2.00."[8] Thus, Mr. Berry, up to this point not even an active member, was informed that he not only owed an entrance fee, but also more money should be sent along if at all possible.

The Pythian Club collected enough dues to make the trip. They departed on August 28, 1867, and divvied up their time in DC as if on a diplomatic mission. They scheduled games with both the Alerts and the Mutuals and made every effort to accept the gestures of hospitality offered. With only so many hours in the day, however, the Pythian leadership had to turn down some invitations, such as the one from Company A, First Battalion, of Washington's City Guard, which invited the Pythian players to attend a promenade at the company's armory.[9]

The Pythians played the Alert first, asserting their dominance from the start by scoring sixteen runs in their half of the first inning. While the Alert regrouped to give up only one run in the second, to their own tally of five, the score stood at 52–25 after the completion of five innings. The skies then again opened up, and a "violent rain storm" ended play. Game statistics show that Cannon, Cavens, Adkins, and Sparrow carried the Pythians, each scoring seven runs. Cannon clubbed two home runs. Despite the lopsided score, the Alert had their chances. They left eight men on base, due in part to excessive caution at the plate. The game's box score revealed that the umpire called thirty strikes on the Alert. This total during a time when many umpires refused to call balls and strikes at all suggests that the Alert were sitting on certain pitches that never came.[10]

Having handily dispatched the Alert, the Pythians looked toward the match with the Mutuals as a chance to avenge the lone official blemish on their record. Trailing after four innings, the Pythians erupted for nineteen runs in the fifth and twenty-one in the seventh. According to the *Mercury*, "The game was intensely exciting, and it was witnessed by a large crowd of spectators."[11] The Pythians' rally withstood the steady flow of runs the Mutuals pushed across the plate. The Pythians emerged victorious 50–43 and left Washington DC, having reconfirmed their preeminence in black baseball circles.[12]

As fall weather pulled the leaves from the trees and pushed afternoon starts even earlier into the workday, the Pythians still found time for a few more challenges. The Pythians met and defeated the Rouen Base Ball Club of Philadelphia by the score of either 30–9 or 30–15, depending on varying accounts.[13] After the Rouen the Pythian BBC met and defeated the Aldridge Base Ball Club, 35–13. Next they took on the Resolute Base Ball Club. The Resolute played out of Camden, New Jersey, the manufacturing city just across the Delaware River from Philadelphia. By all indications the black ballplayers from Camden faced more difficult circumstances than their counterparts in Philadelphia. In November 1864 a violent race riot had erupted in one of Camden's growing black neighborhoods, heightening the already simmering tensions in the city. In 1874 the city would elect a mayor, Democrat John J. Jones, who had campaigned almost exclusively on an antiblack and antiforeigner platform. When Jones took control of the city, he pledged to control the "half-humanized Negro."[14] But even in the midst of such circumstances, the Resolute played on—if not very well. The Pythians played the role of visitors this time, packing onto the ferry for the ride across the Delaware River. The Pythians won easily, 50–6.[15]

When the Monrovia Club from Harrisburg visited Philadelphia in mid-October 1867 (without an expressed invitation from the Pythians), the Pythian Club emptied its coffers once more, although on a bit more moderate scale this time. The Committee of the Monrovia Reception billed the club for $30.63. Still, a new expense arose for this contest. The Pythians for the first time, according to their fastidious record keeping, were forced to pay a fee for the use of a baseball field. The accounting entry shows a debit of $10.00 paid to use the Columbia Park, located at Twenty-Fourth Street and Columbia Avenue.[16]

Here the inequity of the black-white baseball relationship becomes clear. Quite simply, the white clubs, in controlling the baseball land in Philadelphia, as in other baseball cities, held all the bargaining chips. Thus, the fact that the Athletic Base Ball Club had planned to host the Jefferson Club of Washington at about the same time that the Monrovia Club visited the Pythians meant significant problems for the black ball club.[17] The Pythians could not use the Athletics Grounds. Exactly why and how the Pythians were denied use is unclear. Maybe the Athletic Club felt such a show of solidarity with a black club would insult their visitors from the "South." Maybe the Athletic Club's leaders simply did not want the hassle of divvying up field time. Or perhaps the Pythians knew better than to ask for use of the field near the time that the Athletics would be hosting an out-of-town (albeit a minor) club. Regardless, the episode made evident that the Pythians' claims to baseball space in the city and its claim of friendship with the Athletics, who might loan them use of their field, were remarkably tenuous.

Before his resignation, Thomas Fitzgerald had candidly detailed the advantages that the Athletics had in controlling their own field. Noting that nearly half of the gross revenue received by the Athletic Club in 1865 came from admission fees, Fitzgerald explained the value of the Athletic Grounds:

This one fact is highly illustrative of the advantage of a permanent and enclosed ground; for, to say nothing of the advantages accruing from having a ground entirely under club control, and kept in order, the receipts from grand matches not only places a club in a position to make visits to towns and cities, thereby greatly promoting the popularity of the game, but it also relieves those liberal members of every club who usually bear the heavy burdens of expense, from the onus of sustaining the principal expense of an organization by themselves.[18]

A baseball club needed either a rich membership or an enclosed facility in order to flourish in baseball. The Athletics had both, the Pythians neither.[19]

"It is always better for a club to have its own ground. . . . [T]he time will come when there will be no grounds for match playing except enclosed grounds," wrote one particularly prophetic journalist in 1867.[20] Land separated the baseball "haves" from the baseball "have-nots" and, more practically in this Reconstruction era, white clubs from black ones. Between 1865 and 1870 the Athletic Club controlled grounds at Seventeenth and Columbia. Then the club moved to a field located at Twenty-Fifth and Jefferson from 1871 to 1876. Both parks were located due north of the still-under-construction Philadelphia City Hall. The *Spirit of the Times* described the latter grounds as "for natural beauty one of the finest in the country." The paper pushed the club to make improvements as well: "We hope they will put up a nice grand stand for the exclusive benefit of the ladies, or gentlemen who are accompanied by ladies. They took over $25,000 in gate money last year, and therefore the ship ought not to spoil for the proverbial 'haporth of tar.'"[21] Recognizing a sound investment, the Athletics were not stingy. Before the 1866 season the club spent twelve hundred dollars building grandstands and improving the playing surface.[22]

Having nimbly circumvented the challenge of finding an acceptable field, the Pythian and Monrovia Clubs met on a Tuesday afternoon. The Pythians ran up totals of nine, fourteen, thirteen, and ten runs in the first four innings and never looked back. The final score of 59–27 might have been more lopsided had the Pythians kept pressing.[23] The next day the Excelsior Club added to the Monrovia's humbling by trouncing them 82–31. For the Pythians, the convincing victory over the Monrovia closed out a resoundingly successful campaign. The season had few low points—at least on the field.

The Pennsylvania Baseball Convention

While his teammates considered how to effectively host the Monrovia Club without a readily available park, Pythian vice president Raymond Burr made his way to the PAABBP convention in Harrisburg. The Pythians' triumphant season certainly boosted Burr's chances for success at the meeting. The Pythians had been proficient on the field and gentlemanly off it, precisely the mix of behavior espoused by baseball leaders such as Henry Chadwick. Further buffeting the Pythians' odds, state and national baseball associations pushed for expansion rather than exclusivity in the years immediately following the Civil War. The organizations wanted new members. The purpose was to bring more teams into the fold and to codify the rules and traditions of the game. Thus, the National Association made clear in November 1866 that clubs should expect to be admitted:

> The Convention—the following is a letter from the Secretary of the Convention: New York, Nov 8, 1866. To the Base Ball Clubs of the United States; Notice is hereby given, that the regular annual meeting of the National Association of Base Ball Players will be held on Monday, December 12, 1866 at 3 o'clock, pm. . . . Clubs desirous of becoming members, who, from any cause, have neglected to give the [required] thirty days' notice, by sending their application signed by the President and Secretary, they will be received by the Secretary and duly laid before the meeting, *and without doubt they will be admitted to membership.* Let no club that is eligible, who have and feel an interest in the continued and wide-spread popularity of our national game, and who play under the Rules of the Association (from which emanates the laws governing the game) by not claiming the honor of enrolling themselves as one of its members.[24]

The state associations functioned as part of Henry Chadwick's baseball structure. Chadwick wanted centralization; he argued for a strong national organization to govern baseball and set its rules and procedures.[25] But recognizing the chaos that would result from assembling all baseballists at a national convention, Chadwick charged state associations with electing representative delegates. So the Pennsylvania Association represented the Pythians' first step toward inclusion in the National Association. State conventions thinned the crowds. Those players and clubs who achieved sanctioning on the state level could have their say at baseball's national convention.

Pennsylvania had a healthy state association. Due in large part to the statewide barnstorming of the Athletics, the Pennsylvania Association had a sizable rural delegation, in addition to dozens of clubs from Philadelphia, Pittsburgh, and Harrisburg. But the 1867 convention drew an unexpectedly low turnout. *Wilkes' Spirit of the Times* reported that only twenty clubs arrived in Harrisburg for the convention, a total less than the number of baseball organizations in Philadelphia alone.[26] Still, convention planners scheduled the baseball business to stretch across two working days.

Burr arrived without official standing before the PAABBP, but not unpracticed in the skills of high-stakes negotiations. Burr had worked as the personal assistant to Colonel John McKee, often regarded as "the richest colored man in America," for many years. Thus, Burr had seen his share of deal making. The Pythians picked up Burr's expenses for the trip, $5.50 in all.[27] This total included transportation, room, and a per diem. As a responsible advocate and representative of the Pythians' interests, Burr provided a detailed report on his experience at the convention. It is from this report that the clearest picture of what happened at the convention emerges.[28]

Burr arrived in Harrisburg on October 15, the night before the convention began. He settled into comfortable accommodations at the Lochill House, the same hotel where other convention attendees stayed. He reported that the Athletic Club delegation greeted him with special warmth. The connections established on the ball fields of Philadelphia meant something outside the city as well. Hicks Hayhurst took Burr under his wing, introducing him around the baseball fraternity. Then early on the morning of the sixteenth, convention proceedings commenced at the city's courthouse.

Hayhurst introduced Burr to the state association officers before official business began. Burr met association president Rose and secretary Domer. Although things began smoothly enough, Burr's presence did not go unnoticed by his colleagues. Burr recounted that small groups buzzed with conversation regarding the Pythians' request to officially join the association. After the roll call a Committee on Credentials was formed, with Athletic Base Ball Club leader Hicks Hayhurst as a member. This committee took up the task of considering how to handle the Pythians' request, and other clubs' requests, for official recognition. The black club had followed the proper procedure. After enjoying a successful and stable season, it had paid to send its man to the convention and submitted an application for recognition. Thus, there could be no rejection by technicality.

Burr had the uncomfortable role of waiting for a decision on the Pythians' fate. He was not offered the opportunity to argue his case. Still, the convention leadership was not completely insensitive to Burr's position. Hayhurst and Domer informed Burr that they had had discussed the issue the night before. Both, Domer assured Burr, favored the Pythians' acceptance and planned to vigorously canvass their fellow members on the Pythians' behalf. But they also warned Burr that the rest of the delegates were not so progressive. And here the equivocating began. Perhaps, Domer suggested, it would be better to withdraw the application rather than face a formal rejection. "This your delegate declined to do," Burr reported back resolutely to his teammates.[29] Burr had no intention of playing such a game, letting the state leadership off without making a decision.

The Committee on Credentials slowly worked its way through the applications for membership. One club after another gained approval. And still Burr waited. An official read a general report to the convention attendees, informing them of the committee's decisions, but saying nothing about the Pythians' case. As the last words of the report left the speaker's lips, a quick-thinking delegate, Mr. Ellis, sprang to his feet, suggesting that the Committee on Credentials be discharged. The parliamentary maneuver was obviously meant to thwart any discussion on the Pythians' application. But Burr had at least a few friends in the crowd.

Mr. Rodgers, of Philadelphia's Bachelor Club, stated that one application remained and that it deserved consideration independent of the other cases. Rodgers offered no promises to Burr or the Pythians, but stated that the issue had been presented independently so that "the convention might take such action on it as they should deem fit."[30] The obfuscator, Ellis, however, still sought to avoid a direct confrontation. After submitting to a reading of the Pythians' petition, Ellis moved that the motion be tabled indefinitely. Two-thirds of the delegation quickly seconded this motion. Again, it seemed that the Pythians' case would die without so much as a discussion. At this juncture, however, the paltry attendance numbers worked in the Pythians' favor. Hayhurst and Rodgers argued that tabling such a significant issue, with a quorum of only about twenty delegates, would be presumptuous. They suggested postponing any final decisions until after the evening meal when more delegates would likely arrive.

The convention carried on throughout the afternoon, dealing with less controversial matters. The men formed and ratified a constitution and decided on, not surprisingly, a congratulatory motion for the organizers of the convention. A poetry reading soothed the tension in the assembly. Although Burr did not transcribe the words of the poem in his detailed report, he liked what he heard: "It was a beautiful composition, bringing all our name's phrases in, and winding up in a very soothing manner."[31] Backslapping and laughter again filled the room. For Burr, the wait continued. During breaks Burr became the center of attention. According to his report, "the members of the convention clustered around your delegate."[32] Almost to a man, they expressed their sympathy to Burr for the Pythians' plight. But Burr saw through the platitudes to the heart of the matter. "Whilst all expressed sympathy for our club, a few only . . . expressed a willingness to vote for our admission, while a number of others openly said that they would in justice to the opinion of the clubs they represented be compelled, tho [sic] against their personal feeling, to vote against our admission."[33] This passive, noncommittal encouragement did little to assist Burr and the Pythians in their cause to gain full status in the PAABBP.

Even those few (Hayhurst and Rogers among them) who stated they would vote for the Pythians' acceptance continued to push Burr to withdraw his application. "Messrs Hayhurst and Domer again requested the withdrawal of our credentials, and were seconded in their request by most of the members," Burr recalled of his "advocates."[34] Better to withdraw with dignity, they counseled, than to be "black balled." Burr stood at a crossroads. He could take the advice of his tepid supporters and withdraw, realizing that acceptance into the PAABBP remained a long shot anyhow. Or he could force the issue and determine where white baseball's organizers stood in terms of racial integration. It was too significant a decision for Burr to make alone. He telegraphed back to Philadelphia for advice. Burr personally felt disinclined to withdraw the application when even a scant chance remained of its acceptance. His fellow club members felt the same. Across the telegraph wire came the instructions: "Fight if there was a chance."[35]

Burr had hoped that additional convention attendees might sway the vote in the Pythians' favor. Unfortunately, reinforcements never arrived. Burr realized that the present group would undoubtedly reject his proposal. Hayhurst reminded him of this reality repeatedly. Thus, as the delegates gathered for the evening session, Burr did what he had dismissed only hours earlier. "When evening came the delegates were in number about the same as in the morning and as there seemed no chance for anything but being black balled, your delegate withdrew his application."[36]

The rejection made clear the capricious nature of race relations during the Reconstruction era. White support for black baseball existed, but only to a point. Flattering words ("Whilst all expressed sympathy for our club . . ."), whether in print or person, often carried few connections to actions. The manner in which the PAABBP convention rejected the Pythians served notice of exclusionary trends to come. Many a "nonevent" would dash dreams of equality and stealthily shape history. As for the ballplayers, the unified gathering of white members forced the issue off the voting agenda, without ever officially voting on the proposal. The strength of opposition to the Pythians made the club's fight for equal recognition a hopeless cause, and the Pythians took themselves out of the running for a position of equality.

Once the threat of the Pythians' application was removed, Burr again became a popular man. He received a free pass for the railroad ride home, courtesy of Domer. Burr was touched by this practical act of kindness, but the same treatment had actually been arranged for all the conference attendees.[37] The delegates encouraged Burr to stay for the remainder of the convention. He had been neutralized and thus could remain as a spectator. Burr remarked that "all the delegates seemed disposed to share their sympathy and respect for our club by showing him every possible courtesy and kindness."[38] Burr dined with Hayhurst and Rogers in the wake of losing in one of baseball's first racial standoffs and then took in a baseball game (featuring white clubs) in their company. While all accounts of Hayhurst and Rogers suggest that their fondness for Burr and the Pythians went beyond mere meaningless words, neither had been able or willing to persuade the other delegates to support the Pythian Club.

The Pythians, of course, did not collapse upon news of the PAABBP's rejection. Instead, the club carried on as usual, finishing off the remaining games on their 1867 docket with convincing victories. The 1867 season had demonstrated the Pythians' autonomy and revealed the limited scope of white support for black baseball. It had revealed the Pythians' commitment to making black baseball viable (thereby making the best of segregated norms) and to pushing for equality. No records of any postconvention discussions exist, but the Pythians had probably anticipated the opposition from the PAABBP yet still found it disappointing. Opportunities to legitimately petition for integration and equality, such as the one experienced (albeit unsuccessfully) by the Pythians, would disappear altogether for black ball clubs in the United States by the end of Reconstruction.

A Fitzgerald Difference?

What if Thomas Fitzgerald had remained in his post as president of the Philadelphia Athletics? What if Fitzgerald, not Hicks Hayhurst, had represented the dominant Athletic Base Ball Club at the 1867 convention? Might the presence of Fitzgerald, a founding member of the Athletics, an influential newspaper publisher, an education reformer, a former president of the National Association of Base Ball Players (1863), and a seasoned political and race-rights battler, have somehow altered Burr's experience? Such hypothetical (although maybe ahistorical) questions deserve pause, because the PAABBP did far more than simply rebuff the Pythians. This October 1867 convention, with its rejection of the Pythians, established baseball's first segregation precedent.

Fitzgerald had a reputation for getting things done and for providing aggressive leadership. Fitzgerald was also an outlier, not afraid to break or bend social customs. His successors with the Athletics, first Colonel

D. W. C. Moore and then Hicks Hayhurst, did not share these characteristics. The *New York Sunday Mercury*, in 1868, noted the Athletics'
leadership falloff: "There is no questioning the truth of the statement
that the Athletic Club owes its good name and fame to the energetic
and liberal management of its old presiding officer, Col. Thos. Fitzgerald." Things had not been the same since. "His successors, unlike him
[Fitzgerald] have done nothing but talk. . . . [Fitzgerald] talked big,
to be sure, but he acted big." To some it seemed that because of these
weaknesses, the Athletics' time in the spotlight might be closing. "The
powers that have held sway since the Colonel retired—Fitzgerald, we
mean, and no more—have lowered the club's name for liberality; and
allowed its nine to become, in a measure, the mere tools of the 'ring
masters' of the Quaker City."[39]

Hicks Hayhurst played a passive, but still significant, role in laying
the foundation of baseball's segregation framework. Historians should
not necessarily expect that Hayhurst would have trumped the racial
norms of his times, but neither should Hayhurst be lauded for his progressivism. His platitudes changed little. In an engaging and thorough
history of Philadelphia baseball, John Shiffert riskily tabs Hayhurst as
an early Branch Rickey:

> Hayhurst was additionally the Athletics' captain in the mid-'60s,
> a friend of Philadelphia Pythian club founder and Philadelphia
> civil rights pioneer Octavius Catto, and an umpire at many black
> games in and around Philadelphia. . . . Just as it took someone of
> the stature of Branch Rickey to get a single player into the game
> in the 1940s, so would it take someone of Hayhurst's stature to try
> and get an entire team into the NABBP. . . . [D]espite Hayhurst's best
> efforts, the Pennsylvania Association sidestepped the entire issue.[40]

This argument, that a man such as Hayhurst wanted to aid the cause
of black inclusion but could not overcome the biased masses, misses
the point. Hayhurst, regardless of his personal feelings on the matter, refused to act aggressively to champion black baseball. He did not
speak out at the convention or in the newspapers. He did not use the
leverage of Pennsylvania's most important baseball club (by far), the
Athletics, to start a pattern of interracial competition. Perhaps such

leadership tasks were too much for Hayhurst, who won the presidency of the PAABBP at the October 1867 convention. The *Brooklyn Eagle* in 1872, for example, tried later to goad Hayhurst into organizing a building drive for the Athletics ("The club ought to build a handsome clubhouse.... Ten years ago Col. Fitzgerald showed the possibility of this undertaking.... Mr. Hayhurst if he could borrow a little courage and common sense, might carry out these ideas"), but without any results. Hicks Hayhurst, like the vast majority of his contemporaries, abided by social norms. This tendency, though not malignant in and of itself, must be noted in a recounting of the mechanics of segregation in nineteenth-century baseball.

Fitzgerald and Catto: Marginalized but Undeterred

The increasingly conservative tendencies of America's baseball community did not convince either Thomas Fitzgerald or Octavius Catto and his Pythians to give up on the game. The Pythians continued to play after their PAABBP rejection. Fitzgerald accepted the position of president with the Equity Base Ball Club and later supported the *City Item* team.[41] Integrating baseball remained the goal, although baseball competitions (rather than the structures of state or national organizations) became the new target. Catto expressed optimism, in an August 1869 letter, regarding "the probability of our meeting our white brotherhood" on the ball field, and strengthened the Pythian Club's roster in preparation.[42] Fitzgerald and the Pythians worked together toward this competitive end. Fitzgerald, for his part, continued breaking all sorts of social and political norms. He was an Irish Republican, an anomaly given the historically tense relationship between the Irish and black populations in Philadelphia. In Philadelphia politics, as W. E. B. DuBois would observe, "the Irishman had been the tool of the Democrats, the Negro became the tool of the Republicans."[43] Fitzgerald tried to bridge this divide.

Fitzgerald drew public scorn for both his political and his baseball causes. The *Sunday Mercury* continued to pillory him. When Fitzgerald chaired an 1868 meeting of Irish Republicans, for example, the *Mercury* dismissed the effort as "nonsense" and "folly."[44] The newspaper described the Republican Party itself as the "Radical, miscegenating, amalgamating, negro-miring, negro-mingling, negro-worshipping,

negro-reconstruction party." If such hyperbole was not enough to dis-
suade an Irishman from joining the Republican Party, the presence
of former Know-Nothings, many of whom had been committed to
disenfranchising Irish immigrants, did little to foster the image of an
inclusive party.[45]

The same day that he had commented on, for the second time, his
ouster from the Athletics, Fitzgerald reported that the *City Item* would
feature a new and more extensive weekly baseball column. In typical
fashion Fitzgerald celebrated his own importance. He made certain to
note the appreciation that others felt for his newspaper. "The reception of the *City Item* in baseball circles is indeed flattering. We are
constantly receiving letters from all parts of the country praising us
highly. . . . [W]e recommend it to all who are interested in the Great
National Game. It should be taken by every baseball player in America."[46] By featuring baseball prominently, Fitzgerald sought to maintain his influence in the sporting community.

In 1869 Fitzgerald used the *City Item* to carry out one of the most
aggressive and public integration campaigns in baseball history. Beyond
simply expressing banal appreciation for or lukewarm friendship with
black baseballers, Fitzgerald challenged the manliness of Philadelphia's
best white ball clubs—the organizations that Fitzgerald and the Pythians
sought opportunity to compete against. Fitzgerald cajoled and pleaded.
He slandered Hayhurst and other leaders of the Athletics. In his quest
to secure a white opponent for Catto and the Pythians, Fitzgerald did
not always play fair. Roughly a year and a half after the PAABBP rejection, Fitzgerald pushed hard for one of Philadelphia's white baseball
clubs to accept a challenge from one of its black ones.[47]

The effort began harmoniously enough. "The Pythians (colored)
have beaten all the colored clubs, and would like to play a match with
some of their white brethren. What say you, Athletics, Olympics, Keystone, Intrepids . . . ?" the *City Item* prodded on July 17, 1869. Fitzgerald received no response. From this starting point, Fitzgerald gradually unleashed an ever-escalating torrent of rhetoric meant to shame
white clubs into a game with their black counterparts. In the next
issue of the *City Item*, Fitzgerald published a letter to the editor: "My
attention was favorably called to an article in your last issue with reference to a game between one of our white clubs and the Pythian. . . .

Who will put the ball in motion?" Tellingly, however, this same letter acknowledged that whatever interracial games might take place, they had already been thoroughly confined by the National Association decision of 1867 (to be discussed in the next chapter): "According to the laws of our last convention, no association game could be played between such clubs; but, in view of the fact that our most prominent clubs are now frequently playing sociable and friendly games . . ."[48]

A week later the not-so-subtle effort continued. The *City Item* printed another anonymous letter to the editor: "*Editor City Item*; Why is it that the Athletics will not play the colored base ball club called the Pythians? Are they afraid of them? I hear that the Pythians are very strong. I think it quite possible that *apprehension of being beaten by them* is the real cause. Fie, Fie! I call on the Athletic Club to play the Pythians forthwith. Signed, A. Member."[49] This might have been a fabricated account, meant simply to make a point to the Athletics. Although such a tactic would be unusual, the *City Item* waded into the waters of satire and slander more egregiously than most papers. In a profile of Hicks Hayhurst in June 1869, for example, the *City Item* mixed truths, outright lies, rumors, compliments, and seemingly irrelevant details into a comedic sketch. The *Item* portrayed Hayhurst as "a champion smoker," "always opposed to slavery and seldom drink[ing] whiskey," "never without an excuse," "an honorable player," and "[having] had seven wives and [being] the father of forty-two children," and said, "When the Athletics want ten or twenty thousand they go to him."[50] In such scathing jest the *City Item* pushed its causes.

This irreverent tone was evident in an ongoing fictional baseball column that Fitzgerald, the playwright, published alongside the baseball scores on the inside page of the *City Item*. On July 31, for example, this fictional baseball column bore the title "The Playful Pythians," and it taunted the venerable Athletic and Keystone Clubs.

"The Playful Pythians"
> Scene: Fairmount Park. Members of the Athletic and Keystone Clubs in high discourse

KEYSTONE—By heavens, Louise, look—there goes a cussed Pythian!

ATHLETIC—Where? Where?

KEYSTONE—There (pointing scornfully)

ATHLETIC—Ah! (Striking attitude) Horror—Horror!

KEYSTONE—What the thunder does Colonel Fitzgerald mean by wanting us to play the P's? I won't play no d——

KEYSTONE—Hush! *Allez an diable, mon cher!*[51] Remember, we are gents, you know.

ATHLETIC—I knows what I is, but, as Ophelia says, I know not what I may be if we plays them Pythians.

KEYSTONE—You're right, Louise, my pet. If Colonel Fitzgerald keeps this thing up, why we'll . . .

ATHLETIC—What?

KEYSTONE—Why, (whispers), That's what we'll do!

. . . When are the Athletics to play the Pythians? Name your day, gentlemen, and we will be present.[52]

Exactly "what the thunder" compelled Fitzgerald to act as he did and what he believed an interracial contest might accomplish is unclear. During the 1869 baseball season Fitzgerald seemed possessed with the prospect of an integrated baseball game. In August Fitzgerald kept up the pressure. In the August 7 edition of the *City Item*, Fitzgerald addressed the possible commercial appeal of integrated baseball, fingered several members of the Athletic Club who might be holding up a match with the Pythians, and then called for black ballplayers to take on leadership positions in the Philadelphia baseball community. Fitzgerald, it seemed, would not be deterred. "Five thousand persons would pay fifty cents each to see the Athletics play the Pythians," the *City Item* boldly predicted. "Why not give them a trial? Oh—but Fisler, who is a roaring, red-hot Democrat, objects; and so does that Black Republican Reach, and so does Cuthbert, and so does that other fine gentleman—that refined, educated, tasteful young gentleman—who says 'the Pythians are d——d niggers!'" Unwilling to allow the issue to rest even for a few pages, Fitzgerald continued in a subsequent column: "We advise the Pythians to send a polite request to the Athletic, Keystone, and Olympic clubs to play them at an early day. . . . Only three of the Athletic nine object, and they are afraid of the black balltossers." And if all this was too subtle, the *City Item* also, in the same edition, called for the "bottom rail" in the Philadelphia baseball world to be put "on top." "Why not," the question came from the *City Item*, "ask one of the Pythians to umpire occasionally? We are told that every one can read and write, and all have made a careful study of the rules. . . . 'Honor to whom honor is due.'"[53]

Midway through August Fitzgerald's efforts began to bear fruit. Robert T. Murphy, secretary of the Masonic Base Ball Club of Manayunk, Pennsylvania, wrote a letter to the *City Item* editor, expressing his team's willingness to take on the Pythians. Murphy framed the issue as an inevitable one: "There is a desire on the part of a great majority of the admirers of the game of base ball," Murphy wrote, "to have some club, composed of members of the Caucasian race, play a game with the famous Pythian Club."[54] The Masonic Base Ball Club offered to be that trailblazing white club. Fitzgerald wanted more, though, than a game between the mighty Pythian Club and a fledgling (the Masons gathered only once a week and had lost many of their best players to other clubs) white team. Thus, rather than trumpeting the Masonic Base Ball Club's offer, Fitzgerald ignored it. Fitzgerald continued, in the same issue, with his fictional assault on the Athletics. In an installment called "Louise to the Rescue," Fitzgerald conjured up a scene depicting a meeting of resolute Pythian ballplayers doing everything possible to secure a match with the Athletics. The Pythians, for their part in this fictional scene, welcomed a match with the champion Athletics.

A week later Fitzgerald's theatrical assault continued. "Love! or, The Pale Eyed Gudgeon" mixed romance with challenges for racial equality—a potent brew in 1860s America.

> Scene—*Fairmount Park. All is silent save the plaintive murmur of the lone frog and the whispers of love. Member of the Pythians behind a tree.*

LOUISE—Darling—then you will be true to me?
MEYRLE—True to thee? Can you ask it?[55]
LOUISE—I can. And now tell me. Why don't the Athletics and Keystones play the Pythians?
MEYRLE—I don't like to say.

PYTHIAN— (aside) Ha, ha! He trembles?

LOUISE—You must speak. Tell your own Louise, or I'll set Johnny Abel's dog on you the next time I meet you in Johnny's Bower of Bliss.

MEYRLE—Well, then—since you must know all—I will say that—the—the—reason why the Athletics and the Keystones don't p—p—play the Pythians is—is—

LOUISE—Well?

MEYRLE—Because they're—afraid of being beaten!

LOUISE— (with a scream of horror) —Ah!

PYTHIAN—Ha, ha! Ha, ha!

Omnes form tableau.[56]

The pressure applied by Fitzgerald provided impetus to the struggle for baseball's integration that Octavius Catto and the Pythians could not generate. Still, Fitzgerald could not break the Athletics. *Wilkes' Spirit of the Times* noted this failure. "For some time back, Col. Fitzgerald, of the Philadelphia *City Item*, has been striving to get on a game between the Athletic Club and the Pythians, the latter a colored organization," the paper reported in September 1869. "The Colonel's efforts were in vain—the Athletics would have naught to do with the dusky votaries of the bat and ball."[57] Not surprisingly, Fitzgerald did not give up. He could not get the Athletics, and he would not settle for the Masonic Club of Manayunk. So the venerable Philadelphia Olympic Base Ball Club became Fitzgerald's next target. The club had history and a respected place in Philadelphia's baseball community. The Olympic Club by 1869 did not play at the top level of baseball competition, but most all Philadelphians still knew of the club. So, when the Olympic Club agreed to accept a challenge from the Pythians in September 1869, the Pythians and Fitzgerald won a muted, but still significant, victory. The Pythian Club and the Olympic Club met in Philadelphia on September 3, 1869, with Fitzgerald proudly serving as the umpire.

Wilkes' Spirit of the Times, after reporting on Fitzgerald's unsuccessful campaign to get the Athletics on the field, fairly gave Fitzgerald much of the credit for the integrated contest occurring. The paper, in fact, focused on Fitzgerald as much as the pathbreaking Pythians. Fitzgerald's "efforts were crowned with success on Friday, the 3rd inst, for on that day he had brought together the Pythians and the Olympic Club," *Wilkes'* reported.[58] The white baseball press did not give the Pythians any credit for earning the opportunity because of their previous successes. The *New York Clipper* took note of the contest as well, jumping to unfounded conclusions as a result: "The prejudices of race are rapidly disappearing."[59]

On the field the Olympics defeated the Pythians 44–23. This result hurt. Octavius Catto played second base and served as the Pythians' captain for the contest. The Pythian-Olympic game punched a hole in the racial barrier that had prohibited white and black clubs from competing against each other, but also supported suspicions among some baseballists that black clubs could not compete with white ones. Fitzgerald jumped to the defense of the Pythians once again. "There was a little nervousness perceptible in the early part of the game, owing to the novelty of their situation and surroundings," Fitzgerald explained.[60] The Pythians had also, Fitzgerald clarified, let several poor calls by the umpire go uncontested, as "the Pythians, we suppose, were not disposed to be critical or captious under the circumstances."[61] Holding little back in his support of the Pythian Club, Fitzgerald concluded his coverage of the Pythian-Olympic match with a familiar tone and message: "We shall look for the return game with some impatience, feeling assured that it will be won by the Pythians. *We hope the Athletics and the Keystone will play them soon.*"[62]

Only a few days after the Olympic Club defeated the Pythians, another interracial game took place in Philadelphia. The white team taking the field this time was, appropriately, Fitzgerald's City Item Club. Three of Fitzgerald's own sons played against a much-superior Pythian Club. The outcome broke another barrier. The Pythians, tallying twenty-seven runs to City Item's seventeen, recorded the first victory for a black baseball club over a white one.[63]

The Pythians and Fitzgerald pressed on. In early October Catto and his teammates played against a picked nine of Olive Club members. The unfortunately named Olive Club (white) had organized earlier in 1869 and offered little challenge to the Pythians. The Pythians won, 48–28.[64] Then the Pythians ended the pathbreaking 1869 season by playing the Olympic Club once again. That the Olympics not only played the Pythians but also honored the return-game tradition demonstrated a true openness to equality. On the field, though, the Pythians still could not take advantage. Not even Fitzgerald and the *City Item* could explain away the "champion" Pythians' second defeat to the declining Olympic Club. After touting the prowess of the Pythians all summer in the campaign for integrated ballgames, the *City Item* sounded as defeated in its cause as the Pythians had been on the field. "Rematch— The Olympics beat the Pythians more than two to one on Monday," the *City Item* reported. "The Pyths acted like sick men, who had no doctor, no medicine, and no one to sit up with them."[65]

In a matter of two years Philadelphia's baseball community played a vital role in establishing baseball's first official precedent of racial segregation (the PAABBP rejection of the Pythians) and also in experimenting with integrated baseball contests. These dichotomous firsts captured the mechanics of segregation at work and also the reforms of the Reconstruction era. Not surprisingly, different opinions emerged about the significance of these changes—especially regarding the Pythians' contests with the Olympics, City Item Club, and Olive Club. Thomas Fitzgerald and the *City Item* portrayed the games as important first steps. The Olympic-Pythian game was "one of the most interesting ever played," according to the *Item*.[66] Similarly, the *Morning Post* celebrated the Pythians' game against the City Item Club and praised the participants for "having the manliness to grapple with our great social question in a practical way."[67]

But were these integrated games precedents or anomalies? Certainly, the interracial games that took place in Philadelphia during the 1869 season had been successful financially. The crowds had been large and appreciative, and the players had seemed to enjoy their experiences. More pessimistically, however, even the casual baseball fan knew that the Olympics, who were fading badly, and the City Item were mediocre white clubs. The Olives barely registered as an organized club at all. As Eric Foner asserts, the circumstances of integration matter, and in Philadelphia's case the interracial games did not take place even close to baseball's highest level.[68] The Athletic and Keystone Clubs held strong against the entreaties by Fitzgerald to take on the Pythians. Perhaps most telling, the city's *Sunday Mercury*, the most widely read baseball-savvy press in the city, refused to classify the Olympics' game with the Pythians as a game at all. In a recounting of the Olympic Club's 1869 season, the *Mercury* characterized the Olympics' August and September (the period during which they played the Pythians) as a time of rest. Who could play seriously during the long, hot summer? "The Olympics did not play again [after July 15] until two months after the game with the Intrepids. . . . [N]o one seemed to take any interesting in the affairs of the club. On the 3d of September, the Olympics played a social or practice game, at Twenty-fifth and Jefferson streets, with the Pythians, a club of colored men, of this city, defeating them by a score of 44 to 23." Thus, as the *Sunday Mercury* saw it, during a time when no one really cared about the Olympic Club and while taking a break from regularly scheduled games, the Olympic Club played a "social or practice game" with the Pythians. It was a footnote to the rest of the season, nothing more.

Chapter 5

Washington DC

Nationalizing Separation

Beginning immediately after the Civil War, dozens of Washington DC clubs played baseball. Government offices often fielded their own teams. Georgetown University gave rise to the Stonewalls and the Quicksteps, bringing collegiate baseball to the nation's capital. But the game's popularity multiplied in DC starting in 1867. The clubs that took the field in Washington DC in 1867 included the National, Olympic (the two most prominent clubs), Capital, Interior, Union, Jefferson, Empire, Gymnastic, Continental, and two nines representing the Cicero Debating Society. Along with the robust activity on the field, Washingtonians played continual and crucial leadership roles in the emerging game. The District positioned itself for a short time as a rival to New York City and Philadelphia as a center of baseball in America. Thus, 1867 was, by all accounts, a critical year.[1]

The National Base Ball Club opened the 1867 season in robust condition, with ninety-six active members. The club also had more than twenty honorary members, including the esteemed Henry Chadwick. The Nationals' organizing documents had set forth a noble agenda: the "National Base Ball Club of Washington DC" was to "improve, foster, and perpetuate the American game of Base Ball."[2] Here again, in slightly different terms, was the erstwhile commitment of white baseball players to nationalizing the game. New members joined the National Club by referral only. All members paid an initiation fee of five dollars and annual dues of six dollars, limiting potential affiliates even further. Club bylaws mandated a time investment—all members were required to attend monthly meetings and "field exercises." In order to guard against corruption within the club, the bylaws contained an impeachment proviso by which officers could be removed from their positions if two-thirds of the club's membership deemed such a move necessary.[3]

The Nationals' Tour

As mentioned previously, Washington DC's white baseball community had two patriarchs—Arthur Gorman and Nicholas Young. During the 1867 season, though, given his position as president of the National Association, Gorman had pushed past Young into a higher strata of baseball importance. Arthur Gorman's Nationals generally outshone Nicholas Young's Olympics on the field. Cementing his leadership role even further, Gorman announced that the Nationals would get to work nationalizing baseball's popularity. In 1867, with Gorman along for the ride, the National Base Ball Club of Washington DC set out on a "Western Tour."

The point of the tour was to help civilize those areas of the country just getting started in baseball. Ironically, New York City clubs had once viewed the Nationals with these same idealistic, reconciliationist, and somewhat condescending sentiments that the National Club took along on its own extended tour. The summer before their tour, the Nationals had visited New York City. They visited the Excelsior Club in July 1866 and dined at "the most splendid reception ever given by one club to another." The reason behind Excelsior's hospitality was to make the Nationals, a representative of "the Southern portion of the base ball fraternity," feel especially welcome. The New Yorkers intended to show the Nationals how to proceed in the post–Civil War baseball world. "The 'ballplayers policy of reconstruction' is one marked by true fraternal regard, irrespective of all political opinions or sectional feelings. . . . [A]s the Hon. John M. Botts once said—'No North, no South, no East, no West,' but simply the interest and welfare of the game itself, and the cultivation of kindly feelings between different clubs."[4] A year later the Nationals planned to share with the clubs they met along their three-thousand-mile trip this same "ballplayers policy of reconstruction." French, the meticulous secretary of the Nationals, kept a clipping from the club's 1866 trip to Richmond that expressed the National Club's philosophy on baseball diplomacy. "There is one thing we desire to impress upon the

Southern portion of the fraternity; and that is to sincerely repudiate sectionalism in baseball. . . . Let the ball-field be neutral ground. . . . If there is one thing more than another that the Northern portion of the fraternity is determined upon it is that our National Association shall . . ."[5] And then the Nationals' representative quoted Botts's "No North, no South" again.

The Nationals' tour took the club farther west and south than any single club had previously traveled. Before Gorman and the Nationals embarked on their "task of cleaning up the 'Wild and Wooly West,'" the Nationals tuned up against the other clubs of Washington DC.[6] They defeated the Interior, Jefferson, Olympic, Continental, and Union Clubs handily—besting all but the Union Club by at least thirty runs. The pretour contest between the Nationals and Olympics (led by Nicholas Young) had special significance. Not only were they the two best clubs in the city, but the Nationals also chose the occasion to inaugurate their new "National Base Ball Grounds."[7]

The new National Grounds had all the advantages of the Athletics Park in Philadelphia. Situated at Fifteenth and S Streets NW, the Nationals' venue had easy access to the Fourteenth Street trolley. The grounds were "nicely fenced in" and had spectator seating that allowed the club to charge admission. Unfortunately, for all their focus on securing the grounds, the National Club had paid only minimal attention to the field itself. In a swampy city, the low-lying field served as a water-collection area. A drainage system, not fences, should have been the first order of improvement. Thus, a slight rain the day before the game left the field muddy for the contest with the Olympics.[8] Although the Nationals would continue to utilize the White Lot for select games, the "National Base Ball Grounds" separated the Nationals from most of its DC rivals. The Nationals controlled their own land.

The Nationals left Washington DC on July 11, 1867, with a delegation of club officers and reporters accompanying the players. Gorman stayed behind to attend to other business before joining the club in Chicago. Over the course of the tour, the group traveled to Columbus, Cincinnati, Louisville, Indianapolis, St. Louis, and Chicago.[9] The National Club romped through the competition until they reached Chicago, where they met up with the Forest City Base Ball Club of

Rockford, led by a seventeen-year-old future Baseball Hall of Famer, Albert Spalding.[10]

The fact that the tour was an attempt at reconciliation and increasing the national stature of baseball, and that that reconciliation would not come easily, is readily evident when one looks beyond the copious box scores that Chadwick (who traveled with the club) and other scribes produced to chronicle the historic trip. In Louisville the Nationals saw firsthand that Southerners evaluated baseball on their own terms. Southern women booed the National Club heartily, *Wilkes' Spirit of the Times* noted. "Their approbation was for the boys in gray, the National color not being to the taste of the haughty belles of the South apparently." The Civil War lingered in the background of the baseball contest. The Southern crowd appreciated only the ballplayer confirmed as a "red-hot sympathizer with the 'lost cause.'"[11] Visits to Indianapolis and St. Louis in the days that followed produced fewer boos, but still plenty of reminders for the Nationals and Gorman that the U.S. baseball community was far from homogenous.[12]

Chicago, at the tale end of the trip, proved to be more hospitable. Gorman arrived to support the club. Although the "West" had its own baseball culture, there were no Civil War tensions here to be stirred up by the Nationals' visit. Albert Spalding, in his book *America's National Game*, published more than forty years after the match, vividly recalled the Nationals' visit as his introduction to big-time baseball. "It was the first big game before a large audience in which I had ever participated. A great lump rose in my throat, and my heart beat so like a trip-hammer that I imagined it could be heard by everyone on the grounds."[13] In a hard-fought but rain-delayed game, the Forest City Club shocked the Nationals, 29–23.[14]

The Forest City victory so stunned the baseball world that questions arose as to whether the National Base Ball Club had thrown the game.[15] The Nationals erupted in defense of their respectability. The club pointed to its connections with the federal government. Club president Colonel Frank Jones, who had replaced Gorman when he moved up to the presidency of the national association, wrote an editorial clarifying that the Nationals were neither professionals nor gamblers. Gorman followed up by providing the press with a list of his roster and each member's occupation to demonstrate the club's respectability:

W. F. Williams, law student

F. P. Norton, clerk in the Treasury

G. H. E. Fletcher, clerk in the Third Auditors Office

E. A. Parker, clerk in the Internal Revenue Department

E. G. Smith, clerk in the Fourth Auditors Office

Geo. H. Fox, graduate (July 3) Georgetown College

S. L. Studley, clerk in Treasury

H. W. Berthrong, clerk for the Comptroller of the Currency

George Wright, clerk, 238 Pennsylvania Avenue

H. C. McLean, clerk in the Third Auditors Office

A. N. Robinson, clerk, Washington DC[16]

When the club's association with the federal government did not convince the skeptical Chicago press and its readership, Gorman pointed out the Nationals' conservative political connections. The club had members throughout the Andrew Johnson–led Washington bureaucracy, as well as representatives from Washington's wealthiest families: "Regarding the entire party, reference may be made to the Secretaries of the Treasury, Navy, and War Departments; to the Surgeon and Paymaster-General, to the Treasurer of the United States, to the Auditors of the Treasury Department, to the First National Bank, Washington; Jay Cooke and Co, Geo. W. Riggs and Co., Rittenhouse, Fowler and Co.; L. Johnson and Co., and numerous others."[17] Finally, in light of such a potent defense, the *Chicago Tribune* and *Republican* dropped their accusations. The issue subsided. The Nationals received rightful credit for their loss, and the rest of the trip played out uneventfully.

The Nationals returned to Washington DC "weary, dusty, and looking like a party just out of a coal-mine," but also as heroes. Two days after their homecoming, the National ballplayers assembled at the luxurious Kirkwood House for a banquet. It was a lavish affair; "ranged around the room, on three sides, were tables glittering with plate and ornamented with pyramidal cakes, interspersed with handsome bouquets." The president of the District Association, Major Ellerbeck, rose to toast the Nationals and reflect upon the significance of the tour. "No baseball club has ever undertaken an excursion of so great a magnitude and it may never be excelled on this or any other continent. The good name you have left behind you, gentlemen, will be remembered as long as those who participated in the games may live to recall them . . . and I cannot see why it is not an event in your lives that will stand inscribed on the records of time in such glowing letters as to well afford you the greatest pride and satisfaction."[18]

Toasts went late into the night, ranging well beyond the specifics of the Nationals:

"To the President of the United States"
"To the Fair Sex—the patrons of our game"
"To the Press," by, not surprisingly, a member of the press
"To the National Game"
"To the American Field Sports"[19]

The success of the Nationals' tour increased Washington's baseball stature and further promoted the idea (if not reality) of baseball reconciliation.

Charles Douglass and the Alert and Mutual Clubs

While the Nationals worked on nationalizing the game, Charles Douglass and his fellow black baseball players sought to claim part of Washington DC for themselves. Toward this end Douglass fostered connections with white baseball leaders. These were necessary relationships. Douglass boasted that he alone among black ballplayers could secure use of the exclusive National Grounds: "As yet but one game between colored clubs has been played on the National's new grounds . . . and they were secured at my own solicitation," he boasted to a fellow black baseball leader.[20]

Washington DC's black baseball community, as has been mentioned, connected with its counterpart in Philadelphia.[21] Understanding the matches from Washington's side is informative. The Alerts went to Philadelphia and gave the Pythians a good match. The game revealed the localized nature of baseball's rapidly emerging structure of race relations. Even regarding an encounter as innocuous as one prominent black baseball team playing another, Washingtonians reacted more cautiously than Philadelphians had. Or at least the Washington press took a more conservative approach. While the readers of Philadelphia's dailies opened their newspapers to reports of the Pythians and

Alerts, residents of the District read nothing of the game. Washington DC newspapers did not mention the contest. That the match took place at the Athletics' grounds, was washed out by a summer storm, and attracted "quite a concourse" of interested spectators, Washingtonians could know only from reading the *New York Clipper* or *Philadelphia Sunday Mercury*.[22] The *New York Clipper*, which had a record of reporting fairly if sparingly on black baseball (sometimes describing blacks ballplayers as "our colored brethren"), headlined the event "Frederick Douglass Sees a Colored Game."[23]

Washington DC's black ballplayers left behind sparse documentation. Box-scored last names (the Alert nine: Green, Savoy, Cook, Steward, Webster, Douglass, Wormley, Talifero, and Barlow) provide only the scantest of information. Had newspapers given even the ballplayers' first names, tracking their employment through government offices might be possible. But in looking at the few black baseball reports that appeared in Washington DC newspapers, black baseball teams seemed to organize from nowhere, play a game, and then disappear until their next irregularly scheduled match. Quite possibly, the men on Douglass's team held positions in the Freedmen's Bureau, as Douglass did.[24]

Charles Douglass and the Alerts were a part of a burgeoning black baseball community, one that was becoming increasingly difficult, by 1867, for the NABBP to ignore. In Washington, the Mutual Base Ball Club flourished alongside the Alert Club. When the Alerts challenged the Pythians and traveled to Philadelphia, the Mutuals followed closely behind. When the Pythians came to Washington DC in August 1867, they played both the Alerts and the Mutuals. The Mutual Club also had connections in the Freedmen's Bureau. In April 1867 George D. Johnson, secretary of the Mutual Base Ball Club, wrote to his counterpart with the Pythians in order to congratulate the Philadelphia club on its success. As a return address, Johnson simply listed, "George D. Johnson; Freedmen's Bureau, Washington DC."[25]

The Mutuals matched the success of the Alert Club versus the mighty Philadelphia Pythians. On July 19, 1867, the Mutual Base Ball Club won the aforementioned hard-fought 44–43 victory in Philadelphia. The Mutual Club surprised the large Philadelphia crowd, including members of the Philadelphia Athletics who had gathered to watch the two black clubs face off. Philadelphia's *Sunday Mercury* blamed an incompetent umpire for the result. With the Alert and Mutual Base Ball Clubs having both defeated the Pythians, Washington briefly enjoyed the distinction, albeit an unofficial one, of being black baseball's champion city.[26]

The claim did not last long. In keeping with the baseball decorum of the day, the Alerts invited the Pythians to Washington DC for a rematch.[27] Interestingly enough, the planning for the Pythians' visit to Washington DC centered on a picnic. When the Pythians tried to shift the late-August dates around by several days, a near panic broke out among Alert members. Douglass quickly wrote to the Pythians, explaining that the games could not be moved due to picnic plans already in the works. The social aspect of the event could not be compromised: "I am instructed to state to your club that we would like to arrange with you to play the game on the 29th so that the ladies may not be disturbed in their arrangements for a Picnic on the 30th inst which is intended especially for the Pythian Club."[28] The Pythians understood. Pythian Club secretary J. C. White wrote back to Douglass: "We will leave the city on the 28th and play your club on the 29th. This will allow the ladies whose consideration for our Club is so manifest to proceed with any arrangements for the 30th which the kindness of their hearts may have suggested. . . . [W]e have challenged the Mutuals and expect to play them on the 31st."[29] The "ladies" in question were never identified. They were probably the wives of club members. Regardless, the all-important picnic went off as planned. So too did the game.

Negotiations between the clubs flew back and forth in the mail. The exuberance of exchanges, debating rather mundane details, evidenced the centrality of these social organizations in the community. No act in support of club operations, it seemed, was considered drudgery. Rather, an air of freedom and self-reliance emanated from the correspondence. Still, the negotiations were surprisingly drawn out given that no monetary details required settlement. On that front the host club took on most responsibilities. But a suitable date proved difficult to find. Because all the players held jobs, some dates and times were naturally eliminated.

Like the Pythians had done in Philadelphia, and perhaps because they had, the officers of the Alert Club took seriously their role as hosts. A letter from Louis Bell, the Alert chairman for the Committee on Reception, arrived in Philadelphia almost immediately after the challenge had been set, requesting a head count on the Pythians' travel group so that hotel accommodations could be made.[30] Mr. Bell ostensibly had other things to do. His letter came addressed on "Navy Department, Hydraulics Office" letterhead, denoting that he held a respectable job in the gradually diversifying federal government. Arranging a baseball match and taking care of a visiting ball club, however, allowed Bell and the Alert players to claim Washington DC as their own city and to show off its merits to the out-of-towners. In paying for and providing relatively lavish entertainment for their guests, Douglass and the Washingtonians violated a new rule of the NABBP. Clubs were not to spend excessively on entertainment. The baseball game itself, not picnics or banquets, should dwarf all the other activities, the NABBP had mandated.[31]

Just as in Philadelphia, hosting meant a significant financial investment. Charles Douglass had kicked off a fund-raising campaign by requesting a letter from his father that called for the black population of Washington DC to support the Alert Base Ball Club. Frederick Douglass complied and sent along a letter with his own five-dollar donation. Charles circulated the letter himself and called on members of the Alert Base Ball Club to contribute five dollars to the club so that they could entertain the visiting Philadelphia Pythian Base Ball Club in grand style.[32] The members came through, some with donations as high as fifteen dollars. These were significant gifts at a time when a first-class federal clerk might make one hundred dollars per month and many black men struggled to find work and provide food for their families.[33] Douglass urged his father to attend the game. "It is the wish of everybody here that you will come to Washington on the occasion of the visit of the Pythians," Charles explained.[34] Frederick Douglass did not attend.

Again a violent rainstorm interrupted the long-awaited contest, and again the Washington DC press ignored the game—this time a match held in the District.[35] Charles became temporarily pithy in describing the game to his father in a letter. "In the match with the Pythians," he simply wrote, "they were victorious."[36] The Mutual Club hosted a reception for the Pythians, calling for Washington's finest black citizens to come to the Mutual Club's rooms between six and midnight on Saturday night, following the Pythian-Mutual match.[37]

The 1867 National Association Convention

By the time of the National Association of Base Ball Players' 1867 convention, Washington DC's white and black baseball clubs had established themselves as major players on the national baseball scene. The Nationals' tour, Arthur Gorman's tenure as NABBP president, and the Alert Base Ball Club's brief rise to the top of the black baseball world all served notice that the District, not just New York City or Philadelphia, could make a claim of baseball supremacy. The symbolic political relationships and significant connections of Washington DC baseball also helped. In Washington DC baseball games took place on the president's front lawn. Government workers filled baseball rosters. Political dignitaries played ball. Presidents greeted visiting clubs. In short, it was good to be a ballplayer (especially a white one) in Washington DC in 1867. Thus, with these accomplishments freshly celebrated and as one of his final presidential duties, Gorman presided over the National Association of Base Ball Players' convention of 1867.

The convention took place at the Chestnut Street Theater in Philadelphia. The facility had hosted productions of Colonel Thomas Fitzgerald's plays. But the location did not play nearly as important a role as did the presence of Arthur Gorman. The reconciliationist cause Gorman represented dominated the gathering. President Gorman called the convention to order on Wednesday, December 11, 1867. A well-trained speaker, Gorman gave a history of the game and then extolled the delegates of the convention to work toward increasing the respectability and popularity of the game.[38]

As a part of the convention each year, the National Association's nominating committee performed the rather monotonous task of approving membership applications. It was a rubber-stamping task. The committee in 1867 did its work, validating dozens of club applications requesting membership in baseball's national organization. If a club had its documents in order, it received membership.

While carrying out this business, the nominating committee made a decision that clarified the game's policy on race. Certainly, the successes of clubs such as the Pythians and Alerts, as well as the Unique Club of Chicago, and the precedent of the Pythians' rejection two months prior in Harrisburg influenced the decision. The members of the NABBP nominating committee acted aggressively. They issued a jarring and preemptory strike against baseball's racial integration with the following statement: "It is not presumed by your committee that any club who have applied are composed of persons of color, or any portion of them; and the recommendations of your Committee in this report are based upon this view, and they unanimously report against the admission of any club which may be composed of one or more colored persons."[39] Although this statement did not change the NABBP's constitution, as some scholars have claimed, the committee acted aggressively out of a spirit of sectional goodwill and an attempt to avoid controversy.[40] In doing so, the committee established an on-the-record precedent. Having elected Gorman, a "Southerner," at the previous convention, the baseball leaders continued in their reconciliationist ways.

The baseball press explained the rationale behind the decision: "If colored clubs were admitted there would be in all probability some division of feeling, whereas, by excluding them no injury could result to anybody, and the possibility of any rupture being created on political grounds would be avoided."[41] The decision reaffirmed the exclusion of the Pythians at Harrisburg. The statement also furthered baseball's increasingly systematic approach to racial exclusion and put one of the country's first interstate Jim Crow "laws" (albeit a baseball law) on record.

A reporter for the *New York Tribune* provided a report of the convention, particularly focusing on the race decision, that was reprinted by numerous newspapers in the North. The report chided baseball for taking itself too seriously. The baseball leaders convened, "all sitting and deliberating, grave, and wise, and pure as legislators," and produced documents that "exceeded in voluminosity the report of the Committee on the Impeachment of Andrew Johnson."[42] A Cleveland reporter similarly joked that he expected a "National Convention of Players of Tag" next.[43] Regardless of the naysayers, the baseball men took their business seriously. The announcement on "colored persons" set off a blast in what previously had been a mundane processing of baseball business. "Selfishly and cowardly," the *Tribune* reported, "it is resolved that 'No persons of color, or having in its membership persons of color, shall be admitted into the association.' Great applause by the delegates and hisses in the galleries." Here Gorman jumped in. "The President, with more feeling than dignity, declared, as one having much authority, that if these demonstrations were repeated, he would 'order the galleries to be cleared immediately.'"[44] In overseeing and defending the decision to bar black players, Gorman had carried out the ultimate act of Reconstruction-era reconciliation. He had done what his fellow baseball men selected him to do. "With more feeling than dignity," Gorman's tenure thus ended.

The opinions of most baseball men on the momentous decision escaped recording. We do not know what Catto or Douglass thought. Baseball-inclined presses reported the decision, but did not belabor it with much analysis. The decision did not seem to jolt many members of the baseball community. Thomas Fitzgerald, though, once again provided a courageous voice of dissent. Having chosen not to address the initial act of segregation produced by his fellow Pennsylvanians at the Harrisburg convention, Fitzgerald bitterly denounced the National Association's decision. "The Base Ball Convention was a lamentable failure," Fitzgerald seethed in the *City Item*. "The principal business seemed to be opposition to the colored man. The 'toughs' of the assembly were united in their determination to keep, 'the nigger' out in the cold. The following resolution is to the point—Resolved that the d——d Irishman, the d——d Jew, the d——d Dutchman, and the d——d nigger are nowhere just now in our estimate!" Fitzgerald understood the decision as a serious blow struck for strict racial segregation. Fitzgerald had had enough. "Baseball is in serious decline," he concluded, resigned to defeat.[45]

Somewhat surprisingly, many histories have recounted the decision of Gorman and the National Association in 1867 to bar black clubs amid a myriad of factual errors. Mostly, the inaccuracies have resulted from mentioning baseball's segregation in passing, but the problem is still significant. Harold Seymour, as he did in many areas of baseball history, broke ground on the subject of baseball's segregation, mentioning the NABBP decision in his 1960 *Baseball: The Early Years*. In this work Seymour demonstrates that more than a "gentlemen's agreement" existed to explain baseball's segregation.[46] He concludes that the National Association made a broad decision on race, not one particularly aimed at the Pythians. After Seymour, though, the story often got mangled. Robert Peterson, in *Only the Ball Was White*, inaccurately describes the NABBP decision as "the first color line in baseball."[47] This ignores, of course, the Pennsylvania state decision.

Jumping forward from Peterson's 1970 work, Dean Sullivan's oft-cited and extraordinarily useful *Early Innings: A Documentary History of Baseball* distorts the story of baseball's segregation slightly. In his brief introduction to "The Exclusion of African Americans from the NABBP (1867)" document, Sullivan summarizes that "when the Pythians of Philadelphia, an African American club, applied for membership in the NABBP in 1867, the nominating committee unanimously voted to bar any club 'composed of one or more colored persons.'"[48] This is inaccurate. There is no evidence to suggest that the Pythians were one of the eight clubs who had submitted applications to the NABBP only to be rejected.[49] The preponderance of evidence suggests that the NABBP acted not specifically in response to a Pythian application, but rather to preempt any black club from joining. To some this distinction might mean little. One might very reasonably argue that the Pythians, by pursuing membership on the state level, were pursuing membership in the NABBP. After all, the state meetings served as conduits to the national convention, and few clubs outside the South sought state membership without also going after national membership. Still, the subtle difference between the Pennsylvania Association acting very specifically to bar one club (the Pythians) and the NABBP preemptively banning an entire race is another step worth noting in studying the mechanics of baseball's segregation. Only a couple of years later, the *New York Times* would reference the NABBP and race and insist that no club had ever directly petitioned for membership: "If a colored club is good enough to play ball in order to make gate money, they are good enough to enter the National Association. *But as yet, no club has attempted to seek admission to the Baseball Associations.*"[50]

Sullivan's compilation of primary documents rightfully became a source of note for most baseball historians (myself included). Thus, scholars interested in merely mentioning the NABBP precedent or the Pythians as context restated Sullivan's explanation regarding the rejection of the Pythians on the national level. Slowly, the stories of the Pennsylvania convention rejection and the NABBP convention pronouncement have been merged. Historians have improperly inserted

Octavius Catto and the Philadelphia Pythians into the NABBP meeting. Scholars have drawn conclusions not directly supported by the primary resources. Christopher Threston, for example, posits that Catto personally submitted an application directly to the NABBP.[51] Mark Ribowsky places Raymond Burr in Philadelphia, at the national convention, rather than at the Pennsylvania gathering in Harrisburg. Even more egregiously, Ribowsky's Burr, wooed by the differential treatment of Hayhurst, was "only too happy to comply" when asked to withdraw the Pythians' application.[52] John Shiffert contends that the Pythians were "invited" to apply to the Pennsylvania convention, reading far between the lines in Raymond Burr's report.[53]

Getting the facts straight has proved surprisingly difficult. Simple mistakes litter the history of baseball's segregation. I will again start with the dean of baseball historians. While updating his scholarship to reveal the precedent of the Harrisburg rejection, Harold Seymour repeatedly misnames the Pythians' delegate to the convention. In *Baseball: The People's Game* Seymour refers repeatedly to Raymond Burr as "R. S. Bun."[54] It is a minor mistake, undoubtedly caused by the loopy script of the Pythians' records. Other similar errors pile up as one reads various accounts of the Pennsylvania and national conventions. John Thorn emphasizes the role of Jacob White Jr., instead of Raymond Burr, at the Harrisburg convention.[55] Octavius Catto's biographers also miss on several details. One records the pivotal baseball conventions as having occurred in 1868, rather than 1867. The most recent work on Catto, *Tasting Freedom*, inaccurately reports that Thomas Fitzgerald was, and had been since 1862, the president of the National Association of Base Ball Players when the nominating committee made its racist decision.[56] If only. Jules Tygiel, the master of the Jackie Robinson story, writing in *Total Baseball*, inaccurately cites the Pythians' game versus the Philadelphia City Item as baseball's first integrated contest.[57] It was not. Shiffert, citing Tygiel, repeats this inaccuracy.[58]

The point here is not to engage in scholarly "gotcha."[59] I have consulted and used each of the works I just mentioned. This study would not exist without those ones. But the discrepancies point to an important reality. The story of baseball's desegregation—represented most poignantly through the ascension of Jackie Robinson—has received the attention of history's most eminent scholars. Books and articles have abounded. The details have been ironed out. The story of how baseball came to need Jackie Robinson in the first place, on the other hand, has not even been handled to the point where all the details are confirmed. Imagine reading that Jackie Robinson broke into the Majors in 1947 . . . no, maybe it was 1949. And then Robinson played for either the Dodgers or the Giants. And an executive named "Rickey" or possibly "Rooney" helped bring about the acquisition of baseball's first black ballplayer. This would not suffice.

The action of the nominating committee damaged black baseball immediately and also served as a foreboding sign of baseball's future. National reconciliation would trump civil rights, even if the National Association did not have binding control over its members. The Gorman-led National Association simply made black clubs ineligible for baseball's highest organization.

For Arthur Gorman, baseball served as a practice ground for carrying out restrictive racial policy. Gorman would move on from baseball to state and then national politics. After election to the Maryland House of Delegates in 1869, Gorman served as the director of the Chesapeake & Ohio Canal and later in the Maryland Senate. Gorman then won election to the U.S. Senate in 1880. In the Senate Gorman rose through the ranks. He made one of his most indelible marks during his long tenure in the upper chamber by leading opposition to the so-called Force Bill. The Force Bill, introduced by Henry Cabot Lodge in 1890, would have, among other actions, set up an election commission to ensure that blacks in the South could vote.[60] Gorman vehemently opposed the measure and organized political resistance to it. It was Gorman's finest hour, according to the *Baltimore Sun*: "Close upon this came the most memorable parliamentary battle ever witness in Congress, a battle in which this Marylander led a minority party in a victorious assault upon the Force bill, defeating demand of the united Republicans that the South again yield itself to negro domination."[61] As he had in baseball, Gorman oversaw a strategic movement to preserve white exclusivity. Whether at the polls or on the base paths, black Americans had reason to fear Gorman's leadership. Gorman had experience orchestrating exclusion. "Every Democrat, in this crisis, turned to Gorman, as if by instinct," recalled one journalist. "If any man could save the South they believed he could do it."[62]

Readjusting to Rejection

Guided by the ever-stratifying National Association, baseball became more like Washington—more bureaucratic. Forms had to be filled out. Applications had to be processed. Committees convened, and meetings became even more a part of the game's structure. In the midst of this hierarchy, the activities of black clubs came under scrutiny, and black baseball clubs moved further to the periphery of the organized baseball community. But, and this deserves noting, black clubs kept playing.

Washington's black clubs in the 1860s and early 1870s often played on the same grounds as white clubs. The Alerts and Mutuals played regularly on the White Lot, and later the grounds of the Nationals, and at the Olympics' Park.[63] Access did not, of course, mean that black clubs had equal control of baseball space. White clubs set the parameters on when and how black clubs could use their facilities. Still, white clubs were often generous in how they controlled their grounds. The Olympic Club, for example, magnanimously donated use of their facility to the Mutuals for an 1870 match meant to raise funds for a tour through western New York.[64]

In a subtle but significant shift, baseball space in Washington became scarcer for all clubs in 1869 when the District's Commission of Public Grounds restricted use of the White Lot. An order issued in May 1869 summarily closed the White Lot to most baseball games.[65] The decision, which was never explained, scattered baseball contests throughout the city. The measure hurt black clubs most. As baseball land became more tightly controlled, black clubs encountered greater obstacles simply to play a game.

Interestingly enough, the District did not completely enforce the White Lot ban. The field remained partially open to a few clubs—white clubs—for baseball practice. The Olympics, for one, continued to practice at the White Lot in 1869, even as they moved their games to another venue. The Union Club, however, was banned from the property altogether. The Union Club moved their baseball activities to the "Monument Lot," near the Washington Monument. The *Clipper* in reporting this news went straight to the top of the political heap, looking for the culprit. "The Union Club, of Washington DC, has secured what is known as the 'Monument Lot' for practice grounds. At a little expense, these grounds can be made to almost equal the former grounds held by them on the White Lot, of which the Baseball fraternity have been deprived by order of President Grant."[66] Although the particulars remain obscured to the historian, it remains clear that a blanket policy of restriction regarding the White Lot, followed then by selective enforcement, forced black clubs to look elsewhere for ball grounds.

But still black teams played. In Washington DC the Alert Base Ball Club mirrored most other baseball clubs in the city. The Alert Club had government employees on its roster, secured "rooms" in which to meet, elected leadership officers, issued challenges, played matches, and traveled outside the city limits. The differences between white and black baseball clubs were largely a matter of scale. White clubs received more press coverage and had more resources at hand than their black counterparts. The Washington press, for its part, completely ignored black baseball in 1867.[67] The only indications of black baseball in Washington DC in 1867 came from correspondence between Charles and Frederick Douglass and out-of-town newspapers such as the *New York Clipper* and *Ball Players' Chronicle*. And in this respect the *Clipper*'s continual claim that Washington was a Southern city seemed correct.

Charles Douglass eventually experienced a more racially mixed environment at work than he did at play. When drastic staff cuts at the Freedmen's Bureau cost Douglass his job in the spring of 1869, he secured a position at the Treasury Department's Third Auditors Office, joining many of the other baseball players in the city.[68] The Treasury Department, among all government offices, had a special affinity for baseball. So much so that resentment arose throughout the civil service regarding special treatment for ballplayers, as evidenced by one letter to the *Chronicle* editor:

> Now, Mr. Editor, if catching a ball "red-hot" from the bat, or sending a "daisy-cutter" with lightening-like rapidity to "centerfield" constitutes a foundation for reward in the office, I have no doubt the clerks would like to be officially informed of that fact in order to prepare for the future. It would be hard to tell by what law or principle of the public wealth a celebrated "short-stop" who, since he came into the bureau as a messenger, has been promoted to a second-class clerkship, over those who have been there longer

and perform higher grades of duty. . . . The feeling of the clerks burns with indignation to contemplate with what force base ball matters are encroaching upon their rights and the best interests of the public service.[69]

Ballplayers indeed threatened to overrun the burgeoning department. Nicholas Young worked in the Second Auditors Office before becoming the president of the National League. Douglass joined Frank P. Norton, pitcher for the Washington Nationals, in the Third Auditors Office. Nationals G. H. E. Fletcher and Harry McLean worked in the same office as well. The Third Auditors Office had such a proclivity for baseball in fact that it fielded its own team—although no indication suggests Douglass had a chance to suit up for the club.[70]

Although the odds of a black man landing a plum federal appointment (especially without a famous father) were long, Charles Douglass's experience seems to suggest that a black man taking a desk alongside a white federal employee was more likely than his joining a white baseball club. Although less than 1 percent of federal jobs in Washington DC went to black men or women in the 1860s, none of the several hundred positions on Washington DC's white baseball clubs during the same period went to a black man.[71]

Discounted Integration

At nearly the same time he switched jobs, Charles Douglass left the Alert Base Ball Club and joined the rival Mutuals. Charles's older brother Frederick Jr. joined the Mutuals at the same time. By leaving the Alert Club, Charles just missed making history—much as when he stayed behind sick as the Fifty-Fourth Massachusetts stormed Fort Wagner. In September 1869 the Alerts (Douglass's former club) broke the color line in Washington DC baseball.

The *Evening Star* reported on the planned interracial match matter-of-factly: "The Olympics [of Washington DC, not Philadelphia] have received a challenge from the Alert Base Ball Club, (colored) of this city, for a series of home and home match games, which challenge will undoubtedly be accepted."[72] The coolness of the announcement— certainly the Olympics' acceptance of a challenge from a black club was not a given—set the tone for the reaction of Washington's press.

Leading up to the match Washington's newspapers covered the event in a subdued and respectful tone. The broad baseball community monitored the interaction closely: "Great curiosity was manifested in the fraternity to know what action the directors of the Olympics would take," the *Star* reported.[73] Only as the contest neared did the *Evening Star* finally speculate on the significance of the meeting.

September 18, 1869—

The Olympic Base Ball Club of this city, received a challenge from the Alert Base Ball Club (colored) for a series of home and home match games. As a white and colored club had never met in the District of Columbia in a match game, considerable attention was manifested in the fraternity to know what the action the directors of the Olympics would take. On Friday the directors, Motlee, Smith, Hoyt and Young directed the Secretary to return a communication accepting the challenge. . . . [A]s the Alerts play a very strong game it will be both a novel and interesting match.[74]

September 20, 1869—

This afternoon a match game is in progress on the National's grounds between the Olympic Club and the Alert, the former a white and the latter a colored club of good reputation as players.[75]

Before and during the contest, race remained the key descriptor of the clubs involved. But despite this predictable preoccupation, race never derailed the competition or even put it under a cloud of racist apprehension. Fans, both white and black, came in large numbers to witness the groundbreaking event.

The Alert-Olympic game marked the first time that a "major" white club met a black nine, anywhere in the United States.[76] That the Washington's Olympics belonged to the National Association of Base Ball Players, which had denied black clubs admittance, made the event only more significant. And unlike the Philadelphia Olympics who had played the Pythians only a few days earlier, the Washington Olympics were at the height of their baseball prowess. The Olympics would be crowned the "champions of the South" in 1870—temporarily supplanting the Nationals as the premier club south of New York. Thus, the Alert Club had gained an opportunity to play against one of Washington's best clubs.

In this anomalous game the white team won, 56–4. Because of the stature of the Olympics, however, the score did not matter as much as it had in Philadelphia. The *Evening Star*, one of Washington's most baseball-savvy newspapers, did not see fit to mention the final score at all. Although it did express some disapproval of the Alerts' baseball skills ("It seems that as the game progressed their apparent proficiency diminished"), overall the coverage remained positive. "The game yesterday on the National Grounds being rather a novel sight here, that of a white and colored club playing together, attracted a large concourse of spectators, comprising the friends of both organizations. . . . Good feelings prevailed throughout, the game being equally enjoyed by the contestants and spectators."[77] The national baseball press, led by the *New York Clipper*, made note of the contest as well. The *Clipper* alluded to the politics that must have taken place behind the scenes to allow such a match to take place. "The Alert club (colored) of Washington DC, backed by some of the public men of the city, challenged the Olympic club to a series of matches. The challenge was accepted."[78] Unfortunately, the "public men of the city" who had supported the game went unnamed. But Nicholas Young was clearly among those who had supported the match. Still serving as an officer for the Olympic Club, he played right field in the contest.[79] The *Clipper* noted the makeup of the crowd: "a large assembly of both sexes and colors, and quite a number of prominent government officials."[80]

There was some fallout from Washington's interracial match. Only a couple of days after the Olympic-Alert contest, the Maryland Club of Baltimore announced that it would not play against the Olympics in the future. The Maryland Club would not share the field with the Olympics "because [they] played a match with a colored club," reported the *Baltimore Sun*.[81]

Despite the minor backlash, a second interracial game in DC occurred shortly after the first. The Mutual Base Ball Club again followed on the heels of the Alert Base Ball Club. In October 1869 the Mutual Club requested a match with the Olympic Base Ball Club. The Olympics again accepted. The word was apparently out that the Olympic Club would accept a challenge from a "colored" nine. The second integrated game predictably received far less attention than the first. "The game played yesterday between the Olympics (white) and the Mutual (colored) resulted in favor of the Olympic by a score of 24–15 in a game of eight innings," one paper reported.[82] Charles Douglass proudly reported the results to his father. "The club to which I belong in a game of base ball with the Olympics (white) were beaten by a score of 24–15 so you can see we played them as close as the Mutuals of New York did."[83] Although he did not mention it to his father, Charles did not play in the game. His name did not appear in the box score. Thus, he watched again, as he had as a soldier, as history passed by. The *New York Clipper*'s coverage contained a couple of jabs aimed at the Mutuals. It was, the paper reported, "a friendly game of ball," but not one requiring the Olympics to field their best players. "The Olympics were short four of their nine on account of the elections, and had but two men in their regular positions. Their play was of the muffin kind."[84] Still, the white club won.

The *Brooklyn Eagle*, always generous in its baseball coverage, not only reported on the interracial games played in Washington DC, but also pondered their significance. In a column provocatively titled "War of the Races," the *Eagle* suggested that baseball brought questions of race out of the political arena and into the social realm. "On the one side is the Olympic, Caucasian, and on the other, the Alert, African," the paper reported, setting the scene and continuing with its warfare metaphor. "It is not a political or civil right or a privilege of citizenship that a colored base ball club shall be permitted to challenge a white base ball club. . . . [I]t is a purely voluntary matter." The *Eagle* saw the contests as signs of change. Progress had been made; the world was becoming a better and more equitable place. "The Washington of today is not the Washington of the earlier time," the paper concluded matter-of-factly.[85]

Despite the directness of the *Brooklyn Eagle*'s interpretation, evaluating the significance of these integrated baseball matches requires nuance. The task is made difficult by the fact that interracial play happened infrequently. Although historians may in future years unearth additional records of black and white contests, the Philadelphia and Washington games were not complemented by similarly significant events in New York City, Boston, Chicago, or Detroit.[86] The members of a *New York Tribune* baseball team, in October 1869, rejected a friendly challenge from a ball club "composed of American citizens of African descent."[87] Although it probably need not be said, neither did the baseball cities of the South—Richmond, Louisville, Savannah, New Orleans, among others—host integrated matches. Indeed, before 1870 there were no other widely reported interracial contests besides those in Philadelphia and Washington DC. This lack of even a partial pattern defies easy explanation. And why did integrated games occur most prominently in Philadelphia and the District—the two cities most closely linked to baseball's increasingly strict measures of racial segregation?

Certainly, baseball's structure remained in flux. Although the National Association had determined that black clubs could not join their organization, the body made no attempt to control scheduling.[88] So the Alert-Olympic game did not break the ruling of the National Association. Also because of the lack of centralized scheduling, these 1869 games cannot be simply categorized alongside the barnstorming contests of the twentieth century. Barnstorming games were decidedly "unofficial," featuring white rosters thrown together haphazardly. The games took place during the months between the World Series and the start of Major League Baseball's spring training—baseball's off-season.[89] Unlike the barnstorming of the twentieth century, which filled the time between "real" seasons, interracial games in the 1860s were a part of the formal "season." The challenge extended from the Alert Base Ball Club to the Olympic Base Ball Club conformed to standard baseball practices while ignoring the rapidly emerging racial protocol. Thus, as conclusively as anything, the historian can determine that Washington's interracial contests (along with those in Philadelphia) demonstrate the complexity of the mechanics of segregation. The integrated contests meant something. They were positive developments in terms of equal rights for blacks. But they also must be understood as only one volley, and a rather controlled one at that, in the struggle over baseball's future.

Chapter 6

Richmond

Calibrating a Response

Not a single Richmond baseball club attended the 1867 National Association of Base Ball Players' convention. In fact, despite the reconciliationist overtures made by the association in 1866 and 1867, not one Southern club made the trip to Philadelphia for the gathering.[1] Thus, ironically, no club from the former Confederacy witnessed, first-hand, the grand "no colored" gesture made by Arthur Gorman and the NABBP. But notwithstanding their physical absence from the proceedings, Southern baseball players paid attention to the decisions of their Northern counterparts. Not surprisingly, Southern ballplayers (and those reporting on the game for Southern papers) found the developments at Harrisburg and Philadelphia in late 1867 worthy of note.

Southern Response to Northern Exclusion

The news of baseball's increasingly codified racial segregation spread quickly in the South. Of course, the spreading of this news to the South was precisely the point. Savannah's *Daily News and Herald*, not a newspaper particularly concerned with the ballplayers of the Philadelphia area, reported on the Harrisburg decision first. "At the Base Ball Convention, Twenty Clubs were represented, Pythian club (colored), of Philadelphia, was excluded."[2] The paper offered nothing more on the situation, just the basics. White Philadelphia ballplayers had gathered and chosen to "exclude" a black ball club. This was explanation enough.

Several other Southern newspapers printed the exact same paragraph in their pages. The *Columbia (SC) Daily Phoenix* reported the news on October 19.[3] The *Georgia Weekly Opinion* followed a few days later, sharing the accounts of a relatively faraway group of white baseball players making a decision to exclude some ballplayers from their organization based on race.[4] Not all non-Pennsylvania newspapers, incidentally, that reported on the Pennsylvania decision took this same approach. *Wilkes' Spirit of the Times*, for example, covered the Pennsylvania convention, but focused on different details. "The Pennsylvania Base Ball Convention," the *Spirit of the Times* summarized, "met at Harrisburg. . . . Twenty clubs had representatives present. A constitution was adopted and officers elected. Mr. E. H. Hayhurst, of the Athletic Base Ball Club of Philadelphia, was elected President."[5] The Pythians' exclusion did not make the report. Thus, there was obvious precision in the Southern newspapers' reporting. The Southern papers did not mention most of the available details, nor did they overtly support or condemn the Pythian decision.

But the fact that the Harrisburg decision was reported at all in the South helps explain (but not condone) why leaders such as Henry Chadwick espoused shaping baseball into "a pastime thoroughly unobjectionable in every point of view."[6] Southerners, during the Reconstruction era, had a myriad of concerns about how they might rejoin the North—whether in baseball or in more important political terms. If the game was to be national, a long-held obsession of Chadwick and others, a host of potential roadblocks would have to be avoided. And because Southern baseball players noted so carefully what was said on race in the game, reconciliationist policy determined that baseball leaders should pursue "unobjectionable-ism" at the cost of, say, a Pythian application for membership in the PABBP.

News of the decision to restrict "persons of color" made at the National Association meeting of 1867 also moved south. Atlanta's *Daily Intelligencer*, a prominent paper serving Atlanta's rapidly growing baseball community, provided the most explicit and revealing coverage of the NABBP pronouncement. "Among the resolutions introduced and adopted by the Convention was one of significant political importance, *to wit*: 'That no club composed of persons of color, or having in its membership persons of color, shall be admitted into the National Association,'" the *Daily Intelligencer* began. The paper then, proceeding deliberately, noted the allegiances of the decision makers. The delegates were from Northern states, "in every one of which, where elections have recently been held, negro suffrage and negro equality have been scouted."[7]

Concluding the lengthy column, which was telling entitled "Straws Show Which Way the Wind Blows," the *Daily Intelligencer* surmised that the delegates had represented the wishes of the majority of Americans. Only radicals would oppose race restrictions in baseball.

> We would not be surprised to find the elegant Mr. Sumner [Thomas Fitzgerald's politician of choice], or the "Kidnapper Drake," or Impeacher Ashley, or Lodbrog Logan, or some of that ilk bringing forward in Congress a bill to suppress the game of base ball by military interference, as a punishment of the conduct of the National Convention.

The paper suggested that reconciliationism, essentially trading the rights of black ballplayers for the favor of white Southern ones, would certainly work. "We doubt not that this rejection of negro clubs into the National Association of Base Ball Players, will be responded to most heartily by the membership all over the land," the paper surmised.[8] Here it was stated more baldly than ever: the rejection of black ball clubs made possible a truly national following for baseball.

Richmond Baseball

Despite the efforts at reconciliation, baseball remained less popular in the South than in the North. Baseball's popularity in Richmond in particular ebbed and flowed during the Reconstruction era. Although the 1866 season gave rise to dozens of clubs and near-countless games, baseball activity tailed off in Richmond, unlike in Washington or Philadelphia (and unlike in many Southern cities), in 1867 and 1868. Understanding this gradual decline of baseball activity in Richmond might be rooted in the tail end of the 1866 season. The final weeks of the 1866 season in Richmond had provided the city with its first exposure to big-time Northern baseball. The National Base Ball Club of Washington DC came to town to play against Richmond's Union and Pastime Clubs. The visit stirred up reminders of the still-gaping divide between the North and the South. The games took place on the Stuart Hospital Grounds, a part of the city's Old Fair Grounds that had only a few years prior been a bustling military hospital.[9]

Richmonders had put on smiles and welcomed the Nationals. Unlike the clamor that had occurred only weeks before when the Union Club received its rejection from the Richmond and Old Dominion Clubs, Richmond newspapers accepted without complaint the Nationals' arrival. The *Times* broke the news. "The famous National Club of Washington," it reported, "will soon visit this city."[10]

The Nationals had arrived after defeating the Monticello Club of Charlottesville 34–7 in a tune-up match.[11] The Nats planned to instruct the Southerners in the finer points of the game and in doing so fulfill a request from baseball's leadership who encouraged such encounters: "Why cannot some of the Northern Clubs extend their trips to Richmond? Baseball-fever is ragin [*sic*] here, and the material is fine; but some fine playing is needed to teach the players a great deal they never would learn any other way. A few visits from some of the A No. 1 clubs would make Richmond, in a little while, a formidable competitor for the championship."[12] Travel between the two cities was relatively easy, and perhaps, Northern baseball leaders supposed, Richmond's clubs might soon join the National Association.

The Nationals' visit highlighted the raw sectional tensions and general animosity still present in the South. The Nationals understood they were entering hostile territory. E. F. French, the dutiful treasurer of the National Base Ball Club, had closely followed the Union Club scandal. His scrapbook contained numerous newspaper clippings regarding the affair, the most pious of which derided the notion that sectionalism or politics had any effect on the game. French also, however, clipped those articles that argued the exact opposite—that sectional disputes in baseball could undermine the entire Reconstruction process.

> Not only is the above reply [the "we are Southerners" letter] ungentlemanly and uncalled for as a response to a courteously-worded challenge from the Union Club, but an insult to the whole baseball-fraternity, conveyed in the allusion to the Richmond Club not expecting to be members of the National Association. Such pitiful display of sectional ill-will it is, that is doing so much to retard the efforts of the President to restore the Union, and especially is it out of place in baseball-matters, for hitherto politics or sectionalism have been kept out of our national game.[13]

This line of thinking ignored much of what was going on in the Southern baseball world. Not only did baseball clubs still function as political bellwethers, but many Southern clubs also provided an outlet for Lost Cause sentiments.[14]

The Union Base Ball Club of Richmond met the visiting Nationals at the Central Train Station on October 25, 1866, and escorted them to the Ballard Hotel. A tour of the city—including the hallowed Hollywood Cemetery—preceded the 1:00 p.m. game at the Old Fair Grounds. A decent crowd, but far from a record throng, gathered to watch the match. The rout came quickly. After the first inning the score stood at nine runs for the Nationals and two for the Union Club. From that point, the gap widened. The final score was 143–11. The box score listed twenty-four missed fly balls by the Union Club.[15]

A late-night banquet allowed the clubs' players to celebrate together, "locked arm-in-arm." The extravagance of the Unionists' banquet mocked the city's still pressing poverty. "Nothing was lacking to suit the palate of everybody, from the fattest oyster through the list of edibles, down to the choicest of wines and champagnes."[16] The two clubs took turns making toasts to the others' future success. The federal army had its presence at the event as well. The Eleventh Infantry band provided the festivity's music.[17] W. F. Williams concluded his speech with an exhortation to the Union Club—composed of federal employees and soldiers—to "become the champions of the South."[18]

National versus Pastime

The Union-National match served as an undercard for the main event, the Pastime-versus-Nationals contest. Alexander Babcock's Pastime Club had already defeated the Richmond Club soundly, confirming its supremacy in Richmond's baseball circles. The Pastime had also beaten the Union Club a week earlier, 133–35, a total nearly equaling the lopsided score produced in the National-Union game. Thus, the Pastime, it seemed, stood a chance against the mighty Nationals. It would be Richmond's finest versus Washington's best.

The national press fumbled to find the right tone by which to report on the North-South match. One has to read between the lines to appreciate the situation. The *New York Clipper*, with its typical obfuscation, tried to promote good feelings. The *Clipper* searched for common ground between the men. Certainly, the National Club would receive a warm welcome from the Pastime and the Richmond fans because of the moderate political leanings of the National players: "As they are all Johnson men," the New York paper reasoned, "the club will no doubt be received well."[19] Another newspaper followed a similar rationale, offering further specifics. Because the Nationals' president, A. P. Gorman, had recently been dismissed from his long-standing position as postmaster of the Senate due to his "personal relations and close friendship" with President Andrew Johnson, the writer argued, the Nationals would doubtlessly receive a "hospitable greeting characteristic of the Southern people."[20]

The effort to reconcile sectionalist animosity with traditional baseball hospitality led some newspapers to invent connections where they did not exist. Secretary French of the Nationals had scrawled his objection to one such inaccuracy in his diary. "Several of the gentlemen of the visiting club," the *Richmond Times* had claimed, "served gallantly in the ranks of the Southern army in the late war." The paper went on to say, "Mr. [George] Fox, who carried off the palm in batting, which was a perfect model of display, ran away from Georgetown College to enter the Southern army, making three ineffectual attempts, but at last succeeding, and served with distinction to the close." Next to this *Times* clipping, French wrote simply, "Not so."[21] The *New York Clipper* later offered an official correction of the claim that members of the Nationals had fought for the Confederacy.[22]

The game began at 1:00, on a glorious fall Saturday afternoon. Not to be outdone by the Union Club, the Pastime had entertained the National Club during the morning before the game. A large crowd, much larger than for the Union-National match, gathered to witness the contest. Estimates on the exact size of the crowd varied. The *Richmond Times* calculated that a late-arriving crowd multiplied from fifteen hundred spectators at the game's start to between six and eight thousand at the game's conclusion. The *Dispatch*, in contrast, estimated that between three and four thousand fans watched at least some part of the game. Regardless, the event was the biggest baseball contest ever held in Richmond.[23]

The Old Fair Grounds offered a suitable, if humble, baseball diamond. In a telling report the *Times* touted the ground's levelness as its best feature. Such a characteristic could not be taken for granted in

Reconstruction-era baseball. A ten-foot fence surrounded the entire complex. Before the game began, members of the Pastime club staked off the field, using a rope to keep the fans from intruding on the playing space. The scorekeepers and press sat in a reserved section. The city's wealthy residents simply pulled their carriages up to the playing grounds. The bustling gathering reminded the reporters from both the *Times* and the *Dispatch* of antebellum Richmond. "The scene presented was one of a most lively character, reminding the observer of days long past," the *Times* noted. The setting reminded some of the "good old *ante bellum* days."[24] Again, baseball in Richmond harked backward rather than looking toward the future.

The game itself dragged on for more than four hours. The Nationals, apparently only slightly fatigued from the record-setting 143 trips around the bases the day before, tallied 78 runs against the Pastime. The Pastime managed just 10 runs. The score revealed the gulf in baseball experience that existed between the two cities. Richmond was in its first year of organized baseball, while Washington DC had clubs playing since before the war. A postgame banquet, complete with the extravagant menu and the requisite speeches, concluded the Nationals' visit to Richmond. In keeping with the day's custom, Babcock humbly presented the game ball to the Nationals as a prize for their victory. He did so with the request that "it might be received as a token of lasting friendship rather than the symbol of their defeat."[25]

Nearly lost amid the descriptions of the game in the local and national presses is one key description of the diverse group of spectators who took in the game. The *Times* noted the presence of some of Richmond's black residents at the game. The park was, according to the *Times,* "filled with the elite and fashionable, while perched upon the enclosure were hundreds of boys and negroes, and in the distance several of the house tops were dotted with people, taking observation through telescopes and opera glasses."[26] Thus, segregated seating, by race and class, allowed the rich and poor, black and white, to see the game.

As the coverage of the Nationals' visit wrapped up, newspapermen could not restrain themselves from commenting on the apolitical purity of the contests. In an article clipped and saved by E. F. French and the Nationals, an editorialist revisited the Union-Richmond Club controversy even as he provided the particulars of the National-Pastime ballgame.

We are gratified to learn that the action of the Secretary of the Richmond club, some time since, in refusing to play with the Union was repudiated by the club [no record of this repudiation can be found in Richmond's press]. . . . The *Richmond Times*, in commenting on the games, states that several of the Nationals were in the Southern Army. We beg leave to contradict this statement, as those who were in the service fought for the old flag and not against it. However, these things have nothing to do with baseball, which is national and not sectional. We learn that the Union Club, of Richmond—and hope that others will, too—intend joining the convention next month. We can insure them such a reception and hearty welcome will prove to all how little sectionalism there is in the fraternity North, though there is not a club North that had not a representative in the Union Army.[27]

The sheer amount of coverage papers gave to nonsectionalism and nonpoliticism made it obvious that baseball was, well, indeed sectional and political. The prior military affiliations of players did matter. And if anything, the Richmonders seemed to be the only participants honest enough to admit that baseball was a vicarious fight over issues of race and sectionalism.

In one season baseball had become a gauge of Southern resistance to Reconstruction. Richmond's white baseball organizations gained popularity by espousing the city's antebellum notions of what it meant to be a white Southern gentleman. A few days after the Nationals left town, the *Dispatch* commented at length on the rapid rise of baseball in the city. The editor doubted the ballplayers would give up the game even as winter temperatures descended upon the region. "Baseball is not only a fashion, but an enthusiasm," the editor reported. The paper praised the early accomplishments of the city's baseball players, but also reminded Richmond men of the other challenges at hand. "Their 'runs' and 'innings' are great. If their 'innings' could only indicate the financial reconstructedness of the South we would flourish. . . . If the Radicals could only take to 'base-ball,' it would be a national blessing. They would be diverted for a while from deviltry. But let the boys go it on the base-ball game. It won't harm them, while it will help to develop their manhood."[28] The Maryland Base Ball Club of Baltimore arrived in Richmond only days after the Nationals left. Again, the *Richmond Times* referred to political conservatism to assure its readers that the visit was acceptable. "Most of the gentlemen composing the visiting club served in the Southern army during war, and are really exponents of the Southern element of Baltimore, to which element we are indebted for much sympathy and material aid," the *Times* reported on the day of the Maryland Club's arrival.[29] Like the Nationals before them, the Marylanders had their way with the Richmond competition.[30]

1867

While baseball fever seemed only to intensify in 1867 in Washington DC and Philadelphia, Richmonders reconsidered their role in the "national pastime." Baseball games continued, but at a less frequent clip than in 1866. Plans for a grand baseball tournament in the spring of 1867, the first of its kind to be hosted in Richmond, had to be scrapped due to lack of interest from the city's clubs.[31] And by 1868 reports of baseball games in Richmond appeared only irregularly in Richmond papers.

Reconciliationist promises dominated the baseball headlines, but beneath the surface the Southern ballplayers probably also noted the paternalistic and condescending treatment occasionally directed their way by national papers such as the *Ball Players' Chronicle*. It was as if, even while trying to be inclusive, the Northern baseball community's true feelings occasionally seeped out. In late-June 1867, for example, the *Ball Players' Chronicle* printed what it probably considered to be a fair assessment of both the backwardness and the brimming possibilities of the South. "The time has arrived," the *Chronicle* reported while observing a rise in baseball activity in the South, "when we are to see the last, we trust, of the listlessness and love of indolent pleasures which has too long been a blot on the escutcheon of Southern youths."[32] A week later the *Ball Players' Chronicle* pounced on an episode of unruly fan behavior at a Richmond's Pastime game. "We regret to learn," the paper tattled, "that the [Richmond] game was interrupted by a disturbance." Perhaps, the paper mused mockingly, Richmonders would do better to "devote their time to battledore and shuttlecock."[33]

Still, Richmond baseball clubs organized and played. If anything, they became more Southern. The names of these Richmond clubs revealed much about the sectional sentiments of the city's ballplayers and about how the clubs fostered white exclusivity. Richmond's Stonewall Base Ball Club braved forty-degree weather to play the Ashby Base Ball Club in February 1867.[34] The former club had organized in 1866 to commemorate the fallen Confederate hero Thomas "Stonewall" Jackson.[35] The latter played to remember Confederate general Turner Ashby. Simply reading the box scores of Richmond baseball games reminded one of the Confederacy. The Stonewall Club competed against the Confederate, Robert E. Lee, and Mosby (named for Confederate colonel John S. Mosby) Clubs.[36] In 1867 the Secesh (short for *Secession*), Old Dominion, Dixie, Lone Star, South Star, Stuart (for Cavalryman J. E. B. Stuart), and Southern Clubs also joined the baseball consortium in Richmond.[37]

Names mattered. When, for example, a club had organized in late 1866, getting ready for the 1867 season, and chosen the "Keystone Club" as its moniker, the *Daily Dispatch* voiced serious concern. The name hinted at allegiance to Pennsylvania. Of the Keystone the *Dispatch* concluded dourly, "We consider this a sad misnomer for a Virginia club, we would advise a change of the name."[38] The club complied. Few names seemed out of bounds as long as they were associated with the Confederacy. The 1867 season gave rise to the Libby Base Ball Club, presumably an organization in some way commemorating or associated with the infamous Libby Prison.[39] The Libby Prison, of course, was noted for its savage treatment of Union prisoners of war. During Reconstruction occupying federal troops used the facility as a command center. Whether the Libby Base Ball Club consisted of federal army men or former Confederates is unclear.[40] Certainly, though, the name carried distinct connotations.

Club names helped set the racial boundaries of Richmond's baseball fraternity. Richmond club names announced to the baseball community how a club perceived itself. Club names gave hints about the causes supported and the ideals espoused by particular groups of men. To name a club "Dixie," "Confederate," or "Robert E. Lee" was nearly the same as announcing a policy of racial exclusion. Perhaps most compelling on the Richmond name front in 1867 was the organization of the Sic Semper Base Ball Club.[41] The club did not play often or particularly well. But its name effectively hinted at states' rights, violent radicalism, and opposition to federal intervention. Playing off of the Latin phrase "Sic semper tyrannous," this otherwise insignificant baseball club had settled upon a name that meant "Thus always to tyrants." Or more practically, one should turn violent in the face of an oppressive government. Adding further weight to the name, John Wilkes Booth, after shooting Lincoln, had supposedly uttered "Sic semper tyrannous" while fleeing Ford's Theater. The State of Virginia also used the phrase as its official motto.

It Will Be Southern Baseball

While Richmond baseball declined slightly in 1867, in many other parts of the South the game expanded. This incongruity should not come as a surprise. Indeed, in investigating the rise of baseball and analyzing the mechanics of segregation, one cannot allow for the designations of "North" and "South" to be used as exhaustive indicators. Throughout the Reconstruction period, individual states and cities of the South made their own decisions about baseball and race.

The Virginia Association of Base Ball Players met in February 1867. The group elected officers and agreed upon a constitution. Neither the officers nor the constitution made a single statement on the future of black players and clubs in the game. That issue was so clear it needed not be addressed. In the following months state associations throughout the South followed Virginia's example. The desire for organization and for more formalized championship procedures clearly crossed the Mason-Dixon line, even as Southern clubs eschewed the already in place baseball hierarchies of the North. In 1867 Georgia ballplayers discussed how to fairly determine a state champion. Also in 1867 the first annual state convention of baseball clubs of Tennessee met in Memphis. By 1868 Alabama and Louisiana had organized baseball associations as well.[42]

With the Civil War a couple of years in the past, baseball clubs organized and played across the South. The presses of Atlanta, Charleston, Little Rock, and New Orleans in particular gave their city's baseball clubs lavish coverage. Atlanta's *Daily Intelligencer* covered more than fifty games in 1867. The paper described baseball as a "manly and healthful exercise."[43] Atlanta's Gate City Base Ball Club claimed their city championship in 1867, daring other clubs to wrest it away. The Atlanta ballplayers also encouraged competition among Southern clubs. After a flurry of correspondence with the National Club of Chattanooga, Tennessee, Atlanta's best ballplayers engaged in a contest to determine the champion of the South, specifically the champion of "south of the Kentucky and Virginia line."[44] At the same time, black clubs organized and played in the South as well, although tracking their numbers remains difficult due to sparse newspaper coverage. Occasional reports showed up. The black Cumberland Base Ball Club of Tennessee, for example, looked for games in the North and South.[45] In the nether regions of the South, three black clubs organized in St. Louis.[46]

In Charleston black and white baseball clubs flocked to the grounds of the Citadel to play the game. Unlike in Richmond at least one press account confirmed that black clubs had taken to the game. The *New York Times*, squarely in baseball's reconciliationist camp, interpreted Charleston's baseball activity as a sign of a sectional rejoinder. "One of the best evidences that the last spark of rebellion's feelings has died out among the people here may be found in the marked revival of sporting tastes," the *Times* postulated. "The base ball fever has attacked the rising generation of Charlestonians, and there are nearly a dozen clubs, white and black, composed juveniles and children of a larger growth already organized."[47] As an indicator of the city's passion for baseball, one 1868 game between the Alert Club of Charleston and the Forest City Club of Savannah drew more than three thousand spectators.[48]

Arkansas newspapers also gave generous coverage to baseball. Unlike most baseball states in the North, Arkansas produced clubs outside the state's major city (although Little Rock was hardly a metropolis). Arkansas reporters noted clubs organized in Little Rock, Fort Smith, and Pine Bluff, among other cities.[49] This diffusion was not altogether uncommon in the South. With urbanization having taken hold only nominally in the former Confederacy, midsize and small cities meant far more in the Southern baseball world than they did in the North. So Chatawa and Osyka, Mississippi, clubs, for example, traveled regionally to compete.[50] In Mobile and Montgomery, Alabama, clubs organized, as did clubs in Columbia, South Carolina.[51]

New Orleans, along with Richmond, garnered the most attention from the Northern press for its baseball clubs. The Crescent City was home to dozens of clubs, including the Lone Stars, who traveled widely and hosted numerous Northern teams. According to the *New York Clipper*, baseball permeated the entire state of Louisiana. "The national game is insinuating itself into the affections of the residents amid the bayous of the Louisiana lowlands, as it is in the other sections of this enlightened republic," the *Clipper* reported charitably.[52] The Louisiana State Base Ball Association promoted the game in the state from 1868 until 1873. The association encouraged clubs to challenge for the state championship, though without ever really affixing rules to the process.[53] Black baseball also flourished in New Orleans. Dale Somers, in *The Rise of Sports in New Orleans*, notes that black clubs played occasionally against their white counterparts from 1869 until the mid-1880s.[54]

One Game, Two Purposes

When Northern baseball men learned of games in New Orleans or Mobile or Richmond, hopeful prognostications about the future of the game, and nation, often abounded. Henry Chadwick predicted that it might be baseball that would defeat the "spirit of factionalism" in the country.[55] Chadwick went so far as to see baseball as a game that could both be free of sectional animosity itself and also erase such tensions from society. In Chadwick's voluminous scrapbooks, one finds the following passage describing the games in the South:

> In Mobile, Savannah, New Orleans and even in Galveston, they have base ball clubs organized. . . . In fact, quite a furor for the game has sprung up in the South, and it is a healthy sign for the future to see this game becoming so popular. If the fraternity will only introduce the custom of visits among the clubs of the two sections, as did the Nationals of Washington last year [discussed in the previous chapter], in making a base ball turf of Virginia, more good will be done in the way of social reconstruction in a few seasons than the politicians could achieve in half a century.[56]

This report, and others of its ilk, was both optimistic and delusional.

Baseball, along with more traditionally noted Southern activities such as hunting and dueling, "gave expression to the core values of Southern men of honor."[57] Southern baseball did not typically function to mend fences with the North. Just as Cubans would later use baseball "both as a means to nationhood and as a metaphor for nation," Southerners used the game as a means of keeping alive memories of the recently defeated Confederacy.[58] Antebellum times and traditions and Civil War glories stayed in the present through baseball. So too did concerns about racial separation. As with Richmond the most obvious manifestation of this use of baseball surfaced in the club names. While Northern papers waxed poetic about baseball ending sectional divides and doing more in a few years than Reconstruction politicians could do in decades, baseball clubs in the South repeatedly identified themselves with the former Confederacy.

There were a few baseball teams in the South named the Nationals or the Alerts or the Olympics—the most common of club names in the North. Some Southern clubs did choose innocuous names that connected them to their city or neighborhood, such as the Gate City Club of Atlanta or the Montgomery Base Ball Club.[59] Dozens and dozens of other Southern clubs, however, chose more pointedly. There were Robert E. Lee Base Ball Clubs all over the South—in Galveston, Little Rock, New Orleans, Richmond, and Russellville, Arkansas, to name a few. Similarly, Dixie and Southern Base Ball Clubs abounded. An 1860s ballplayer mentioning "the Dixie Club" might have been referring to an organization in Athens or Little Rock or Pine Bluff or Richmond. The same multiplying effect plagued "Southern" Base Ball Clubs. While one Southern Base Ball Club claimed the championship of Baton Rouge in 1868, for example, another similarly named team struggled to win even a single game in Richmond.[60] Likewise, Richmond's Confederate Base Ball Club also had counterparts throughout the South.[61]

Beyond the most common Southern-commemorating names, some clubs were more creative and pointed. In Columbia, South Carolina, the Chicora Base Ball Club linked itself to the css *Chicora*, a Confederate ironclad.[62] The Pickwick Base Ball Club of New Orleans referenced a social club known for both its race and its class restrictions. Only rich white men joined.[63] In Charleston the Germania Base Ball Club formed in 1868. The club's name, though not virulently racist, made direct reference to European bloodlines.[64] In Memphis a Pride of the South Base Ball Club played a handful of games. The club's members not only played baseball but were also rumored to run with a newly formed Ku Klux Klan (KKK) unit.[65]

The Ku Klux Klan provided perhaps the most extreme and direct association for a club to draw upon. Just as the Pythians of Philadelphia selected their moniker because many of the club's members held positions in the Knights of the Pythias, some baseball clubs highlighted their connections to the radical and violent KKK—a group that made no pretenses about its desire to keep black and white Americans apart. There were Ku Klux Klan baseball clubs in both the North and the South. Some clubs, such as the Pride of the South Base Ball Club of Memphis, only flirted with the KKK association. Others clubs equivocated far less. During the Reconstruction period, there were openly and unapologetically named "Ku Klux Klan Base Ball Clubs" in, at least, Arkansas, South Carolina, and Tennessee.[66] The mechanics of segregation here need little explanation. Obviously, no black ballplayer or club would need question the racial politics of a club openly associating with the KKK.

Combing through baseball records (admittedly skewed by more vigorous coverage of the game in Northern newspapers), one finds more instances of KKK Base Ball Clubs in the North than in the South. Indiana, Maine, New Hampshire, and New York each had Ku Klux Klan Base Ball Clubs.[67] Although perhaps some newspapers refused to give KKK baseball clubs coverage, the short articles that do exist show only an occasional note of disapproval. In most cases the lack of a critical comment from the press on the name is jarring. "Challenge! The Ku Klux Klan Base Ball Club of Bangor," the *Bangor (ME) Daily Whig and Courier* announced, "do hereby challenge the 'Katabdin' Base Ball Club of Hampden to play a match game of base ball."[68] The matter-of-factness of the Ku Klux Klan Base Ball Club reports did not, of course, limit the message sent to black players by the name. Ku Klux Klan clubs, whether baseball or otherwise, sent clear messages of exclusion.

Richmond Reconsiders

By the close of the 1867 season, Richmond's *Daily Dispatch* had shrugged off its role as the promoter of baseball in the city. "We have no very special admiration for base ball," the paper reported simply.[69] If losing the support of the *Richmond Daily Dispatch* was not enough, Richmond's baseball community lost the *Times* altogether. In 1867 the owners of the *Richmond Daily Dispatch* purchased their main competitor and combined the major dailies in the city.[70] The merger cost Richmond baseball one of its most committed supporters and resulted in baseball virtually disappearing from the press.

Adding to the contraction movement, the city government of Richmond also began withdrawing its support for baseball at the tail end of the 1867 season. Similar to the closure of Washington's White Lot, the Richmond City Council voted to limit baseball activity on the city's most active ball ground. The city council had previously designated the Old Fair Grounds, a place steeped in Civil War memories, as the domain of ballplayers.[71] This council decision had placed baseball at the top of the recreational spectrum in the city. Boxing, due to its semi-legal status, took place on the heavily wooded islands on the James River. The city's horse racetracks were also located on the outskirts of city limits.[72] All the while, baseball players gathered on a central and memory-soaked parcel of land.

In August 1867 the council switched directions and approved a three-year commercial lease on the property. The city council promised that the city's baseballers would be kept off the land. Buried in the details of the agreement was a proviso that explained the city council's authority in the case: "The Base Ball clubs occupy the ground at the pleasure of the council."[73] The loss of land changed everything for Richmond's baseball clubs. Baseball games in Richmond as a whole declined by nearly 75 percent, from their 1866 and 1867 levels, beginning in the 1868 seasons.

Explanations regarding this decline are mostly speculative. Certainly, Richmond's continual Reconstruction trials (including race riots, the drawing down of Freedmen's Bureau rations, and hosting the Jefferson Davis trial) created difficult circumstances in the midst of which to play ball.[74] Poverty continued to grip Richmond and many Southern cities. On this front the ballplayers tried to do their part. Alexander Babcock and the Richmond Pastime, for example, played in numerous charitable games, especially for orphans.[75]

Confederate causes still mattered as well. One of the few widely reported matches involving a Richmond club in 1869 pitted the Pastime Club of Richmond versus the Pastime Club of Baltimore. The game raised money for "the expenses of re-interring in Hollywood Cemetery."[76] Still, baseball dropped off the pages of Southern newspapers. In

Atlanta stories about baseball in the *Daily Intelligencer* dropped from more than fifty in 1866 and 1867 to just a handful in 1868. Searching for something to report about the formerly robust baseball scene in Richmond, *Wilkes' Spirit of the Times* and Philadelphia's *Sunday Mercury* reported on the April 1869 reelection of Babcock as president of the Pastime Club. "Mr. A. Babcock," the papers reported, "an old Atlantic, has been elected President of the Pastime Club, of Richmond."[77] Still pursuing reconciliation, the papers avoided mentioning Babcock's traitorous past. Certainly, the story of Babcock leaving the Union army for the Confederacy would have outraged many in the patriotic Northern baseball community. It was not reported.

Violence Down South, 1869

Southern journalists did not report on the interracial games in DC and Philly of 1869. The South, however, had its own interracial baseball moment at about the same time. The happening was not an interracial game, like the Pythian-Olympic contest, but rather a "race riot" surrounding a high-profile Southern baseball contest. The violence confirmed for many Southerners the long-unstated maxim that black and white (and thus Northern and Southern) ballplayers should not mix.

On July 26, 1869, the Savannah Base Ball Club visited Charleston, South Carolina, to take on the Carolina Club. The game commenced at 1:00 on the Citadel grounds. A large concourse of black and white fans attended the game. The Savannah Club quickly seized the lead and never let up. The final score, 35–17, reflected the disparate talents of the two clubs.[78] The better team had won.

The racial complexion of the event, unlike the outcome on the field, defied an easy tallying. The Savannah Club brought with it to Charleston a band—the "Washington Band"—composed of black musicians. The events that occurred after the game, especially involving the Washington Band, supplanted the contest itself in terms of press coverage and lasting significance. Shortly after the Savannah Club's victory, the two clubs, apparently not ready to end the competition, decided to have a throwing contest. Thus, the police force present at the game worked to clear the field of spectators, many of whom had crossed the ropes onto the playing ground after the final out. This proved to be a difficult task. At least one fan, one black fan to be precise, objected to the police's tactics. Rafe Izzard, a man heavily intoxicated according to the Charleston paper, resisted. Words were exchanged, and fighting broke out. Working to get control of the situation, the police arrested Izzard. They led him away from the field.[79]

At this point Charleston's black residents sensibly intervened on behalf of Izzard. Certainly, the specter of law enforcement officials taking away one of their neighbors rightfully concerned the black attendees, regardless of Izzard's state. The policemen had made their arrest, but then things got worse. "The riot spread," the *Chronicle* explained. News circulated throughout the city of escalating conflict. What had started as innocent fun turned violent. Black residents came running to the ball grounds. Interestingly, with the situation rapidly escalating, the target of the "about three thousand negroes" shifted. The Washington Band, composed of black musicians "who were said to be Democrats," became the object of the black Charlestonian crowd's hurled insults and rocks.[80] With the police and military escorting them, the Savannah ballplayers and band members took refuge in a hotel. The planned meal and speeches went off as scheduled, but with the din of protests throughout the city in the background.[81]

Rather than quietly heading for the docks and escaping out of town after their meal, the Savannah men and their conservative Charlestonian counterparts made an ill-timed stand for Southern pride. The Washington Band blared the tune "Dixie" as the ballplayers, protected by armed officers, headed to their awaiting steamer. A "mob of infuriated black-skinned hell hounds" pushed and taunted as the white Savannah ball club and its strangely united black band headed for the river. The ballplayers and band made it. They left the city.

For all the bluster in its reporting, the *Charleston Courier* could come up with only minor bumps and bruises for its injury report. Wounds from sticks and stones (quite literally) made up the tally of injured. The *Courier* made it clear, though, that it felt the black fans turned protesters deserved worse. "It was rumored," the paper reported, "that one of the mob was shot, but unfortunately that rumor turned out to be incorrect."[82] The white press's condemnation did not come strictly along race lines. Charleston reporters noted that many black policemen performed well in the crisis. The problem stemmed just from the aggressive and radical African Americans of the city. White

Charlestonians were put on alert. "The result points plainly to one fact. That there is in our city a number of idle, vagabond, lawless negroes, who must be put down; and if the Mayor of the city, elected partly by them, and the police force, composed of men of their own color, cannot make them behave in a decent, respectable manner, the citizens of the community must prepare themselves to keep the public peace."[83] Interestingly enough, the *Charleston Courier Tri-Weekly*, whose reporting on the Savannah-Charleston "riot" read like an angry, barely controlled rant, turned back to baseball at the end of its long column on the incident. "The Savannah boys played well," the writer concluded, regaining control. The visitors had deserved to win. Then a promise was made: if Savannah's white baseball players returned to Charleston, they would be protected. "We can safely promise," the *Courier* ended, presumably speaking for Charleston's white baseball community, "that we will be better prepared to entertain [the Savannah Club] and defend them too."[84]

The Savannah players gave their account of the conflict in the days that followed and in doing so shed some light on why black Charlestonians had reacted so strongly to the Washington Band. "Their especial cause of enmity against the band," explained a Savannah player, "seemed to be because [quoting a black Charlestonian] 'they were a d——d Democratic crowd,' and played 'Dixie' for those 'd——d rebels in gray uniforms.'"[85] Here the symbolism of Southern white baseball shone through clearly. The mechanics of segregation emerge more transparently than usual, and historians gain a source that comes the closest to explaining how black Southerners understood white Southern baseball. The Savannah ballplayers, in the eyes of black Charlestonians, were "damned rebels in gray uniforms." Baseball simply provided a reason for the visit. The message of the Lost Cause and racial segregation were too omnipresent to ignore, in this case without a clever name such as the Confederate or Lee Base Ball Club being necessary. And the fact that a group of fellow black Southerners would support these former Confederates, even if they were playing ball rather than fighting to uphold slavery, led to violence.

Reports of Charleston's race-based baseball violence spread quickly north and south. The *Columbia (SC) Daily Phoenix* estimated that nearly 1,000 black Charlestonians were in attendance when the fracas broke out. The capital paper then cited most of the *Charleston Courier*'s report on the details.[86] The *Southern Watchmen* of Athens, Georgia, attempted to clarify that the lack of mortal violence should not minimize the alarm to the Charleston situation. White Southerners should still be concerned. The *Atlanta Constitution* covered the story for several days. The *Constitution* projected a more reasonable estimate of 250 black men having been involved in the struggle but also noted that the affair caused "intense indignation among the whites."[87]

The reporting by Northern baseball presses on the incident did not sound much different. There was no condemnation for the mixing of the tune "Dixie" and a sporting event. The *New York Times* printed the same copy as most Atlanta newspapers and a couple of days after the incident printed the entire biased account from the *Charleston Courier*.[88] *Wilkes' Spirit of the Times* voiced nearly as much concern about the decidedly nonfatal conflict as Southern papers. "The blacks thereupon raised a fight," *Wilkes' Spirit* reported, "which, if it did not end in bloodshed, was a disgrace to the city."[89] Some Northern newspapers did attempt to classify the conflict as a "disturbance" rather than a "riot," but readers got essentially the same jolt of alarm. Ohio's *Newark Advocate*, evincing the growing frustration of many Northerners with the Reconstruction effort in general, simply headlined its coverage "Negro Riot? 'Let Us Have Peace.'"[90] Thus, the baseball grounds that had previously been considered a paradoxical place of reconciliation ("The Citadel-green, erst the Campus Martius of Confederate battalions, is now daily the scene of the peaceful pastime") had turned violent.[91]

E. L. Godkin's *Nation* provided the most balanced coverage of the incident. Breaking the clash down to its simplest components, the *Nation* pointed out several realities. Southerners did care about baseball (as opposed to cricket). The nationalizing efforts of white baseball leaders had succeeded to a point. Because of this interest in baseball, people showed up for games. Because of the interracial crowds, violence was more likely to occur. Regarding "the recent riot in Charleston," the *Nation* concluded: "It was a base ball club; the throng was immense; the riot ensued; and thus did a little game of ball affect the great game of Reconstruction."[92]

White Charlestonians, embarrassed at reports portraying their city as one controlled by angry mobs, begged the Savannah Club for another chance. And, breaking the tradition of return games being played at the opposite site of a first match, Savannah agreed to come back. Baseball was the pretext, but demonstrating white control of Charleston's streets was the main order of the day. The plan for bringing peace once again to Charleston's baseball world involved an overwhelming show of white military force. Thus, nearly two thousand white Charlestonians greeted the Savannah ballplayers when they arrived back in Charleston on August 16, 1869. The police force was on hand as well, "armed with Winchester rifles and bayonets."[93]

The game itself, barely mentioned in press accounts, went off without a hitch. The key had been to remove the black residents of Charleston from the equation. "The negroes generally kept within doors, and very few were to be seen on the streets," reported the *New York Times* approvingly.[94] Black citizens, even the baseball fans among them, stayed inside their homes because they likely feared overwhelming violence. The scene smacked of exclusion and hostility: "The march from the wharf to the hotel was attended with much confusion and excitement, the procession being accompanied by armed police and two companies of United States troops." The city was "very feverish" as it waited for further violence.[95]

Thus, by the end of this incident, the U.S. military had provided the most direct show of reconciliation that Southern white baseball players had ever experienced. The duly noted selection of Arthur Gorman and the decisions of the PAABBP and NABBP had been statements of support for Southern conceptions of proper race-mixing restrictions. But an armed response to the relatively minor conflict in Charleston provided something more tangible. When Southern white baseball players were threatened by black fans, there were no questions about what might have been done to illicit such a strong response. Instead, rifles and bayonets appeared in support of orderly white Southern baseball competition.

PART 3

New Realities
Entrenched, the 1870s

Chapter 7

Philadelphia

Permanent Solutions

Although many clubs played, there was no question about which baseball club was Philadelphia's most powerful; the Athletics reigned supreme. The club won more games, brought in greater revenues, and had more influence in the baseball world than any other Philadelphia club. The Athletic Club also served as the unlikely catalyst for discussions about race relations and baseball. Thomas Fitzgerald, as president of the Athletic Club, had emerged as a vocal proponent of racial equality. This radicalism likely led to his ouster from the Athletic Club in 1866. Still, in 1869 Fitzgerald, working with Catto, helped organize an interracial baseball game in Philadelphia for the first time. The Athletics, for their part, refused to participate in such contests.

As the decade of the 1870s dawned, the traditions of baseball became more entrenched. Rules and laws on race began supplanting customs and unspoken norms.[1] Whereas in many cases complex factors continued to coalesce and shape race relations in Philadelphia, simple violence also pushed segregation forward.[2] Philadelphia's racial violence stemmed, in part, from blacks and whites living in close proximity. Although the Pythians, as members of the upper crust of black society in Philadelphia, faced fewer direct violent threats than most black Philadelphians, it took only one pointed instance of violence against a black baseball player to severely undercut the progress that had been achieved by the Pythians.

Catto's Success

By 1870 Octavius Catto had secured his place in Philadelphia society. Playing for the Pythians made Catto an accomplished, and somewhat famous, athlete. Teaching at the Institute for Colored Youth allowed

Catto to work toward improving the black community. Membership in organizations such as the Liberty Hall Association certified Catto as an intellectual.[3] In short, Catto had an impressive résumé. To know Octavius Catto was to respect him—at least until race was considered. Thus, it made sense that when officials in Washington DC began their search for a superintendent to lead their embryonic black school system, they targeted Catto. Catto's reputation and credentials made him a desirable hire.

The question of whether to leave Philadelphia for Washington DC was a complicated one for Catto. Catto had strong ties to Philadelphia, not the least of which included the Pythian Base Ball Club. He also had a decadelong tenure at the ICY and had risen to the position of assistant principal.[4] Less tangibly, Philadelphia had provided Catto with the educational opportunities and relative freedom to flourish once the Civil War ended. And certainly Catto had close friends in the city. When Catto traveled outside of Philadelphia, for example, he frequently wrote to Jacob C. White Jr., often urging that his longtime friend "drop me a line immediately, will you?"[5]

The task of reforming Washington's black schools would take a Herculean effort. But it was a noble challenge. Catto did some preliminary research on the position and the Washington DC school system for black children. He found black Washingtonians to be passionate about education, but also uncovered some troubling trends, such as $1,859.77 in unaccounted-for expenses in the previous year's budget.[6] Further complicating Catto's decision, a groundswell of opposition against his candidacy arose in Washington DC. Politics and partisan turf came into play here. A handful of prominent black Washingtonians, probably led by John F. Cook, backed another candidate. Catto received "threatening letters" that made him question the safety of relocating to DC. Reports also came to Catto that a contingent of black men who "had sold themselves body and soul to the Devil and the Democratic Party" would complicate the reforming process.[7]

After much consideration, Catto accepted the Washington DC position—sort of. Catto wanted the job. The new post was a significant promotion and presented to Catto the opportunity to shape black education in the nation's capital. Unfortunately, though, Catto could not convince the ICY to allow him to break his contract. So, strangely,

Catto signed on to serve for one month as the educational czar of black Washington. Catto accomplished much in this short tenure. According to the *New National Era*, Catto "organized the Washington schools completely, graded them," and placed everything "upon a firm footing" during his one month of service. Then Catto went back to Philadelphia.

Although his situation was not nearly as egregious as the labor contracts being used to keep former slaves working on Southern plantations, Catto's inability to extricate himself from his own employment contract in order to accept a better and important job was a sign of the times.[8] In a letter printed prominently in the *New National Era*, Catto explained his predicament: "At the time I accepted this position I had no doubt of the immediate acceptance of my resignation from the situation I then held. Precedents to that effect had been established. Finding, however, that I could not be immediately released, I concluded to do whatever I could, with the generous permission of my managers, in freeing the commencement of your schools from the embarrassment under which it would otherwise be placed."[9] In baseball terms Catto's inability to pursue a better offer foreshadowed the "reserve clause" (introduced in the National League in 1879) that would keep players under the control of one club throughout their careers.[10]

The Pythians, perhaps energized by the near loss of Catto, experienced a rebirth in 1871. The club opened its 1871 campaign with a match versus their cross-river counterparts, the DeWitts of Camden, New Jersey. The Athletic Club agreed to allow the black clubs to use their facility for the game.[11] The *New York Clipper*, in an increasingly common declaration, termed the game "the championship of colored clubs." The designation, which had little to do with the recent records of the clubs, became a near prerequisite in describing black matches. The Pythian Club prevailed 28–13 over the DeWitts. Catto did not take the field for the contest.[12] Shortly thereafter, the Pythians engaged in another series of games with the Washington Mutuals, the first of which took place on the Athletic Grounds on August 12. More than eight hundred spectators gathered to watch two of the country's most famous black clubs play for the same prize, at least according to the white press: "the championship of the colored clubs of the United States."[13]

The Pythian-Mutual game turned out to be a fiasco. The umpire (Theodore Bomeisler of the Olympic Club) was hit and injured by several errant pitches. Lengthy delays eventually gave way to a hard-fought Pythian victory, 20–15.[14] Providing more than the bare essentials about black baseball for the first time in several years, Philadelphia's *Sunday Mercury* praised the two black clubs' first-rate uniforms. The Pythians appeared in blue pants, white shirts, and blue and white stockings.[15] The full box score also revealed a relatively cleanly played game. The Pythians committed only seven errors, compared to the Mutuals' fifteen—commendable tallies for the times.

The two clubs met again two weeks later. The second contest attracted even more attention than the first. Nearly a thousand spectators watched as the clubs played again at the Athletics' grounds. The Mutuals improved their performance nearly enough to pull out a victory. The Pythians barely prevailed, 17–16.[16] Both the *Sunday Mercury* and the *New York Clipper* gave the game generous coverage. "The fielding of the Pythians was visibly improved, and although the Mutuals fielded about as well as in the previous game, yet some very loose play in the sixth innings lost them this. The most noticeable features of this game—which was wonderfully exciting towards the close—was the fine catching of Adkins and first base play of Henley, of the Pythians, and the splendid throwing to bases of Tyler, the catcher of the Mutuals, and the fine second base play of Jordan."[17] This return game, not surprisingly, also bore the designation of a "colored championship game."[18]

Making sense of this emerging trend—that of labeling games between prominent black clubs as "championship" matches—involves considering several realities. The baseball press had long used the "championship" designation loosely. In 1866 especially, an ambitious club could claim the championship of its city simply by declaring they had yet to lose to another club in the area. This loose championship process, however, was rapidly changing by 1871. The establishment of the National Association of Professional Base Ball Players in 1871 (to be discussed subsequently) emphasized that championships were to be earned through a predetermined slate of games. The NAPBBP also emphasized national rather than local championships. Thus, the labeling of black matches as championships took on a different meaning as baseball became more hierarchical.

In raising the specter of a national "colored champion," white newspapermen voiced increasingly fixed ideas about the organization, scope, and separateness of black baseball. The colored-championship designation acknowledged that black baseball clubs were numerous and well established. More important, though, the colored-championship designation also clearly emphasized separation. There would be organized championships for whites and de facto championships for blacks.

Black baseball continued to develop in the United States in the 1870s in an uneven, patchwork manner. Boston, Chicago, and New York City, along with Philadelphia and Washington DC, were home to numerous black baseball clubs. Reports surfaced in newspapers regarding clubs organizing and games, but at an irregular clip.[19] Plans for "colored tournaments" (such as one planned for July 1871 in New York) were sometimes announced, then ignored, leaving the historian to question whether the planned event transpired and was ignored or never happened at all. Integrated games also went off occasionally. News of an 1870 contest in Boston, for example, between two clubs, "both Resolute by name," one white and one black, caught the attention of the nation's press. The "sons of Ham" won the game and kept the Resolute name. Similarly, Cleveland reported on a black-versus-white contest of its own in 1874.[20]

In Chicago the Blue Stocking Club organized in the mid-1860s and led an emerging black baseball community in the Windy City.[21] Composed primarily of waiters from city hotels, the Blue Stockings struggled initially to find a place to play. Like most cities Chicago had a marquee (if still roughly developed) baseball park. Ogden Park, located along the shoreline of Lake Michigan, served the same function in Chicago as the White Lot in DC, the Athletics' facility in Philadelphia, and the Old Fair Grounds in Richmond. Those looking for a game of baseball in Chicago knew where to find one. The park hosted numerous games, including some to raise money for the orphans of fallen Union soldiers.[22]

The Chicago Blue Stocking Club, and other black baseball teams in the city, faced a "rowdy element" that kept them out of Ogden Park during the 1860s. White toughs guarded the lakefront land as "a white man's park."[23] By 1870, though, resistance to the presence of black ball clubs at the facility had lessened somewhat. In August of that year a game between the Blue Stockings and the Rockford Club finally brought black baseball to Chicago's baseball center. The *Chicago Tribune* commented at length on the contest and on the scope of black baseball in the city. Its reporting was at once insulting, paternalistic, and supportive. The *Tribune* decried those racists who somehow supposed that Reconstruction reforms should not seep into the social (baseball) arena. The paper then used a handful of descriptors to remind its readers repeatedly of the Blue Stockings' race. The athletes were "dusky," "colored," "amendments," and "of African persuasion." The whites in attendance, on the other hand, were of the "un-adulterated race." The paper praised the play of the Blue Stockings and Rockford Club as skillful. But the paper also noted that the black ballplayers did not start their game on time (a violation of baseball decorum) and had an "irresistible propensity for tumbling head over heels when in the act of running." The *Chicago Tribune* denounced these shortcomings.[24] The mix of acceptance and derision experienced by the Chicago Blue Stockings mirrored the broader national race relations surrounding baseball.

Beyond Baseball: The 1871 Election

Octavius Catto did not play for the Pythians during the 1871 season. He left behind no explanation for this absence on the ball field. Perhaps the onset of middle age or Catto's busy schedule kept him from manning his position in the Pythian infield. Regardless, Catto remained a leader in the organization. As irony would have it, just as Octavius Catto seemed to be disappearing from the public baseball community, events unfolded that placed his name on the lips of civil rights crusaders across the nation. And in this instance the mechanics of segregation at work were bluntly simple and effective.

Catto had always mixed politics, education, and baseball. Known as a political organizer, Catto found himself drawn into the simmering tempest surrounding the election of 1871. The election, held on October 10, 1871, took place two years after Pennsylvania had ratified the Fifteenth Amendment, guaranteeing voting rights for all men. From the start most black Philadelphians backed the Republican candidates. Some Democrats, the party dominated by Irish Americans in Philadelphia, threatened violence in return. Catto rallied black voters particularly to the cause of district attorney candidate William B. Mann. Catto canvassed his home turf, Philadelphia's Fifth and Seventh Wards, urging his black neighbors to vote.[25]

The races for mayor, district attorney, and city controller in the fall 1871 election were the most significant contests in what would otherwise have been a nondescript election.[26] But given the new political climate created by the Fifteenth Amendment, black and white voters flocked to the polling places. City leaders predicted unrest and violence. On election day the Fifth Ward, located about a half mile southeast of Philadelphia's half-built city hall, broke into violence first. Skirmishes arose between black voters, the city police, and white "roughs" almost immediately on election morning. Black voters complained that the police favored the whites, often bumping a black man from the voting queue in order to make room for a late-arriving white voter.[27] In an act of panicked irresponsibility, the chief of Philadelphia's police, concerned about the safety of his own men, called for all available white civilian men to come to the Fifth Ward to control the burgeoning crowd.[28]

In the tense atmosphere of the Fifth Ward, interracial trust was virtually nonexistent. Black voters felt disenfranchised. Many whites in turn viewed the black ballot as nothing more than a bought vote, for the Republican Party. The *Philadelphia Inquirer* described the volatile situation in its issue that came out the day after the election. The paper detailed how individual tussles turned into widespread violence.

> A pretext was afforded about half-past eleven o'clock, when a colored man presented himself at the window, Sixth and Lombard, and offered to vote, presenting a tax receipt dated 1870. It was stated that he was not registered, and his vote was challenged. . . . Angry words ensued, and he insisted upon his right to vote. The parties holding the window-books loudly demanded that his vote should not be deposited in spite of the efforts of the police the crowd, attracted by the high words that passed, surged up towards the window, and in confusion a blow was struck, and almost instantaneously a shot was fired from a building on the opposite side of the street.[29]

The violence left dozens injured. Then the killings began. Isaac Chase, a black man, got caught in the fray. Mistaken by a group of white men as a black voter they had been arguing with, Chase was wrestled to the ground. A hatchet blow crushed the back of Chase's skull, killing him immediately.[30]

As these events had transpired on election morning, Octavius Catto taught his classes at the institute as usual. With news of riots breaking out, the school dismissed students early. Catto then went to vote.[31] Chase had been murdered about one hour earlier. The events that followed, after Catto left the relatively safe confines of the ICY, are disputed. Something relatively close to the following occurred. Catto left the ICY and headed toward a polling place. Shortly thereafter, he became involved in a minor altercation with a cadre of white men. Catto emerged from the scuffle relatively unharmed but shaken. At this point Catto obtained a pistol for protection.[32]

Continuing on his quest to vote, near the intersection of Eighth Avenue and South Street, Catto encountered one particularly aggressive white "peacekeeper" (probably Frank Kelly) amid a larger group of white vigilantes. An argument ensued. Someone in the area called out to Catto, prompting him to turn in response. Kelly then drew his pistol and fired at Catto. Catto immediately raised his hands. Kelly fired again. Catto fled, darting behind a passing streetcar.[33] According to a witness, Catto bounded off the sidewalk and sprinted down the middle of South Street with Kelly close behind. Kelly fired two more shots at Catto, both of which found their mark. The witnessed recalled that after the last bullets hit, Catto "whirled around and threw up his hands" before crumpling to the ground.[34]

Neighbors rushed to Catto's side. Bleeding profusely, Catto stubbornly clung to life as his friends transported him to the Fifth District Station House. Unfortunately, nothing could be done. Octavius V. Catto, having suffered wounds to the "heart, in his right arm, left shoulder, and left thigh," died. He was thirty-two years old. Catto had recently become engaged to marry Miss Caroline Le Count.[35]

Catto's death reverberated on several levels. Philadelphia lost a respected member of its community, and the nation confronted another example of Reconstruction-era racial strain. The national and local press responded to Catto's murder with an avalanche of coverage. The tenor of the treatment varied considerably. The *Philadelphia Inquirer* provided extensive detail regarding the murder and following investigation. The paper falsely accused Catto of firing the first shots and initially described his murder as an act of self-defense on the part of Kelly. "In the heat of the argument, [Catto] drew a revolver and fired one shot from it, but whether at the white men or merely to intimidate them could be ascertained."[36] The white man then fired back in response. The *Inquirer* dug itself deeper into its fallacy by further reporting that police found a revolver with one barrel discharged in Catto's pocket. The account was wrong on almost all counts.[37]

The African American *New National Era* unabashedly lauded Octavius Catto as a martyr. The paper praised Catto for the life that he had lived ("a quiet, inoffensive gentleman . . . who had devoted himself to the amelioration and elevation of the condition of his race") as well as for his ability, in death, to bring attention to the injustices incurred by blacks. "The murder of Catto in Philadelphia," Frederick Douglass's paper reasoned, "has apparently produced a stronger revulsion of feeling there than all the other outrages of the riot during the recent election."[38] The *Washington Chronicle*, a Republican newspaper, had no doubt that Catto had been assassinated "because he was one of the fearless champions of his race."[39]

The *Sunday Mercury*, Philadelphia's most vocal baseball press, not surprisingly, presented the events surrounding Catto's death, and the murder itself, in a different light than the *New National Era*. Initially, the *Mercury* ignored the story entirely in its October 11–14 editions. This decision broke all journalistic codes. While its competitors covered the story aggressively, the *Mercury* acted as if nothing had happened. Finally, on the fifteenth, five days after the murder occurred, the paper gave in and addressed Catto's death. The *Sunday Mercury* did so in an edition that also editorialized about the violence by raising a simple rhetorical question: "What American . . . could witness the scenes exhibited in parts of our city last Tuesday, without feeling disgusted at the attempt to foist political equality between the descendants of Europeans and Africans?"[40] Thus, while tepidly disavowing violence, the *Mercury* mostly blamed Catto's death on radical efforts to achieve racial equality. Had Catto (and the Pythians) stayed in his place, the paper argued and many white Philadelphians undoubtedly felt, such violence would not have occurred.

The editors of the *Sunday Mercury* lambasted what they perceived as the illegitimate martyrdom of Catto and the political hay that the

Republican Party reaped from the event. The *Mercury* fixated on the public response to the murder rather than the murder itself. The paper begged all parties involved—the city's government, populace, and political parties—not to exaggerate the significance of one black man's death. "While we deplore the murder of Mr. Catto, the colored school teacher, during the excitement incident to the election, on Tuesday, we must say that the action of Councils, in resolving to close the city departments, on the day of his funeral, and to attend his funeral in a body, was somewhat surprising.... [T]he object evidently is to make political capital out of this Catto calamity, and the Republicans are willing to make themselves ridiculous for this purpose. Their conduct is a wretched mockery of woe and a sorry simulation of respect."[41] The paper had no choice but to condemn the death of an innocent man. But at the same time the newspaper voiced significant concerns about the city extending its highest honors to a black man.

The *Philadelphia Press*, often sympathetic to the city's black population, ran a lengthy obituary. The obituary highlighted Catto's education, civil rights activism, and baseball activities. In a rare physical description of Catto, the paper described the befallen as "medium size and rather inclined to be stout." More important than his dimensions, however, was his legacy. The *Philadelphia Press* touted Catto as "the pride of his race in this city" and the "ablest and best educated among the colored men reared in Philadelphia."[42]

Reverend William T. Catto, the preacher who had brought his family north in search of new opportunity, could barely cope with the news of his son's death. Nearly bedridden with the ailments of old age, William Catto displayed once again the strength that had fueled his family's success. He did not remain cloistered in his grief. Rather, he attended the impaneling of the grand jury that would investigate his son's murder, his very presence a show of resilience. Observers noted with compassion that the old man "appeared overwhelmed with grief, and, when looking on the inanimate form of his murdered son, wept as though his heart would break."[43]

The city's official response to Catto's death was unprecedented. Because of his military service, Octavius Catto received the posthumous honor of lying in state at the City Armory. On October 16 thousands of Philadelphians gathered to view the body. After an hour the crowd became so large that the police, who had failed to protect Catto when he was alive, were called to maintain order. An honor guard, composed of men from the Fifth Brigade, surrounded the body during the proceedings. Catto lay in a stately black coffin with silver mountings. Muskets were stacked at both ends of the coffin, draped with the colors of the National Guard of Pennsylvania.[44]

The Philadelphia City Council closed all city departments on the day of the funeral so that city employees could attend the ceremony.[45] A vast assembly gathered at Lebanon Cemetery shortly after one o'clock on a drizzling afternoon. Members of Catto's former regiment served as pallbearers. They carried the coffin through the crowd to the grave site. Special friends and relatives followed the coffin. Next members of the Banneker Institute and the Pythian Base Ball Club, two organizations that had shaped Catto's professional and social lives, were seated. Then a delegation of "prominent colored men from Washington" took their places around the site. Finally, the crowds filled in the few remaining empty spaces. A Christian service followed, conducted by Catto's Episcopalian minister. When the grounds were cleared, military formalities closed the occasion. "The firing party, consisting of twenty men, from the 11th, 12th and 13th regiments, fired three volleys over the grave. This was the last act of honor that could be paid to the remains of the fallen soldier."[46]

In typical nineteenth-century fashion, public condolences and resolutions regarding Catto's death appeared in newspapers by the dozen. The Pennsylvania Peace Society issued a statement of sympathy.[47] The Law Department of Howard University, led by the esteemed John M. Langston, linked Catto's death to the fledgling Reconstruction effort in the South. Langston estimated that more than fifty thousand black men, "whose only crime was devotion to free and enlightened government," had been killed because of racial conflict.[48] The men of the Banneker Institute met as well. They celebrated their former colleague and attended the funeral en masse.

The New National Era devoted significant column space, even as October gave way to November, to discussing the meaning of Catto's life and death. Letters to the editor (Frederick Douglass) came from across the United States. The paper printed a sampling. From Washington DC a boyhood friend of Catto remembered "the brilliancy of his intellect" and Catto's "integrity, affability and gentleness."[49] From Cincinnati a letter came expressing "a deep feeling of sympathy" and explaining how significance of Catto's death went far beyond the limits of Philadelphia.[50] A one-thousand-word epistle came from the Far West, Denver, Colorado, tying Catto's death to the Ku Klux Klan, warning blacks across the country to "make note of this" and predicting that "as sure as Judas betrayed Christ, just as surely will the Democrats betray you."[51]

Back to the Ball Field?

Clearly, Octavius Catto was more than "just a ballplayer." But he did play in and organize baseball games. The Pythian Base Ball Club was a significant part of Catto's portfolio of activism. And after Catto's death the Pythian Base Ball Club fell apart. Philadelphia's newspapers stopped reporting on the club's activities, if they occurred at all. The Pythians attended Catto's funeral. Then, in their last public act, the Pythian Club, one week after Catto's death, issued a series of resolutions. Typical of the club's insistence on formality, the membership selected a "Committee on Resolutions" for the task. The five club leaders then articulated three major points. First, the club had lost its heart and soul when Catto died. "Resolved, That in the death of Octavius V. Catto our organization has lost its most active and valued member," the statement began. Second, Catto had died for the causes of "truth, justice, and equality."[52] Third, Catto's quest for equality would be carried on by his former teammates. The Pythians pledged themselves to an "earnest effort to carry out what was his life-chosen work by striving earnestly to raise ourselves still higher above all vile calumny and unholy prejudice."[53] Then the club disappeared from Philadelphia's baseball community.

This pointed act of violence against a black baseball leader effectively crippled black baseball in Philadelphia. This is not to say that the two happenings are perfectly linked; the causal relationship is indeed difficult to gauge. But the fact remains that after Catto's death, the presence of black men in Philadelphia's baseball community was considerably less prominent than before. Determining why the Pythians disappeared falls largely to conjecture. The club might have folded in tribute to its fallen captain. Or perhaps most of the original players had, like Catto in 1871, reached the point where they no longer wanted to play competitive baseball. Perhaps a new generation of Pythians had not been prepared to take the place of the founding generation. Still, it is curious, in light of the calls after Catto's death to continue the struggle for racial equality, that the Pythians did not reemerge following the murder as, at least, a testament of perseverance.

Post-Pythians

No box scores or announcements appeared in the Philadelphia newspapers in 1872 or 1873 to confirm the presence of any black baseball organizations in the city. A slight rebirth in black baseball and its coverage by the white press occurred in 1874. Nearly one month after again trying to find some support for the colonization of the United States' black population, the *Sunday Mercury* made mention of the visit of the Washington Mutuals to Philadelphia.[54] The "colored champions" of DC came to Philadelphia to take on the city's Williams Club. The contest was set to take place on August 24, 1874. With the Athletics touring Europe, spreading the American gospel of baseball, the Athletic Grounds were conveniently available.[55]

Before meeting the Williams Club, the Mutuals played Philadelphia's white Americus Club—a promising team that played dozens of games during the 1874 season. Interestingly enough, the only way to discern that an interracial game occurred is to trace the career path of one of the players involved. Americus catcher Tim McGinley played with the Americus Club in 1874 before joining the Philadelphia Centennials for the 1875 and 1876 seasons. With the 1875 Centennials, McGinley made it briefly into the NAPBBP—an all-white league.[56] Thus, for the first time, and with little fanfare, Philadelphia welcomed a black club from another city to play not only its "colored" clubs, but also one of its white ones. The Americus Club defeated the Williams Club, 28–9.[57] The *Mercury* never made mention of the outcome of the "colored championship" game between the Williams Club and the Mutuals.

The Williams Club, described rather generously by Washington's *Sunday Herald and Weekly National Intelligencer* as "the famous Williams Club, of Philadelphia," did not achieve nearly the success or stability enjoyed by the Pythians. The Williams Club did, however, travel to Washington in 1875, a trip that went unmentioned by the

Philadelphia press. Even with the presence of the Williams Club, black baseball in Philadelphia sputtered badly in the mid-1870s, appearing only one line at a time, a few times a season, in the city's newspapers. The *Washington Sunday Herald* inadvertently noted a shift in status of Philadelphia baseball when it declared that the Williams Club was "able to cope with any club south of Philly."[58] Philadelphia had always looked north to judge itself in baseball terms. The fact that the city, when considering race relations or baseball, was better only than the South got it about right.

By 1876 even the "famous" Williams Club had descended into near obscurity in Philadelphia. The *Sunday Mercury*, paying credence to the long tradition of baseball-friendly presses serving as a post office of sorts, had received a challenge from a black Canadian baseball club. The *Mercury*, however, had lost track completely, or so it claimed, of the black baseball clubs in the city. So the paper issued a general announcement: "There were several excellent colored clubs in this city last season, the most successful probably being the Williams, of West Philadelphia. If the Secretary of this organization will call at this office, he will find a communication from a club of Kingston, Canada, on business of importance. If the Williams club is no longer in existence the letter is intended for the best remaining colored clubs."[59] Such obliviousness from the baseball press had become the fate of black baseball clubs. This fate did not necessarily deter black participation in baseball or negate the communal gains that came from black men creating cooperative organizations that gathered for baseball. But the near invisibility of black baseball clubs in the larger Philadelphia baseball community made baseball's segregation more complete.

When coverage of black baseball did appear, it usually emphasized separation rather than camaraderie. The *Sunday Mercury*, always either a latent or an outright hostile opponent of black ballplayers in the city, in 1876, with congressional Reconstruction waning, described two "kullud" men discussing taking up baseball. "'I say, Sambo, let us join de baseball club.' 'What fo, nigger?' 'Well, Sambo, kase it larn you how ter ketch fowls on de fly—a much easier way dan stealin' 'em from de roost.'"[60] Here again, the mechanics of segregation lacked much in the way of nuance and undoubtedly delivered a clear message of exclusion.

The National Association of Professionals

As the Pythians navigated the choppy waters of Reconstruction-era baseball, the Athletics celebrated the status quo. The "Athletic Machine" had dominated the city's baseball community for nearly a decade, providing baseball leadership, battling for championships, and winning the large majority of its games.[61] In 1868 the club finished with a record of 48–3; made a triumphant "western" tour to Chicago, Cleveland, Detroit, Indianapolis, and St. Louis; and won the *New York Clipper*'s "gold ball" for the season.[62] In the year of Fitzgerald's integration push, 1869, the Athletics fell off only slightly, still compiling a record of 42–7.[63]

The Athletics' success did not ensure that its members would oppose racial change. The club did not spew racist language or insert bigoted passages into its club constitution. The club did not particularly concern itself with the political and legal reforms proposed by congressional Reconstructionists. Such overactions were not necessary. Instead, the Athletic players played ball and focused on their own success. Civil rights questions remained far in the background.

During the 1870s the Athletics promoted professional baseball over the amateur game. The Athletic Club sent a delegate to the March 1871 inaugural meeting of the National Association of Professional Base Ball Players (referred to simply as the National Association by contemporaries). The other nine delegates at the meeting represented the cities of Boston, Cleveland, Chicago, Fort Wayne, New York City, Rockford (Illinois), Troy (New York), and Washington DC (two delegates). The major difference between the professional and amateur associations would be simple: money. Players would no longer be forced to pretend that they did not receive compensation for their play.[64]

The Athletic Club thrived as a member of the National Association. The Athletics won the first professional baseball championship in 1871. While Harry and George Wright's Boston Red Stocking Club won the championships in the next four seasons, Philadelphia rivaled New York City and Boston as baseball's premier city throughout the early 1870s. With open professionalism baseball, of course, became more about money, profits, and revenues than ever before. Profitability, however, proved to be an elusive goal, even for the Athletic Club. Even as the Athletics claimed the first National Association championship banner in 1871, the club lost money.[65] Competition for the city's best players and paying fans became even fiercer when the Philadelphia White Stocking Club (later known simply as the Philadelphia Club) joined the National Association in 1873.

White ballplayers in Philadelphia had every reason to protect the increasingly gaping split between white and black baseball clubs in the city. Profits loomed tantalizingly for both white clubs and white individual baseball players. The Athletics returned to profitability, by a razor thin margin, in 1872 and 1873. The latter season proved financially successful despite the panic of 1873.[66] Members of the Athletic Club in particular used baseball as their entry point into business. Al Reach's baseball shop came first and became a hub for white baseball players throughout the city.[67] On a smaller but still profitable scale, Athletics Ned Cuthbert, Wes Fisler, Ferguson Malone, John Sensenderfer, and Fred Treacy all opened Philadelphia businesses that traded on their baseball reputations and served baseball clientele during the 1870s.[68]

The Athletic Club incorporated and invested heavily during the early 1870s in improving its ballpark. The club had a winning record every season between 1871 and 1875. The organization hosted President U. S. Grant for one contest.[69] As if these successes were not enough, the Athletic Club also went across the Atlantic Ocean in its quest to spread the gospel of baseball. An 1874 tour took the club, along with the Boston Red Stockings, to England. The Athletic players played games and convened with their European counterparts. The A's then returned to Philadelphia and reveled in their status as baseball diplomats.[70] With all these successes, the issue of whether the Pythians or any other black baseball club could join the ranks of white clubs such as the Athletics became less and less a subject for serious conversation as the years passed.

White Casualties of Exclusion

By the end of the Reconstruction era, Philadelphia's press covered only white baseball. Segregation along racial lines seemed complete. But then baseball exclusion itself diversified. When the National League formed in the winter of 1876, Philadelphia had two prominent white clubs—the Athletics and the newer Philadelphia Club. Both had played successfully in the National Association of Professional Base Ball Players. But since the NL formed to fix the problems that had made the National Association volatile and unprofitable, NL founders determined that only the Athletics would be given membership. The NL constitution mandated that no NL club could be located within a five-mile radius of another club.[71]

This five-mile rule determined that the Philadelphia Club would be excluded from the new baseball venture. The NL constitution further curbed competitive freedoms by mandating that "no visiting club, member of the League shall play any club in a city in which there is a League club, except the League club."[72] Thus, with the race question effectively decided, exclusion spread along new lines. Sounding a protest that echoed those of Thomas Fitzgerald and the Pythians in the 1860s, the Philadelphia Club condemned the NL's arbitrary selection process. The club drafted a letter to the "President and Members of the So-Called Professional Baseball League."

> Your action of the 24th inst., in holding a convention composed only of such clubs as you desired represented, to the exclusion of others who possess an equal right in the deliberation of said organization, is looked upon as a most extraordinary and singular proceeding, calculated to ignore the national game, and tending to diminish the interest and attendance of those who are its admirers and supporters. . . . The presence in your organization of a representative from the "Athletic Club" is amply sufficient to show the selfish and mercenary motives of this act.[73]

The irony of this letter of complaint is rich and inescapable. "Selfish and mercenary motives" had, of course, long caused "manifest injury" to less powerful clubs—particularly those composed of black ballplayers.

Even as the Philadelphia Club protested the news that it had been summarily excluded from the NL, the Athletics took the opportunity to twist the knife in the wound, so to speak, using one of its favorite tools of supremacy—the Athletic Grounds. The Athletics announced that, given the turn of events, it would not allow the Philadelphia Club access to its field for the upcoming season.[74] Landless and league-less, the Philadelphia Club occupied a position analogous to the 1867 Pythians. The club was successful, well known, without its own baseball grounds, and barred from competing at baseball's highest level.

Ironically, the Athletic Club would quickly take a Robespierrean fall. In their first NL season, the Athletics failed to generate enough revenue to offset the costs of paying its players and traveling extensively. The club won only thirteen of fifty contests. Already far behind in the 1876 season standings, the Athletics refused to make a costly western tour that had been scheduled by the league. As a result the *New York Clipper* called for the Athletics' immediate expulsion from the NL. Additionally, the *Clipper* argued that, in the best "interests of baseball," the Athletics should not be allowed to rejoin the NL for the 1877 season. Athletic leaders claimed the collapse had been "not of its own fault," that the Centennial Fair of 1876 had "absorbed the whole attention of the public in Philadelphia" and cut into its gate receipts.[75]

The NL's clubs gathered in early-December 1876 for their annual convention. The future of the Athletics (and the similarly collapsed New York Mutuals) headed the list of topics for consideration. The gavel had hardly fallen opening the convention when the clubs from Chicago, St. Louis, Louisville, and Cincinnati introduced a resolution calling for the permanent expulsion of the Athletics from the league. The measure received unanimous ratification; the Athletic Base Ball Club was expelled.[76]

Trial for Catto's Murderer

Frank Kelly, identified by several witnesses as Octavius Catto's murderer, finally came to trial in April 1877—more than five years after the baseball world had last heard from either Catto or the Pythians. Kelly had successfully avoided trial by fleeing to Chicago. In early 1877, though, police finally located Kelly and hauled him back to Philadelphia, and a trial commenced. Kelly had lived near Catto in Philadelphia, making his residence only a block away from Catto's home at Ninth and South. Kelly and Catto had likely crossed paths before their fateful final meeting. At the trial witnesses testified to the brutality of the murder. Several witnesses verified that Catto had not fired a shot. The conductor of the train that had crossed through the incident recalled that Catto seemed confused by the white man's aggression. "What are you doing, What are you about?" Catto had asked. The conductor resolutely fingered Kelly as the murderer.[77]

All told, the lawyers contesting the case introduced thirty-five witnesses, all of whom had a slightly different account of the shooting.[78]

More than a dozen black and white witnesses, however, tabbed Kelly as the shooter. Jacob Purnell, a former member of the Pythians, had no doubts about the identity of the killer. "I was on my own doorstep; I saw the prisoner that day and recognized him at the time I saw him as Frank Kelly." With this testimony still ringing in their ears, the all-white, all-male jury retired to consider a verdict. Thus, for one final time (albeit posthumously), Octavius Catto—a man whose baseball career had revealed a vigorous commitment to both black autonomy and social equality—was left waiting for assistance from white men in his quest for just treatment in Philadelphia. Catto would not get it. The jury came back swiftly with a unanimous verdict—Frank Kelly: "not guilty."[79]

Chapter 8

Richmond
The Final Tally

Alexander Babcock, the New York City ballplayer turned Confederate rebel, had led Richmond's post–Civil War baseball development. Richmond never rivaled Philadelphia or Washington in terms of baseball prowess, but Babcock, as a player and team president, had shaped baseball into a pastime that promoted the values of most white Richmonders. The game became popular, for a time, because it provided a recreational outlet for the men of Richmond. It also gave Richmond men a means by which to express their opposition to federal Reconstruction and, more generally, to the meddling North. Babcock was by any standard a unique baseball organizer. Northern baseball writers respected him due to his status as a former member of the Atlantics of Brooklyn.[1] Richmond baseball players in turn admired his "résumé" as a Confederate hero and Conservative Party political leader.

Babcock oversaw the development of Richmond's strictly segregated baseball community without ever explicitly professing his feelings on race. Babcock and Richmond baseball leaders achieved racial exclusion instead by emphasizing a euphemistic cause—the "memory of the Confederacy"—and by describing baseball activities using Lost Cause verbiage.[2] Babcock directed the Richmond Pastime to honor the memory of the failed Confederate States of America as they played and raised funds for nonbaseball activities. Honoring fallen white soldiers, most everyone in Richmond and the South more broadly understood, meant adhering to racial segregation.

Despite the overtures of Northern baseball leaders, Babcock and the vast majority of Southern white baseball players expressed little interest in using baseball to bridge sectional divides. Thus, the reconciliationism of Gorman and the National Association mostly failed. Still, creating a Southern white game did not guarantee baseball a permanent place at the top of Richmond's recreational hierarchy. Rather, baseball's popularity ebbed and flowed as Richmond men gravitated toward those pursuits they found most satisfying. Pastimes such as boxing and horse racing predated baseball. In the wake of criticism from Northern baseball leaders and a string of defeats from visiting Northern clubs, Richmond men seemed to lose some of their enthusiasm for baseball. The loss of the Old Fair Grounds also contributed to the decline in baseball activity.

The End of the Pastime

Richmond's Pastime Base Ball Club appeared in the pages of the *Richmond Daily Dispatch* for the final time on July 2, 1871. Alexander Babcock had the last word. The *Dispatch* reprinted a letter from Babcock to the Brotherhood of the Southern Cross, a group dedicated primarily to ensuring proper burials for fallen Confederate soldiers. Babcock's public letter served as a eulogy for the Pastime Club:

> Dear Sir, Some time since the Pastime Base Ball Club of Richmond and the Pastime Club of Baltimore played a series of matches, the proceeds of which were to be devoted to the removal of the remains of our gallant Confederate dead to such southern cemeteries as might be selected for the purpose. In this way $240 was realized, and has been sacredly set apart for that object. Believing now, however, that the effort of the S.C.B. [Brotherhood of the South Cross] in this direction offers a proper and legitimate channel for the appropriation of the fund referred to, I enclose a check for $240. With best wishes, A. G. Babcock, President Richmond Pastime Base Ball Club.[3]

The chairman of the Brotherhood of the Southern Cross responded to the gift with a grateful return letter.

The Babcock letter highlighted for a final time the Pastime's almost religious commitment to preserving Confederate memory. The letter's pious language (play "devoted" to the burial of the "gallant" dead, a task set "sacredly" apart) promoted societal values, not simply the game of baseball itself. Baseball mattered most for the support it could yield to white men's causes. Babcock passed the club's hard-earned money along to another white men's organization. The baseball men had done their part in creating a social setting in Richmond that honored white men and excluded former slaves. Thus, in its end as in its beginning, the Pastime emanated white Southern pride.

By way of comparison, baseball clubs throughout the South served white men in the 1870s in the same manner that the increasingly popular Ladies' Memorial Associations served Southern women. The organizations provided social outlets to honor the past. They helped reconfigure Southern ideals to fit in the new postwar world.[4] And regardless of the exact sentiments spoken, the racial agenda that emerged from these organizations was understood by all. The Babcock-led baseball community in Richmond had remained "unstained" by black participation because it celebrated those organizations and causes easily associated with racially exclusive behavior.

After turning over the remains of its coffers to the Brotherhood of the Southern Cross in 1871, the Pastime never again appeared in Richmond's papers or the *New York Clipper* or *Wilkes' Spirit of the Times*. Babcock stayed in Richmond, though, as did Alexander Tomlinson and most other members of the club.[5] The historian at this juncture is again left to draw inferences from incomplete records regarding what happened. One might reasonably conclude that the chaos of 1870, often referred to as the "Year of Tragedy," halted recreational activity altogether in the city. In 1870 Richmond's statehouse collapsed, killing dozens, and the city flooded. Then the panic of 1873, which crippled the railroad industry, nearly shut down Richmond's Tredegar Iron Works. Unemployment rose. Richmond banks collapsed by the dozen. The Freedman's Saving and Trust Company, commonly referred to as the Freedman's Bank, failed in 1874.[6]

The end of direct congressional Reconstruction in Virginia also brought new controversy and instability to Richmond. Frederick Douglass, for one, deemed Virginia unready for autonomy: "Virginia is today as thoroughly rebel and as completely unreconstructed as at any former period."[7] Nevertheless, Virginia's new government took over. Racial tensions were heightened by the influx of black migrants to Richmond. The 1870 census revealed an increasingly black city: of the fifty-one thousand people living in Richmond, twenty-three thousand were identified as black.[8]

Fledgling Baseball, Shooting, and Riding

Baseball had never completely supplanted some of the more traditional Southern sports in Richmond or in other formerly Confederate cities. Shooting and riding contests in particular remained ensconced in Southern life. Thus, it was not surprising that after the Pastime Base Ball Club folded, Alexander Babcock joined the Richmond Shooting Club. This organization, unlike Richmond's baseball clubs, needed no explanation as a thoroughly Southern endeavor. No one needed to assert that only white men could participate. There was no Northern-based organizing structure to address or avoid. Richmond men deemed this lack of a national structure as a positive characteristic.

Examples of what could go wrong with bisectional cooperation abounded, at least in the eyes of many white Southerners. In 1871, for example, a Richmond temperance organization experienced a telling reversal of Northern reconciliationism. This was the constant fear—Northerners would speak in reconciliationist terms and then use any cooperative organization to change the racial norms of the South. "The resolution adopted by the National Division of the Sons of Temperance," the *Richmond Daily Dispatch* reported ". . . by which the doors of the order throughout the country were thrown open to all persons 'without distinction of race, color, or condition,' has caused not a little excitement among the Sons of Richmond." Promises had been made that the cause of temperance would not be compromised by discussions of racial politics. These promises had been prerequisites for Southern chapters rejoining the national organization. "The Grand Lodge of Virginia would never had resumed its organis [*sic*] relations with the National body since the war but for the positive assurances . . . that the question of color should not be introduced into the Order."[9] When the situation changed, it took the Richmond temperance men less than one week to withdraw from the national organization.

Thus, traditional Southern recreations had their appeal.[10] Going far back into the roots of the American South, Southern men, described as "hot-blooded and trigger-happy" by historian John Hope Franklin, had taken guns, marksmanship, and hunting seriously. In the years leading up to the Civil War, the white men of Richmond had armed themselves and organized—establishing militia groups such as the Dragoons, the Light Infantry Blues, and the Rifle Ranges.[11] Shooting competitions in Richmond, like baseball contests, suffered from the economic depression of the 1870s but still went on. In one bizarre competition in 1876, for example, a pigeon shortage cost Babcock outright victory. After shooting seven birds in eight attempts, Babcock had to set down his rifle without a chance to break a first-place tie when the competition organizers ran out of birds to release. When not testing his marksmanship, Babcock also tried his hand at horse racing, but without much success.[12]

Billiards also became immensely popular in Richmond in the 1870s. The Southern press reported eagerly on championship billiard matches, bestowing the title of "champion of Virginia" as haphazardly as it had in baseball.[13] Roller-skating and shuffleboard also gained new participants. Racial segregation was the norm in each of these activities. Putting bricks and mortar to this segregation, Young Men's Christian Associations (YMCAS) opened throughout the city, with separate facilities and organizations serving white and black men.[14] With segregation even more firmly entrenched, Richmond's white press gave more favorable coverage to black recreational organizations. Rather than ignoring black societies that arose, as had been its tradition, the *Daily Dispatch* began providing in the 1870s a regular record of "colored societies" in the city.[15]

A mild pushback against baseball surfaced in several Southern cities after 1870. One Louisville paper joked about baseball and the benefits of early death: "To the parent whose son dies in infancy, there most be something peculiarly soothing in the thought that no matter what may be the fate of the child in the next world, it can never become a member of a base ball club in this."[16] Similarly, the *Atlanta Daily Sun* mused, "What a blessing it would be if base ball were played only by the Japanese."[17]

Even without the Pastime Club, Richmond baseball did not disappear altogether. On July 4, 1871, Richmond clubs gathered to celebrate America's independence while still mourning the South's failed attempt at a similar goal. Richmonders flocked to the Old Fair Grounds for a baseball game meant to raise funds "for the removal of the remains of the Confederate dead from Gettysburg to Hollywood [Cemetery]."[18] Baseball teams representing Richmond and Petersburg competed for a quixotically conceived "championship of Virginia."[19] Clubs, including the Swan, Virginia, Old Dominion, Atlantic, and Athletic, formed and played during the first half of the 1870s in Richmond. Most of these teams, however, played just a handful of public games before disbanding or easing into inactivity. Richmond's *Daily Dispatch* gave the clubs and baseball in the city only sporadic coverage.

As Reconstruction waned New Orleans surpassed Richmond as the center of Southern baseball, but in a less hierarchical manner than had been evident in the years immediately following the Civil War. The ballplayers of Atlanta, Macon, Montgomery, and other Southern cities did not write to their counterparts in New Orleans looking for leadership, as they had to Richmond earlier. The baseball clubs of New Orleans simply played more often and better than those of most other Southern cities. Led by the Lone Star Club, the city's oldest baseball organization, New Orleanians hosted tournaments and watched hundreds of ballgames annually. In 1872 nineteen clubs entered a chase for the city and state championship.[20] New Orleans, not surprisingly, was among the first Southern cities to support professional baseball.[21]

Babcock and the Conservative Party

Many of Richmond's baseball players transitioned from baseball to more direct involvement in politics. Virginia's Conservative Party mirrored the aggressive sectionalism that had surfaced in Richmond's baseball community. The party had formed in 1867 as a Southern-based faction of the Democratic Party. The Conservatives opposed the Republican Party, especially the "mushrooming" radical faction of the GOP that supported equal rights for former slaves.[22] Although the stakes were considerably higher and the politics more direct, the activities of the Conservative Party in Richmond still fit within the patterns established by Richmond baseball clubs emphasizing sectional and racial separation.

As Richmond ballplayers spent less time shagging flies and more time wrangling votes, Alexander Babcock still provided leadership. Babcock emerged as a full-fledged member of Richmond's conservative political movement. Babcock provided public commentary on the

1872 presidential election. In 1875 Babcock was elected treasury pro tem of the city's Conservative Committee and chosen as a delegate to the Senatorial Convention. The *Richmond Daily Dispatch* urged residents of the former Confederate capital to patronize Babcock's ice business; Babcock's service deserved support.[23] The Old Dominion (Base Ball) Club joined Babcock in the political fight. Names that had previously surfaced in only box scores—James M. Tyler (Arlington Base Ball Club) and Daniel Wren (Mechanic Base Ball Club)—began to appear in print attached to conservative political causes.[24]

That baseball for the Old Dominion Club fit with prosegregation, anti-Reconstruction politics was evident as the club played and politicked on a nearly equal basis during the 1874 and 1875 seasons.[25]

Black Baseball and Violence

Black men continued to play baseball in the South as Reconstruction wound down. In 1875 in Louisiana a dozen black clubs formed a "Colored Base Ball Association."[26] Black clubs played and organized throughout the South, from Galveston to Little Rock to Richmond.[27] Although these clubs did not ever acquiesce to the inequalities of segregation, they focused mostly on building the best black clubs they could. Integrating baseball did not concern most black ballplayers on a day-by-day basis. There were too many other obstacles to face.

As the ten-year anniversary of the Civil War's end neared, black players faced an onslaught of negative press. Racial separation was further entrenched in the baseball world by linking black baseball activity to violence and instability. Surveying Southern newspapers during the 1870s makes evident this slandering pattern. The mechanics of segregation in this case reverberated against the idea that baseball was an especially gentlemanly game and that proper ball games needed white female fans.

To be sure, baseball (black and white) had its share of violence during this period. In 1870 in New Orleans, for example, an umpire grew tired of taunts from a catcher questioning his calls. When the offending catcher was knocked to the ground during a play, the umpire picked up a bat and clubbed the catcher in the head, killing him.[28] Other, mostly random, acts of violence happened throughout the nineteenth century. But given the general roughness of the games and instability of the times, one must conclude reports on fights and violence at *black* baseball games received an inordinate amount of attention from the white press. The ratio of reporting on uneventful ballgames involving black ballplayers versus sensationalized accounts of "near riots" connected to black baseball became increasingly skewed. Baseball-centric newspapers led the charge. *Wilkes' Spirit of the Times*, for example, wrote of "dark and swarthy" ballplayers from Williamsburg hosting a black club from Philadelphia in 1870. Rather than baseball, however, "wrangling, disputing, bullying, charging, denying, cursing, and countering" dominated the event. "A general riot took place," the sporting press reported.[29] Similarly, the *New York Clipper* reported on a match between the Excelsior Club of Philadelphia and the Uniques of Brooklyn, both black clubs, where something *could have* gone wrong. "The prospect seemed pretty fair at one time for a riot," the *Clipper* reported, connecting black baseball to violence despite the fact that no actual confrontation occurred.[30]

Relatively isolated incidents of black baseball violence did occur in both the North and the South, but they were wildly exaggerated by the press. The Charleston-Savannah baseball conflict of 1869 seemed to spark a press vigilance movement in reporting on the perceived unruliness of black baseball. The steady stream of stories involving black ballplayers fighting and black fans storming fields certainly served the cause of whites who wanted baseball to remain racially segregated. Reading just a sampling of this type of stories gives one a feel for the effect they had on ballplaying communities. A partial sampling: In 1869 a black baseball club riding a steamer across the Potomac River "commenced fighting . . . and in a short time the row became general."[31] In 1870 in Cleveland, a "murderous affray" took place on the field of the "Colored Base Ball Club of Van Wert." Two black men argued, called each other names, and fought. One hit the other with a "terrible blow on the head" with a baseball bat.[32] In 1871 in Atlanta, a white woman crossed through a baseball field at dark, only to be attacked by black man who demanded, "Give me a kiss."[33]

An 1874 game in Memphis, involving two black teams, turned into a shoot-out. Violence, so it seemed according to many white newspapers, threatened to break out anytime black clubs met. "During a game of [black baseball] in the suburbs of Memphis on Wednesday evening, a negro man, who was in the way of Peter Meath, the catcher, was ordered out of the way, to which he responded with an oath, and drawing a pistol fired at Meath, who ran to his coat, and getting a pistol returned the fire. Some half dozen shots were fired in the melee that ensued, the negro firing at other members of the club. Finally he was shot in the back and then beaten terribly."[34] Similarly, two clubs in Holly Springs, Mississippi, in 1876, fought over field rights. In a strikingly common act of baseball violence, one player struck the other on the head with a baseball bat, "killing him instantly."[35] The men involved in the fight were not just ordinary players: "They were the leaders of the two clubs, and quarreled about their right to a certain field." In Madison, Florida, a few years later, an even more salacious account emerged. An argument arose during a game between two black clubs; it escalated quickly due to the fact that the players had come armed. By the time police responded, "one man was shot and another cut, both perhaps fatally." The police arrested sixteen ballplayers.[36]

The imagery presented in these and other similar accounts undoubtedly frightened many white baseball players and fans. The stories fed prejudices. The difference between the baseball environment presented through stories of violence involving black players versus those of the gentlemanly, controlled, and respectable setting often conveyed regarding white baseball contests could not have been more striking. For example, one might read of the player-crowd interaction at a game involving two black clubs in Chattanooga, Tennessee: "The Olympics [who had lost] . . . grew angry and malicious and tried to embroil the Atlanta crowd in a fight."[37] This image, on some level, would then be compared to highly glossed accounts of white baseball's unique respectability. A not atypical story: "It is to be hoped that all will endeavor to encourage the attendance of their lady-friends, who by their presence will give a refining influence to our national game. In Boston, Hartford, Chicago, St. Louis and Cincinnati, the ladies always turn out in full force and it adds greatly to the interest of both players and spectators."[38] Thus, to the nineteenth-century baseball fan who read enough accounts of, say, black catchers going to the bench to get their pistols and then shooting and beating an adversary, the gulf of respectability (and even safety) between white and black baseball became obvious. Segregation seemed like the only reasonable policy.

The 1875 Season

Baseball experienced a rebirth in Richmond, and in the South generally, in 1875. The worst of the financial crises had passed, and a second generation of white ballplayers took to the baseball fields. Alexander Tomlinson, a former member of the Richmond Pastime, led the revival in Richmond. During the early 1870s when men such as Alexander Babcock concentrated more on politics than baseball, a team from Petersburg, the Old Dominion Club, had emerged to claim the championship of Virginia.[39] Thus, as the first order of business, Tomlinson fired off a challenge to the Old Dominion Club and the rest of Petersburg's baseball community at the start of the 1875 season. Tomlinson asserted that his recently assembled "nine" would face any nine men from Petersburg for "a Ball and the Championship of the State of Virginia."[40]

Richmond's baseball men still perceived themselves to be the finest in the state. Tomlinson's challenge also made evident, again, Richmond's rejection of national baseball standards. Although Richmond could not expect to place a team in the NAPBBP circuit, Tomlinson might have at least acknowledged the more hierarchical nature of baseball competition. He might have admitted that the practice of new teams mandating themselves challengers for a particular championship had long since ceased. He did not. The men of Richmond would continue to play the game and compete for championships on their own terms. Richmond challenged the men of Petersburg to a championship match. The Richmond nine traveled to Petersburg and won. And thus with one hastily arranged game, Richmond regained the unofficial top spot in Virginia baseball.[41]

In 1875 Richmond's newspapers once again gave baseball regular coverage. At least twenty-five publicized contests took place during the 1875 season. Although some overlap occurred, new players and clubs dominated the city's baseball scene. Henry Boschen became one of the new baseball leaders in the city.[42] Through Boschen Richmond baseball gained a Doubleday-esque creation (or at least rebirth) story of its own. According to tradition, Boschen's Richmond doctor recommended that he get more exercise. Following these directions, Boschen went to a vacant lot with a bat and a ball. There he hit the ball and retrieved it, hit the ball and retrieved it, until he grew fatigued. Tired of chasing his own hits, Boschen organized his own baseball team, the Pacific Base Ball Club. For his actions, Boschen would become known, somewhat mythically, as the "father of *organized* baseball" in Richmond.[43]

Boschen, like Babcock before him, was a leader in Richmond's business community. He owned a shoe factory, and many of his workers soon doubled as ballplayers. Boschen did not pay his workers to play ball, but he was known to offer a talented baseball player a job in his factory.[44] The white ballplayers of the 1870s were similar to those who played in Richmond during the 1860s. They came from a variety of backgrounds and held many different jobs. They were factory hands in Manchester and on Belle Isle, saloon owners, hotel clerks, printers, newspapermen, and cigar sellers, among other things. They were mostly political conservatives. Several Richmond ballplayers (including Alexander Tomlinson, James M. Tyler, and Daniel Wren) worked for the city's police force.[45] This commingling, of the police department and baseball, served as another warning for blacks to stay away. The black residents of Southern Reconstruction states complained regularly about the unfairness and, at times, brutality of the white police forces.[46]

Boschen's Pacific Club had a successful inaugural season in 1875. One of the club's first games came on the Fourth of July, a traditional baseball day in the city. The Pacific Club took on the Atlantics, also of Richmond, for the benefit of the St. Joseph's orphanage.[47] Supporting an orphanage did not ring quite as symbolically loud as playing to pay for proper burials of fallen Confederate soldiers, but the cause was still one related to losing the Civil War. The Pacific Club won most of its games and gained a reputation, along with Tomlinson's club, as one of the city's finest. The Washington Nationals took notice and invited the Pacific Club to Washington for a game. The Nationals by this time had fallen from their lofty perch of the 1860s. Still, the club held some lingering influence and cachet in the baseball world. The Pacifics traveled to Washington in August 1875, hoping to demonstrate that Richmonders were finally ready to compete with clubs from beyond their own state. The Pacifics lost, 22–5. The divide between the baseball men of Richmond and those in Washington DC still remained wide.[48]

In all about twenty white clubs played in Richmond during the 1875 seasons. The list included some familiar names (the Richmond,

Old Dominion, Arlington, and Olympic Clubs), as well as a dozen or so new ones. Richmond College fielded a team. Other clubs included the Mount Vernon, Virginia, Swan, Atlantic, Athletic, Eagle, Mutual, Figaro, Eureka, and Excelsior. At first glance the Richmond game had a less sectional tone. The names had softened. Perhaps, however, because political representation had been restored and white men had seized control of the city's government, names such as the Confederate Club and Robert E. Lee Club were no longer as necessary. The Lost Cause connections, however, remained. Boschen would eventually lose control of his ball club to a group of prominent Confederate veterans. Renamed the Virginias, the club joined the Virginia Base Ball Association and raised money for a Jefferson Davis Memorial and the "Lee Camp" soldiers home.[49]

A Northern Humbling

The Red Stocking Club of Boston visited Richmond in 1875 and in doing so illuminated, with some finality, the failure of white baseball's attempt at sectional reconciliation. The Boston club had recently toured Europe with the Athletics of Philadelphia and had won the three prior National Association championships. In 1875 the Red Stockings would win seventy-one of their seventy-nine games.[50] Demonstrating just how wide the gap had become between the best clubs of the North and the best clubs of the South, the Red Sox chose not to challenge any Richmond club to a game. "It is possible that a picked nine of this city will be induced to play the Red Stockings a game, through they can scarcely do so with hope of success," one Richmond paper concluded.[51] Thus, instead of engaging one of Richmond's clubs, the Red Stockings brought the Washingtons, of Washington DC, with them to Richmond. The clubs met at the Richmond Old Fair Grounds on April 29, 1875. It would be the only professional match played in a former Confederate state during the 1875 season.[52]

The Red Stockings–Washington tilt went off as planned. The significance of the event—a Boston club and a Washington DC club meeting for a match in Richmond—had little to do with the score. Boston won. Rather, the game more significantly demonstrated the failure of baseball's reconciliation campaign. White baseball leaders had rejected black clubs and black ballplayers in order to win favor from Southern white ballplayers. And for nearly a decade, Northern white baseball leaders had tried to induce their Southern counterparts to play baseball, to join the National Associations, and to keep overt sectionalism out of the game. Only on the first emphasis did the effort bear some fruit.

The *New York Clipper*'s coverage of the Red Stockings–versus–Washingtons game revealed the Northerner's frustration over the continuing obstinacy of the Southerners to acquiesce to reconciliation. The Richmond crowd did not cheer politely for all the ballplayers, as was the baseball custom. Instead, "[Southern] prejudices were shown in their exhibition of favoritism for Washington, or what they considered as the 'Southern nine' against the Northern or Massachusetts players." The game was, the *Clipper* reported, "about as partisan a gathering as any country village could present."[53]

Perhaps finally recognizing the futility of the reconciliation effort, the *Clipper* let loose and openly belittled baseball in the South. Richmond was a "country village," not a true baseball city. The fans lacked civility. The "better class," the *Clipper* complained, was outnumbered. "The minority of the better class present, of course resented this rural style of things; but the shouts of the majority ruled supreme." Also, Richmond's field was subpar, "rough," and "below the standard exhibited on our local field." The game should have thrilled Southerners, by the *Clipper* estimation. "The play was so infinitely superior to anything ever seen in Richmond, that the spectators were delighted."[54] The *Clipper* concluded its report on Richmond by warning clubs from the North to "keep away" from Richmond. The *Clipper* signed off by again expressing amazement that sectionalism and politics had a place in the baseball community. "We thought that in the baseball arena sectional ill-will was something all would refrain from."[55] In a way both sides had stayed consistent. Northern leaders had always wanted Southern clubs to conform to fit into a national community of baseball players. Southern players had always wanted to remain separate.

Black Baseball in Richmond

Finally, in July 1876, a brief notice in the *Richmond Daily Dispatch* confirmed the existence of a group of men who had been pushed to the far periphery of Richmond's baseball community—black baseball players. In a remarkably nondescript announcement, the *Daily Dispatch* reported on July 22, 1876, that a game of baseball between two black clubs had taken place one day earlier. "Colored Base-Ball Clubs—A match game was played between the Lone Star and Reindeer Clubs yesterday, resulting in a victory for the former by a score of 46 to 5."[56] There was no further comment. Instead, the *Richmond Daily Dispatch* simply announced the game as an everyday occurrence. Indeed, it probably was. The revolutionary nature of the black baseball game in Richmond, in 1876, was not that black men took to a ball field, but rather that Richmond's white press finally chose to acknowledge the event.

Black baseball had almost certainly existed in Richmond long before July 1876. The fact that the *Richmond Daily Dispatch* detailed a match between two black clubs strongly suggests that black baseball had been a part of the city's recreational landscape for some time. The paper did not report on the formation of a black club. Nor did it record two "nines" taking part in an informal game. Rather, two black clubs, at the very least, existed in the city and were ready for action. In September the *Dispatch* reported on a second game involving black clubs, this time the Reindeer and the Lookout Base Ball Clubs.[57]

In assessing Richmond baseball after the Civil War, absence of certain phenomena is important. No grand demonstration existed against black baseball. Instead, complete avoidance relegated black baseball clubs even further to the periphery of the baseball community than if they had been castigated as inferior or unworthy on a daily basis in the press. This avoidance was typical of racism in Richmond. The process is informative in understanding the mechanics of segregation. Countless examples of brutal unacknowledgment, avoidance, and nonrecognition often preempted confrontation, making black baseball players' fight for a position in Richmond an invisible one until 1876.

The End Game

Richmond's baseball history is characterized by continuity rather than change. The white segregationists did not merely emerge victorious at the end of the Reconstruction era, as had been the case in Philadelphia and Washington. Rather, segregation defined Richmond's baseball community from the moment it arose. Racial exclusion always reigned as supremely important among Richmond's white baseball players. Southern baseball had always reveled in the memory of the

Confederacy. As a manifestation of this, Richmond's white clubs had chosen names that made their allegiances clear—the Secesh, Confederate, and Robert E. Lee Clubs, and so on. Baseball at its height in Richmond (in 1866 especially) had also been a vicarious fight against Northern influence in Richmond. Beneath squabbles of sectional allegiances, most prominently those involving the men of the Union Club, was the question of how white and black men would interact in Richmond. White exclusion won out, in a rout.

The reconciliatory gestures made by white Northern baseball leaders—including drawing the color line in baseball associations—were not enough to convince Richmond's white ballplayers to join a national consortium. Broadly speaking, Southern baseball clubs had played their proverbial hand well. Although individual clubs and particular regions acted differently, collectively white Southern baseball players leveraged the *perceived* prospect of joining with the North and making possible the long-desired dream of a truly "national game" into a policy of thorough exclusion of black baseball players from the game's highest levels. Then, most Southern baseball clubs still rejected the National Associations and, to a certain extent, the "national game." The South roundly won baseball's peace.

Chapter 9

Washington DC

Professional Separation

"Base ball is business now, Nick, and I am trying to arrange our games to make them successful and make them pay," Harry Wright, the manager of the professional Boston Red Stockings, wrote to Nicholas Young in 1872.[1] The concept of "making baseball pay" was not, of course, an entirely new one. Gate receipts, gambling revenues, and covert payments to players had long been part of the game. The broad acceptance, however, of a club paying its players for their baseball services represented a departure from the game's long-held ideals of amateurism. The acceptance of professionalism in baseball changed the game forever, paving the way for the National League (and later the American League), the World Series, and the modern game of baseball.

That baseball's professionalization served also to entrench racial segregation in the game might seem contradictory. With market forces unleashed, wouldn't white baseball club owners take advantage of all available baseball talent? Yes, eventually.[2] But during the 1870s describing a ballplayer as a "professional" became another, new, way of saying he was white. Building on the decisions and customs of the 1860s, the NAPBBP set an example of racial segregation that would be adhered to by more than 99 percent of white ball clubs, for the next eighty years. While the National Association of Professional Base Ball Clubs itself was composed of only a few clubs, the organization became the focus of the baseball press and baseball fans.[3]

Professionalism bolstered racial exclusion in many arenas of American society. Specialization and certification often begot separation. When the American Library Association (ALA), for example, formed in the mid-1870s, the move to create an organized, hierarchical, and respectable profession led also to a declaration on racial separation. Reconciliationist overtures, in the name of creating a national (white) body, quickly surfaced. Meeting in Atlanta in 1876 to encourage the growth of librarianship in the South, the ALA leadership decided against allowing noted bibliophile W. E. B. DuBois to speak, reasoning that there existed "the need to be very careful and conservative on the negro [sic] question at this time."[4] The ALA did not allow black membership. Professional, ALA-credentialed librarians would not only possess training and codified skills, but be, without exception, white.

The baseball community for its part did not give up on amateurism easily. The *New York Clipper* had long worried about the influence of money and gambling on the game. Henry Chadwick weighed in frequently on the topic. Chadwick did not object to professionalism per se, but rather feared that professionals would be the "tools" of politicians and gambling rings.[5] As the first NAPBBP convention approached in March 1871, the *Clipper* opined that professionalism meant a decline in equal opportunity. The dominance of professional clubs, the *Clipper* editorialized, would create a situation of "arbitrary control exhibited by a small minority over a large majority." The paper denounced this "abuse of power" and warned that professionalism would ruin the game.[6]

The rise of professional baseball clubs made baseball more like the rest of the working world. Movements toward specialization and certification in professional associations—trends that would be borne out further during the Progressive Era of the late nineteenth century—resulted in higher wages but also new barriers of entry for one seeking to join a profession. To become a paid, expert baseball player became more difficult with the establishment of the NAPBBP. Again, the reality of money changing hands between club owners and players was not the most important change—indeed, these transactions had been occurring for many years. Rather, the establishment of a profession was, at least to an extent, the monopolization of certain skills, resources, and opportunities.[7] Professional baseball created a "closed shop" of sorts.

Many black ballplayers had experienced workplace discrimination. Charles Douglass's brother Lewis waited nine months for an up-or-down vote on his application to the Columbus Typographical Union. The union never rejected his application outright; instead (dealing with the issue in a somewhat similar manner to the way in which the Philadelphia Base Ball Association dealt with the Pythians), the organization tabled the application indefinitely.[8] Similarly, the District of Columbia Medical Association denied three black physicians from Howard University membership in 1869. To then enforce its segregation stand, the DCMA decided shortly thereafter recommended that two Georgetown University doctors be fired for associating with Howard University.[9]

In terms of unskilled laborers, "muffins" in baseball jargon, blacks looking for union representation also faced rampant discrimination. When the National Labor Union—supposedly open to all laborers— refused to address the needs of black workers, the Colored National Labor Union emerged. Lewis Douglass served as secretary for the organization, and Frederick Douglass accepted the presidency of the CNLU in 1871. After a lengthy debate on the issue, the Knights of Labor also adopted segregationist policies.[10] So although it has been argued that professionalism created a tendency for an industry "to organize itself less and less in terms of territory or race or hereditary status, and more and more in terms of function," in baseball and many work arenas precisely the opposite reality emerged.[11] Professionalism did not diminish racial bias in baseball; it became another layer of separation.

New Precedents of Baseball's Racial Segregation

During the final months of 1870, it became increasingly clear that baseball's strictly amateur days had ended. Not coincidentally, several additional nails in the coffin of baseball's racial segregation were also pounded home during this period. On the latter front, in mid-September 1870 Chicago baseball organizers rejected an application from the city's African American Blue Stocking Club to participate in a citywide tournament for reasons of race. Officially, Chicago's white baseball leaders excluded the Blue Stockings "because the Blue Stockings were not deemed of sufficient strength to be entitled to consideration." The *Chicago Tribune* also admitted, however, that "[the Blue Stockings'] social standing had somewhat to do with the matter."[12] The decision became another precedent supporting the increasingly ubiquitous idea that white and black baseball clubs should not commingle in organized events or associations.

Two months later the New York State Base Ball Association made waves for its own dealings with race. The NYSBBA was in decline. Only a handful of organizations made the effort to attend the November 10, 1870, meeting. The meeting agenda centered on selecting delegates for the upcoming NABBP convention. According to the New York Times, however, dissension arose due to the fact that the "leading professional club of New-York [the Mutual Club] was enabled to control the entire business of the convention in the interests of the professional class."[13] The amateurs had lost their positions of leadership. In this context and with the rise of professional baseball seeming inevitable, the role of black baseball somehow entered the discussion. The professional clubs used their disproportionate influence "to introduce a bone of contention into the councils of the fraternity," reported the New York Times. A delegate representing the Star Club of Brooklyn pushed to clarify, further than had ever been done before, that black clubs should be kept out of white baseball associations.[14]

The Brooklyn Star Club delegate, a Mr. MacDiarmid, proposed a statute: the "prohibition of the admission of colored clubs into the National Convention."[15] A majority of the present delegates agreed; the motion passed. This policy undoubtedly went beyond the segregationist decisions of the 1867 conventions. The Pythians had been individually excluded by the Pennsylvania Association, but without the matter ever coming to an official vote or the issue of black clubs in general being addressed. Similarly, the nominating committee at the national convention of the same year, with their "it is not presumed by your committee that any club who have applied are composed of persons of color" statement, provided something less than an official measure delineating segregation. New York State's sparsely attended convention, dominated by newly ascendant professional baseball clubs, wanted to make racial segregation more official.

National reaction came swiftly, decrying the proposal. The New York Times exhibited a schizophrenic sense of disbelief over the development. "Hitherto this subject [segregation] has been prevented from being breached in the Convention," the Times declared, falsely. Never before had "questions of political bearing" been so directly introduced. The Times correspondent further worried that a truly candid discussion of racial segregation might mean the end of the National Association altogether. "One effect of this partisan and political action by our New-York Convention," the Times predicted gravely, "will be the introduction of an acrimonious and exciting discussion at the National Convention, which will result in divided and discordant councils, if not the entire breaking up of the National Association."[16]

The white baseball community, here given voice by the *New York Times*, evidenced a strange understanding of the day's racial climate and the game's racial history. In 1870 the "torrent of public opinion" favored "the equality of every human being before the law," according to the *Times*. Therefore, the influential newspaper conceived of a formal ban on black participation as "a return to the usages in vogue in the days of human slavery."[17]

In a description that echoed the British Parliament eighteenth-century claims that the American colonists had not needed official delegates or recognition because they had "virtual representation," the *Times* also puzzlingly claimed that "colored clubs" had been "practically recognized as being on an equal footing before the law of the ball field."[18] After all, black clubs had played against their white counterparts in Washington DC and Philadelphia (as mentioned in previous chapters). This "practical representation," according to the *Times*, was all that had been necessary or possible.

"Political questions" caused dissension, which had always scared baseball organizers. Additionally, no black clubs, according to the white press, had proved themselves worthy of joining the white baseball community. The Pythians had failed to impress on the ball field against white opposition, as had the Washington Alerts and Mutuals, so the rationale went. Thus, again using the *Times* as a barometer (since white baseball leaders did not elaborate on why they acted as they did in terms of race relations), the possibility for future inclusion hypothetically existed. "If a colored club is good enough to play ball with in order to make gate money, they are good enough to enter the National Association. *But, as yet, no club has attempted to seek admission to the Base-ball Associations, and therefore this premature refusal to associate with them comes as a needless and gratuitous insult.*"[19]

The reaction to the Star Club's overt opposition to black inclusion in the National Association was dichotomous. There existed a seemingly progressive condemnation of overtly offensive statements toward black clubs, but also a fierce desire to avoid discussing baseball as it related to civil rights at all. Slavery had lost; new times mandated that black Americans enjoy similar freedoms and protections as whites. The conviction that discussing the issue of black baseball clubs' place in the white baseball hierarchy should be avoided at all costs, however, reigned supreme. Even with the reconciliationist agenda having largely failed to bring the South fully into the fold, a paranoid fear still existed about introducing political dissension into the ranks of baseball. A paradoxical consensus emerged: statements of direct discrimination against black clubs should not take place *because* the discussion of black ballplayers' place in the National Association should be avoided.

Recognizing the firestorm its delegate had created, the Brooklyn Star Club quickly tried to make amends. The club had a reputation to protect. The Star Club had formed in 1856 and won many National Association games. Among its historic contributions, the Brooklyn Star helped introduce the curveball to baseball and also the box score. Thus, the club disavowed its delegate for introducing a "question of political nature." Agreeing that the move "cannot fail to prove prejudicial to that harmony which is so essential to our success as an organization," the Brooklyn Star Club put forth a public resolution stating that it did not sanction the discriminatory measure.[20]

Heading toward the already scheduled convention of the National Association of Base Ball Players, further reaction to the New York State snafu arose. The *Brooklyn Eagle*, relatively supportive of black baseball in the past, bristled at the notion that the story deserved coverage at all. "Considerable unnecessary agitation" had been created by "political agitators," the *Eagle* complained.[21] The decision on black baseball had already been made. "It would have been better, perhaps, if the subject had not been broached, especially in view of the fact that the question had been fully disposed of in the National Convention of 1867, in Philadelphia."[22]

The difference between the coverage of the NYSBBA meeting in these two influential newspapers, the *New York Times* and the *Brooklyn Eagle*, is worth noting. The *Times* argued that racial issues should be avoided because no black club had ever tried to join one of the major white baseball associations anyway. The *Eagle*, coming closer to getting its facts straight, concluded that the issue should be avoided based on the precedent of the 1867 national convention when Arthur Gorman had taken his stand for reconciliation. The common ground between the two reports, however—that segregation should be observed without its mechanics being discussed—accurately captured the racial climate of baseball in 1870.

The National Association of Professional Base Ball Players

The National Association of Base Ball Players, baseball's premier organizing body since 1857, breathed its last breath of relevant air on November 30, 1870. The national convention that had been eyed by the New York State Association and the impulsive Brooklyn Star delegate went off as planned. The convention attendees never addressed the controversy that had arisen over "colored clubs" only a couple of weeks prior. There was no need to make a statement on racial exclusion when no obvious cracks in the dam of exclusion could be sighted. Mr. MacDiarmid, the testy Brooklyn Star delegate who had caused the controversy at the New York State gathering, lost his seat at the national meeting. He was replaced by another, ostensibly more responsible, member of the Brooklyn club.[23]

Instead, the all-pervading issue at the national convention was the unstoppable rise of professional baseball. Professionalism included more than just the NAPBBP clubs. As had been the case at the New York convention, the outnumbered professionals dominated the majority of amateurs. The end had come: "This convention, and the remarkable proceedings which characterized it shows that the last feather had been placed upon the camel's back, and under the pressure of the control of a clique of professional managers the National Association gave up the ghost," a *New York Clipper* reporter mourned.[24] A fracturing along professional and amateur lines would quickly come to complement the firm racial line of separation. Even as the 1870 national convention was under way, amateur clubs moved to reorganize as the National Association of *Amateur* Base Ball Players, "with a constitution and a code of playing rules which will repudiate every phase of the system of playing base ball for money."[25]

The fact that a rare public debate erupted over race and baseball at almost exactly the same time that a separation formally occurred between professionals and amateurs should be noted. Although the causal link is far from absolute, the last-ditch effort to keep white ballplayers somewhat united probably figured into the public reaction against the Brooklyn Stars' motion. In the relative anonymity of the NYSBBA meeting, white baseball voted to officially exclude black clubs. When the motion became public, however, new considerations arose. The national brotherhood of white baseball players was falling apart, the logic seemed to go, and certainly issues of race should not be added to the equation. In the end it did not matter. Professionals and amateurs separated. Black ballplayers remained excluded.

Nicholas Young—Guiding Professionals

Washington's Nicholas Young played a vital, if somewhat unintended, role in the rise of baseball's first professional association. Taking note of the split that had occurred at the fourteenth annual National Association of Base Ball Players convention, Young called for a meeting of professionals. Up to this point white baseball leaders had been unable to facilitate a fair and logical championship system. The amateur association's funds had been raided by incompetent treasurers.[26] Infighting and bickering, along with constant rule changes, had often dominated National Association conventions.

Nicholas Young thought professional baseball could do better. Thus seeking to facilitate a new organizing structure, Young organized a meeting of baseball leaders on March 17, 1871, St. Patrick's Day, in order to devise a scheduling plan that would result in an undisputed champion. The gathering became something more, leading to the formation of the National Association of Professional Base Ball Players. The meeting launched, once and for all, open and organized professional baseball in the United States.[27] Clubs from baseball's major cities, including New York, Boston, Chicago, and Philadelphia, sent representatives to Young's meeting. Washington got two seats (for the Nationals and Olympics) at the table, probably because of Young's role in the proceedings.[28] The delegates quickly agreed upon a playing schedule (involving each team playing a best-three-out-of-five series with the other nine clubs, but scheduling these contests on their own), a ten-dollar entry fee, and a constitution. The rules of the game, on the field, would be the same as those of the previous association. The precedents and traditions of racial segregation were passed on as well.

After the meeting Young went to work securing an improved roster for the Washington Olympic Base Ball Club. He traveled to find and sign players, going to Buffalo, for example, to recruit catcher Myron Holly.

When not on the road, Young conducted his baseball business from his desk in the Second Auditors Office at the Treasury Department.[29] In the coming years Young would serve on the NAPBBP's Championship and Judiciary Committees and as secretary. When the National Association failed, Young took leadership posts in the National League, eventually becoming NL president. Young organized clubs not only in Washington DC, but also in Chicago and Baltimore. Along the way Young earned a stellar reputation in baseball circles, enjoying "the confidence and respect of the management of all the professional nines."[30] One baseball scribe went so far as to call Nick Young one of baseball's most vital administrators ever: "No man ever connected with the game has had a longer or more respected career than Mr. Young."[31]

Young's role in forming and supporting the National Association of Professional Base Ball Players is informative. Young had experience in government organization, working at the Treasury Department for more than twenty-five years. Young provided leadership to the baseball community, not on the basis of his own playing proficiency, but rather due to his "mathematical mind" and talent for organization. Young took the reputation and position of the game of baseball seriously. He acted judiciously. "Young commands the profound respect of his officials in council," wrote one newspaper in 1892, "by his wise parliamentary rulings and his keen insights into the requirements of the game."[32] The point here is not to deify Young—a well-meaning and organized but not really transcendent leader. Nor is formation of the National Association of Professional Base Ball Players to be understood as a singularly defining moment. Indeed, the association never operated as a truly cohesive league and fell apart after only four seasons. Rather, at issue still is how baseball's mechanics of segregation continued to unfold. Young said almost nothing about race over the course of his career in baseball. Yet Young, through his commitment to organizing professional baseball, played a role in the game's increasingly codified segregation.

The Prerequisites of Professionalism: Money, Land, and Whiteness

The divisive effect of baseball's professionalization became evident almost immediately in Washington DC, as it had in Philadelphia. The plans of the Olympics and Nationals diverged significantly for the first time. Although both clubs attended the National Association's founding meeting, the National Club opted not to join the new association. In the midst of restructuring its membership and finances, the Nationals simply could not commit to the ambitious schedule (a five-game series against each other club) proposed by Young and the other leaders. The cost was too high for the Nats, who only weeks before the founding of the NAPBBP had been sued for delinquent payment by a lumber company.[33]

The financial resources necessary to field a professional baseball club—to pay players, improve grounds, and travel extensively—kept most clubs from participating at the highest level. In order to raise funds, Young's Olympics organized as a stock corporation.[34] The *National Republican*, among other Washington newspapers, quickly picked up on the connection between financial strength and baseball success. In the Olympics' case, the *Republican* assured its readers that the club would be "second to none in the country," because its stockholders were "leading businessmen" and the club's stock was "a very profitable investment."[35]

Professional clubs also needed powerful financial backers. George W. Riggs, one of Washington's most prominent bankers, invested heavily in the Olympic Club. He held the title for the Olympic Grounds, which were on the outskirts of the city proper, on the block between Sixteenth, Seventeenth, R, and S Streets. By way of contrast, there were very few black men in the 1870s who could have devoted their land and money to professional baseball on the scale that Riggs did.[36] Before the 1871 National Association season began, Riggs directed that a ten-foot fence be built around the Olympic Grounds. Baseball's "enclosure" determined that no longer would fans or players be able to wander onto the grounds or even enjoy a glimpse of a game without paying for a ticket. Riggs also built a clubhouse for the players and seating for three thousand spectators. He outfitted each of his players with a new, expensive uniform: "a white flannel Zouve suit, trimmed with blue; hat instead of cap, close-fitting knit shirt, over jacket, corded pants, blue stockings, and white canvas shoes, with leather trimmings."[37] Finally, the club spent nearly four thousand dollars leveling and resodding its field and installing drainage. Riggs also had a forty-four-foot club flag draped from one of the foul poles, displayed the club emblem on the grandstands, and hung two club pennants from the club's new and improved seating rafters.[38]

The costs of professional baseball nearly bankrupted the Olympic Club right out of the gate. In January 1871 an audit had found the club's finances to be in order. By the end of the inaugural NAPBBP season, however, the club was "$3500 behind" in its finances and engaged in an unseemly public dispute with the National Club regarding the use of baseball facilities.[39] Tensions arose between the Olympics and Nationals in 1871 regarding the use of baseball space and over the question of which organization would be *the* Washington club. When a June rainstorm washed out the National Grounds, the spat between the two clubs spilled over into the press. The Nationals' leadership had assumed that hospitality, long a hallmark of the baseball community, would compel the Olympics to share their grounds. But after negotiating back and forth, the two clubs could not reach an agreement.[40] The Olympic Club (probably Nicholas Young, since he still served as secretary) released a letter of explanation to the press, clarifying that times had changed. The Olympics had gone "from a second-rate club to the *front* rank of baseball" and thus had to disassociate themselves from some of their prior friends.[41] The struggle over land had intensified, as baseball grounds became symbols of prowess and chips in the escalating contest for baseball supremacy in the city.[42]

Black and Amateur

As Nicholas Young spurred on professional baseball, the Mutual and Alert Clubs continued to play in Washington as amateurs. In Washington a new black (and therefore amateur) club emerged late in the 1870 season. The black Metropolitans organized with an "excellent board of officers" and "eye for business."[43] The "Mets," ignoring baseball's 1870 fracturing, announced it planned to compete with the District's best clubs, regardless of race. The club purchased a twenty-five-foot pennant and urged all clubs in the District "desiring to wrest this pennant from the Metropolitans" to send along their challenges.[44] No white clubs took the bait. The *Evening Star* and *Sunday Herald* perverted the ambitions of the Metropolitan Club. According to the *Star*, the Mets' pennant was "to be held by the champion (colored) of the District" and the newly purchased pennant as "symbolic of the District colored championship."[45] The Mets themselves had made no such distinctions.

The Washington Mutuals in 1870 traveled to Maryland and New York to compete against other top black clubs. The Mutuals' tour was "the most extensive trip that any colored club has ever undertaken."[46]

The Mutual Club stopped first in Baltimore, defeating the Enterprise Club by a score of 51–23.[47] After Baltimore Charles Douglass and his teammates headed for New York. The trip captured the attention of the *New York Clipper*, a paper that continued to give black baseball sporadic coverage. The paper matter-of-factly reported on the stellar ballplaying of the Mutual Club. "The Mutuals, of Washington—a colored club—recently on a tour through the western part of the state of New York, beat the Arctic Club, of Lockport, on August 19th, by a score of 26 to 0, the Rapido Club, of Niagara Falls, on the 20th by a score of 64 to 10, the Mutuals of Buffalo, on the 21st, by a score of 72 to 10. On the 22nd they played a picked nine, at Rochester."[48] The Mutuals faced a stiffer challenge in Rochester, but still prevailed 23–19 to cap off a successful tour. The trip featured no forays into interracial play, just high-level competition between black baseball clubs.[49]

The Mutuals returned to Washington DC to meet their upstart rivals, the Metropolitans, in September 1870, just as the Blue Stockings were experiencing rejection from the year-end Chicago baseball tournament.[50] The game pitted two evenly matched clubs. The score remained close until the ninth inning. Then, in the last inning, the umpire made a controversial call. The Metropolitans' first baseman objected vehemently to the decision, then quit, refusing to play if the decision stood. The game halted. Finally, "after considerable talk" with no resolution, the game was discontinued and called in favor of the Mutuals, score 36–34. Walking off the field in protest was unheard of in nineteenth-century baseball circles, and the resulting press coverage of the event used the same shocked and paternalistic tone as those stories commingling black baseball and violence. "We regret," one reporter concluded somewhat smugly, "the M's should have met trouble in their first important match."[51] Not surprisingly, the Metropolitans disappeared following their abbreviated 1870 season. Black clubs, mostly lacking financial backers, came and went often during this fluid period.

The Mutual Club Plays On

As the 1871 season began, the black Washington Mutuals had reason to worry about more than just exclusion from the newly formed NAPBBP. Washington DC was abandoning civil rights. After having elected black men to hold nearly one-third of the seats in the city's legislature between 1868 and 1870, black and white Washingtonians alike lost the rights of "home rule" in 1871. In a shocking reversal of democratic fortunes, the U.S. Congress determined that the District of Columbia should be put back under congressional control. While the citizens of Washington maintained the right to elect the twenty-two members of the lower chamber of the District council, the president appointed a governor of the District and the eleven members of the upper council.[52] The best days of Reconstruction-era civil rights progress had passed for Washington DC.

In the midst of setbacks in the city's civil rights, Charles Douglass and the Mutuals followed up their undefeated 1870 tour by planning an even more ambitious slate of games for 1871. Using the Third Auditors Office of the Treasury Department as a return address (Nick Young worked in the Second Auditors Office, and dozens of other players were employed throughout the Treasury Department), Douglass sent out a broad baseball challenge.[53] Black clubs from New York City, Albany, Troy, Boston, Fitchburg, Newport, Philadelphia, and Baltimore responded.[54]

But even with his respected government position, baseball prowess, and famous father, Charles Douglass could not escape the increasingly racist realities of Washington DC during the 1870s. Official rights, where they did exist, were often negated by social pressures. Douglass's position in the government, for example, angered many whites. The *New National Era*, a newspaper begun in Washington DC by Frederick Douglass in 1872, reported with notable detachment on the discrimination faced by Charles. "A Southern delegate, in passing through the Treasury Department, and noticing a colored clerk (son of Fred. Douglass) engaged in slinging his quill, gave forth unmistakable signs of disgust, and walked off with the remark, 'Thank God! When Uncle Horace [Greeley] comes in office there will be a stop put to that work.'"[55] Such scenes and sentiments were commonplace.

Interracial games did not stop entirely in the 1870s, but those that did take place meant considerably less than the first such contests in 1869. In both 1871 and 1872, the Mutuals competed against Washington's white Creighton Base Ball Club.[56] The Mutuals beat the Creightons in 1872. Still, the *Sunday Herald*, the only paper to report on the game, mentioned the event only perfunctorily: "On Friday a match game of base ball was played on the White Lot between the Mutual and Creighton Clubs. The former won by a score of 19 to 14."[57] In 1873 the newly formed Monumental black baseball club defeated the white Capital Club.[58] Again, only the *Sunday Herald* reported on the event, and then only the score. This approach of making light of those integrated interactions that did occur had become, it seemed, part of the fabric of segregation itself.

The *New National Era* (which had become a Douglass family affair) reported the Mutuals' first contest of 1873, a match against the Monumentals on July 24, 1873.[59] The Mutuals lost, but the clubs covered some of their costs by charging twenty-five cents for admission. When the Mutuals and Alerts renewed their rivalry (one of the oldest in black baseball), Frederick Douglass sided with the Alert Club, since he was still an honorary member of the organization. Thus, even though Charles Douglass had jumped from the Alerts to the Mutuals, Frederick Douglass remained loyal. The Mutuals defeated the Alerts in a tight match, 19–13.[60]

When the upstart Washingtons, a white club that emerged as one of the District's finest in 1873, played two games each against the Mutual and Alert Clubs in 1873, it became clear that black-versus-white games no longer had much societal impact. The amateur-professional divide relegated integrated contests to sideshow status. And further adding insult to perceived irrelevancy, the *Sunday Herald* used the *exact* same banal language to describe the 1873 interracial game as had been used four years prior to describe the 1869 Olympic-Alert match. The game was, the *Sunday Herald* reported, once again "novel and interesting."[61]

The *Sunday Herald*'s style of reporting on black baseball illuminated some of the new barriers that had come with professionalism. According to the *Sunday Herald*, one game pitted the "Washingtons (professionals)" against "the Alert (colored)."[62] Thus, professionalism had become another demarcation of whiteness. The paper assumed that its readership would understand that "colored" meant nonprofessional and that "professionals" meant white. For its part, the Washington Club evidenced a remarkable ease in playing black clubs. Having defeated the Alert and Mutual Clubs, the club wrapped up its season with a game against a "picked nine of colored ball players."[63] The black all-stars nearly defeated the Washingtons. The game ended 13–10 in favor of the white professionals. This time the *New National Era* picked up on the action. Douglass's paper, like the white press, made a distinction between professional baseball players and black baseball players. "Though not defeating the professionals," the *New National Era* wrote, "the colored young men, who do not make ball playing a business, succeeded in calling out the utmost exertion on the part of the professionals to save themselves from a defeat at the hands of unprofessionals and colored men."[64] Had the upset occurred, it would have apparently been a double disgrace for the white professional club.

The White Lot

Although the lack of inclusion of black clubs in the professional National Association probably surprised very few black ballplayers in the District, the increasing segregation of baseball land in the city came as an unexpected blow. Land, of course, was central to Reconstruction-era debates. In Washington progress on this front had been slow, but not insignificant. In 1870 Washington DC's city council passed a comprehensive antidiscrimination bill that forbade restaurants and theaters from prohibiting black patronage. In June 1872 Lewis Douglass, then serving on the council, introduced a bill to strengthen the city's non-discrimination statutes even further. This bill passed, only to be struck down by the District Supreme Court in the same year.[65]

The battle for control of the White Lot brought baseball firmly into the civil rights struggle over land. The White Lot had been the birth-place of competitive baseball in the District. Its location on the front lawn, essentially, of the White House made it a political place as well. In 1869 General Michler had ordered that baseball cease on the White Lot. Michler gave no explanation for his edict, but the order was largely ignored anyhow. Games still occurred on the grounds periodically in the 1870s, and the grounds remained mostly open to the public.[66] Black Washingtonians used the grounds for recreation and occasionally for political gatherings. In September 1871, for example, black residents gathered at the White Lot to commemorate Lincoln's "one-hundred-day" freedom proclamation. The celebration included a parade as well as a salute by the Stanton Guard, a black militia organization named after former attorney general and secretary of war Edwin M. Stanton. Standing within a few hundred feet of the White House, the Stanton Guard fired off several salutes throughout the daylong celebration.[67]

4. White House grounds. Library of Congress, Geography and Map Division.

As part of a wave of infrastructural improvements in the 1870s, the City of Washington DC refurbished many of its public spaces, including the White Lot. Baseball players and park patrons were thrilled. The *New National Era* celebrated the upgrades to the White Lot in particular. "To General O. E. Babcock," the *New National Era* gushed, "the citizens and visitors of Washington are indebted for the splendid resorts to avoid the heat and dust, furnished by our parks. . . . Lafayette Square and the White Lot have been great improved, and are now beautiful and fashionable resorts."[68]

The improvements to the White Lot made it even more valuable and contested public space. Not surprisingly, the increased value of the property drew more attention to the activities that played out in the shadow of the White House. By 1873 the Creighton Base Ball Club played most of its games, and the most of any club, on the grounds. It was the Creightons who had hosted the Mutual Base Ball Club on the White Lot in 1872, allowing the black ball club to secure a victory on the field. In 1873 the Creightons had also met the middling Arlington and Irvington Base Ball Clubs, among others, on the grounds.[69]

After nearly a decade of postwar baseball on the site, change came quickly. The White Lot's status as a parcel of land open to nearly any ball-throwing man ended on September 6, 1874. The *Sunday Herald*, with its typical reserve, announced a drastic change in policy regarding the previously open space. "The White Lot has been closed to all ball players except the Creightons," the paper reported. "The gangs of lazy negroes and other vagrants infesting the grounds made this action necessary."[70]

This exclusionary policy essentially partitioned off the land to the Creighton Base Ball Club.[71] It was a strange choice. From a baseball perspective, the Nationals or Olympics would have been more logical recipients of this segregation-inspired gift. The Creightons had only a modest record of success. Douglass's Mutual Club was among the many clubs that had defeated the Creightons in the years leading up to its acquisition of Washington's best baseball land. In fact, the Creightons' only significant achievement had been staying afloat. They had one of the longer tenures in the city, playing somewhat continuously between 1867 and 1873. Furthermore, no record of a lease agreement with the District exists to suggest that the Creighton Club had negotiated for the rights to the grounds. Thus, in the District's desire to expel the "gangs of lazy negroes" who were apparently compromising the highly prized White Lot, city officials awarded a mediocre, second-tier, but politically connected white baseball club full control of baseball's most powerful address.[72]

The closing of the White Lot made a mockery of Frederick Douglass's praise of civil rights progress in Washington DC. In 1873 Douglass had professed great appreciation for the District's protection of black rights, presenting the nation's capital as a beacon of hope in the still wavering process of Reconstruction: "Probably to a greater extent than elsewhere in the country is the equality of the citizens in the matter of public rights accorded in the District of Columbia. This is, no doubt, due to the fact that the Congress of the United States meets here and exerts a great influence immediately over its citizens than is true of other sections of the country."[73] Unfortunately for black baseball players in the city, neither Congress nor any other government authority saw fit to intervene in the closing of the president's baseball grounds for black residents of the city.

Finally, Representation

Still, and this is a constant theme in studying black baseball during the Reconstruction era, the Mutual Base Ball Club of Washington kept on playing ball. The club held its annual preseason meeting in March 1876 to elect a slate of officers and a board of directors.[74] As this meeting occurred, white professional baseball was again experiencing a significant shift. The NAPBBP folded and the National League arose. Nicholas Young served as secretary and treasurer of the new organization from its inception and then as president from 1885 until 1903.[75] Despite its time seeming to have passed, the National Association of Amateur Base Baseball Players continued to meet as well, albeit with very little fanfare. Therein the Mutuals saw an opening to make a step toward baseball integration. Thus, in 1876 the Mutuals sent two delegates to the amateur convention to apply for membership. And surprisingly, the convention nominating committee approved the Washington Mutuals' application for membership.[76]

The presence of black delegates in the previously all-white amateur convention stirred no reaction, positive or negative, from the press.

No cries of outrage arose from whites. No black advocates touted the breakthrough as significant. Rather, the limited attendance of the convention largely muted the effect. Professional baseball had rendered the older, fraternally based game mostly irrelevant. Integration occurred, but it did not matter.[77]

Still, the Washington Mutuals took advantage of the opportunities that arose. In what should have been a significant milestone, one of the club's members, T. L. Brooks, won election as vice president of the National Association of Amateur Base Ball Players in 1877. If only someone had been paying attention. To all but the most ardent baseball fans, the names involved meant nothing. The Confidence, Flyaway, and New Rochelle Clubs were among those in attendance. The bar of admittance had been so low that one club at the 1876 convention had yet to even choose a name for itself. In this low-stakes, rather anonymous environment, baseball's organizing structure was integrated. The *New York Clipper*, still broadly considered the voice of baseball, dismissed the convention altogether. The *Clipper* described the convention by noting that, "the attendance of the delegates being limited," the business transacted was "of but little importance."[78]

After electing a new leadership class (without a Douglass among them) and sending two delegates to a previously all-white baseball association, the Mutuals again looked forward to taking the field. The club considered the possibility of taking another extensive baseball tour. After dismissing the significance of the amateur convention, the *Clipper* touted the Mutuals, reporting that the club was "in excellent condition." The paper predicted that 1877 would be the finest Mutual season ever.[79] The *Clipper*'s optimism proved unfounded.

Black baseball, in Washington DC and elsewhere, failed to produce a second generation nearly as prominent in the game as the first. The Mutuals gradually died out as a baseball organization, making only a few appearances after 1877. The decline of the District's black baseball community resulted, at least in part, from organizations such as the Mutuals and Alerts being pushed further and further to the periphery of the game. With ever-decreasing opportunities to play against the best white clubs and in the city's best baseball facilities, black baseball lost its relevance within Washington's black community. The city's press stopped reporting on black baseball with any consistency. Not until the

Homestead Gray Club began playing many of its home games at Griffith Stadium in the 1930s would black baseball bloom once again, albeit with the bounds of segregation fully entrenched, in Washington DC.

The National League

The National League of Professional Baseball Clubs began play in 1876, just as congressional Reconstruction sputtered to an end. In the National League, "all of baseball's formative characteristics that had appeared in antebellum New York reached their final stage of development," argues National League historian Tom Melville.[80] Professionalism triumphed. Competition emerged ahead of fraternal bonds. The game was manly yet respectable. Northern cities dominated the circuit. Certainly, baseball historians have appreciated each of these trends finding their resolutions in the National League. So too, however, did the National League bring to its "final stage of development" racial segregation. No black ballplayer, recognized as such, played in the National League before Jackie Robinson.[81] Although Moses Fleetwood Walker played in the rival American Association, and Bud Fowler and a relative handful of other African Americans played in baseball's Minor Leagues, a dam of segregation had been erected. Leaks would, over the coming years, be systematically plugged. The resolution was so complete that the National League's leaders (including Nicholas Young) eventually stopped addressing the racial question at all. By the end of the nineteenth century, with the National League firmly entrenched and setting an overarching example, racial segregation in baseball was the norm.

Epilogue

In 1999, more than fifty years after Jackie Robinson broke baseball's color line, the *New York Times* ran a story on declining black participation in organized baseball. The piece, "Out of the Ball Park: For Black Americans, Baseball Loses Its Luster," reported on young black men living in the shadow of New York City's Yankee Stadium (on the very land once occupied by the Polo Grounds) who did not play, or even watch, the supposedly "national pastime." The article highlighted an obvious historical irony: baseball, which played the most important role of any sport in the civil rights struggle, had (and has) become increasingly devoid of African American participation.[1] At the start of the 2012 season, black players made up just 8.05 percent of all Major Leaguers, the lowest percentage since integration.[2] Ricky Clemons, the vice president of public relations for the National League, points to a barrier to black baseball in urban areas that harkens back to Reconstruction: "It takes a lot of equipment and a lot of space."[3]

But the racial changes affecting modern baseball are, of course, very different from those at the root of baseball's segregation during Reconstruction. Opportunity exists for black ballplayers and fans to participate in twenty-first-century baseball. Thus, the choices made by many black men to play and watch other sports are truly voluntary. In contrast, during the Reconstruction era—in the span of little more than one decade—baseball's first generation of modern ballplayers created a game that fostered white exclusivity. Black choice and opportunity steadily declined. The patterns of segregation set in the 1860s and '70s laid down the tracks for the subsequent eighty years of baseball history.

What followed Reconstruction-era baseball should not surprise us—in light of the baseball patterns revealed in this study and due to what we know about the Jim Crow era. Black baseball did not go away. Talented black teams proved that they could compete with all comers. A few African Americans played in baseball's Major Leagues. But the gulf between black and white players and clubs widened. Contact continued to occur, but always with the firm understanding that segregation reigned supreme. Interaction did not necessarily breed equality, just as it had not during the 1860s. Examples abound demonstrating this dichotomous state of contact and cooperation coinciding with constant reminders of the differences between black and white ballplayers. Two case studies deserve particular mention: the Cuban Giants and the Negro Leagues.

Both the Cuban Giants and the Negro Leagues hinted at a widespread acquiescence to baseball's firmly segregated culture. That is not to say—to be clear—that black ballplayers accepted inequality during Reconstruction or after. They did not. But the realities of baseball between 1876 and 1947 made investing in a parallel black-only baseball community a more fruitful day-to-day experience than pushing for inclusion in organized professional white baseball. As the National League flourished while denying entry to African Americans, black baseball players carved out new avenues of success. The Cuban Giants, often called black baseball's first professional team, organized in 1885. The club's name, particularly the *Cuban* part, was another in a long line of purposeful baseball monikers. In this case it was purposely deceptive. The players did not hail from Cuba, although they occasionally "chattered" in a Spanish-like gibberish to please the crowds, but rather the club's leaders used the designation as a means of obfuscating the race line.[4] The club traveled widely, won frequently, and mattered—at least in terms of baseball's National League—only tangentially.

The Cuban Giants continued the trend of the Pythians and Alert and Mutual Clubs, probing for opportunities and making the best of segregated realities. Some cracks, however, developed in the wall of near-universal exclusion of black players from white club rosters during the end of the nineteenth century. Moses Fleetwood Walker, a graduate of Oberlin College, played in baseball's "other" major league, the American Association, in 1884.[5] He was not alone. Weldy Walker (Fleetwood's brother) also played several games for the Toledo club in the the same season. Dozens of other black players, including Bud Fowler, Frank Grant, and George Stovey, played in the Minor Leagues. Only their skin color kept them from moving up. As Fowler stated, "My skin is against me. If I had not been quite so black, I might have caught on as a Spaniard or something of that kind. The race prejudice is so strong that my black skin barred me."[6]

As had been the case during the Reconstruction years, hostility against black ballplayers increased as they traveled to the South. In Walker's case Richmond's baseball community provided the greatest opposition. In 1884 Walker had to be held out of the lineup in Richmond upon receiving word that a riot would break out if he played.[7] Such opposition to integrated events was the rule in Richmond. The city's leaders opposed a possible visit from the Cuban Giants in 1889 based on the mere possibility that the club might play an exhibition against a white club. The *New York Age* reported, "A number of the citizens of Richmond requested Mr. R. H. Leadley to cancel the game [between the Cuban Giants and the Detroit Base Ball Club], as they do not want colored and white clubs to play there against each other."[8] Eventually, revealing a departure from men such as Octavius Catto, Walker called for blacks to leave the United States and establish a "Liberia" in Africa.[9]

By the 1890s the few black players had been mostly removed from all levels of white professional baseball. The *Sporting Life* reported in 1891 on the public backlash that had occurred when the International League (a well-established professional league) had allowed a handful of black players in its midst:

> Probably in no other business in America is the color line so finely drawn as in base ball. An African who attempts to put on a uniform and go in among a lot of white players is taking his life in his hands. . . . [T]he latter team [Buffalo] had an African named Grant playing second base. . . . "Well, boys what'll we do to him? Put him out of the game," in a chorus. . . . Crane was going like the wind. He ducked his head after measuring the distance and caught Grant squarely in the pit of the stomach with his shoulder. The son of Ham went up in the air as if he had been in a threshing machine. They took him home on a stretcher, and he didn't

recover for three weeks. . . . "[T]here were no more darkies in the League after that."[10]

Thus, by 1898, white baseball leaders had added further nuance to the game's segregation, determining that even a smattering of black men mixed into white rosters, at the minor league level, would not be allowed.

In the wake of this near-total exclusion by whites, black ballplayers once again invested in their own baseball organizations. The Negro Leagues, which persisted from 1920 until the 1950s, were a notable instance of black autonomy.[11] Building on the economic foundations established by nineteenth-century black ballplayers, the franchises of the Negro Leagues became some of the largest black-owned businesses in the United States during the first half of the twentieth century.[12] But what has been missing from the increased historical discussion of the Negro Leagues is an acknowledgment that they too were a continuation of patterns set during the Reconstruction era. The Negro Leagues formed due to white exclusion and from the commitment of black men to continue playing baseball in the face of such opposition.

The Negro Leagues were not second rate, just as the Pythians were not during the 1860s in Philadelphia. As the ninety-four-year-old Negro Leagues legend Buck O'Neil resolutely told a class of elementary students who had listened to his presentation on black baseball, "I can see the way you look. Oh Yeah. You listened to that and you think that the Negro Leagues was inferior. The Negro Leagues was not inferior."[13] Although most Negro Leaguers desired the opportunity to join the white Major Leagues, the black-led clubs mattered to the players on their rosters and to the communities in which they competed.

The Mechanics of Segregation

This study overlooked many compelling anecdotes and multitudes of always tempting baseball statistics in order to focus on the mechanics of segregation. The patterns that emerged from this scope are informative. White leaders such as Arthur Gorman, Nicholas Young, and Hicks Hayhurst created organizational structures that made black entry into baseball's highest levels increasingly difficult. Reconciliation and dreams of a national game drove these early decisions. Organizational structures made more formalized segregation possible. It was at the Pennsylvania Association of Amateur Base Ball Players, after all, that white baseball rejected Raymond Burr and the Philadelphia Pythians. "With no chance for anything but being black balled," Burr reported to his club, "your delegate withdrew his application."[14] Then at the 1867 National Association of Base Ball Players convention, the nominating committee issued its preemptive declaration: "The report of the Nominating Committee in which they decided not to admit clubs with colored delegates, was adopted."[15] The measure sacrificed black civil rights in pursuit of sectional reconciliation. The New York State Base Ball Association and Chicago baseball community followed suit in 1870. The New Yorkers claimed that race was simply too controversial: "The motion of one of our delegates [the Brooklyn Star Club] to the late New York State Convention of Base Ball Players in regard to the admission of colored clubs to the State Association, involving, as it does a question of political nature, the introduction of which, in this club, cannot fail to prove prejudicial to that harmony which is so essential to our success as an organization, does not meet with our sanction or approval."[16] Generally speaking, the more organized baseball became, the more thoroughly white baseball leaders were able to enforce segregation rules.

Oftentimes, questions of race were addressed circumspectly. In Richmond segregation resulted from the efforts of Alexander Babcock, who helped make baseball into a white Southern game. Club names such as the Confederate, Dixie, and Secesh communicated white exclusivity without ever having to mention race. The close identification of baseball with white Southern ideals and sectionalist rhetoric made baseball a racially divisive game. Press accounts associating black players and games with unrestrained violence served the same cause. Richmond was not alone in using baseball as a tool to promote white Southern ideals. New Orleans, among others, had a robust baseball community too, with clubs similarly named after Robert E. Lee and other Confederate heroes.[17]

This study attempts to balance national trends with both regional and local nuances. After the Reconstruction era the baseball fortunes of Philadelphia, Richmond, and Washington DC diverged, tellingly. In Philadelphia black baseball remained vibrant. Sol White, the first black historian of black baseball, organized the Philadelphia Giants in 1902.[18] The Giants won informal black baseball championships (fair scheduling and league play still remained elusive) and had a loyal following in Philadelphia's black community.[19]

In 1923 the Hilldale Club, a black team located in nearby Darby, succeeded in acquiring what the Pythians and most other black clubs desperately wanted: its own field. The park was humble—the wooden stands held about 5,000 spectators. A huge tree overhanging the center-field fence served as its most defining feature and was, according to ground rules, in play.[20] The historian, however, must consider the pride (if a lack of exact precision) evident in the recountings of Hilldale players about their own field: "The dirt—I don't know what it was, but it shone something like silver. . . . A ball would very seldom take a bad hop unless someone dug a hole with his spikes. You could just smooth it over and you wouldn't have any trouble."[21] Ownership of a field did not solve all financial problems. The Hilldale Club folded in 1932. The final straw had been a weekend series attended by only 295 paying fans.[22]

In Philadelphia's white baseball community, the distinct dichotomy between soft support for racial progress and commitment to actual change remained evident into the twentieth century. The news of Jackie Robinson's call-up to the Major Leagues prompted a call from the Philadelphia Phillies to Branch Rickey of the Brooklyn Dodgers, warning him "not to bring that nigger here." Additionally, the Philadelphia Phillies, every bit the representative of the "Up South" city, were the last of the National League clubs to integrate (1957) and maintained segregated spring-training facilities until 1962.[23]

Washington DC became home to the Homestead Grays, "the greatest baseball dynasty that most people have never heard of," in 1937.[24] During the club's tenure in DC (1937–48), the Washington Homestead Grays won nine straight Negro National League pennants (some Negro League experts contend it was eight out of nine) and two consecutive Colored World Series.[25] Griffith Stadium, at Seventh Street and Florida Avenue NW, served as the District's primary baseball site from 1891 to 1961—for both black and white clubs.[26] Although white owned, the stadium sat in one of Washington DC's most vibrant black neighborhoods. Black ball clubs frequently leased the venue, drawing capacity crowds of more than 27,000 for games featuring Josh Gibson and the Grays. Only when white clubs played did the stadium have segregated seating.

The success of the Homestead Grays made the record of Washington's top white club, the Senators, even more embarrassing. After winning the World Series in 1924 behind the pitching of Walter Johnson, the Senators had winning seasons in only two of its final twenty-five seasons in the District.[27] Clark Griffith, however, could not bend to sign black players, even those already playing in his own stadium, who might have helped the Major Leagues' most "Southern" town field a winner.[28] In what might be classified as a fitting outcome for the many black ballplayers who had struggled for baseball space in the District, Howard University—a product of the Freedmen's Bureau—purchased the site of Griffith Stadium in 1975 and built a hospital on the grounds.

Richmond's black ballplayers, in contrast to Philadelphia's and Washington's, never fielded a club in the Negro Leagues. The city did not have much success in white baseball, either. Richmond had only a brief "cup of coffee" in the big leagues. Richmond's opportunity to play in the American Association came when Washington dropped out midway through the 1884 season. Thus, the Richmond Virginians played at baseball's highest level from August to October 1884, the same year that Moses Fleetwood Walker played in the association. The Richmond club played forty-six games, winning twelve, losing thirty, and failing, apparently, to finish four games. The club dropped back into the Minor Leagues for good in 1885.[29] When Moses Fleetwood Walker's Toledo Blue Stockings planned to visit Richmond in 1884, a group of Richmonders threatened "much bloodshed" if Walker took the field. Walker, when in Richmond, stayed on the bench.[30]

Beyond outright racism baseball in Richmond continued to be linked to the memory of the Confederacy and the Lost Cause. When it came time to finally unveil the city's Robert E. Lee statue in 1889, for example, tens of thousands of Richmonders marched to the ceremony—arriving at the city's main baseball grounds where the statue had been placed.[31] Racial integration in baseball finally came to Richmond in 1953, six years after Jackie Robinson made his debut. Whit Graves, a black ballplayer from Richmond, joined the Richmond Colts—the city's Piedmont League team.[32] Integration came to Richmond's top club the same year the Washington Senators signed their first black ballplayer and three years before the Philadelphia Phillies placed a black man on their roster.

Reconstruction and Segregation

Part of the intrigue of the Reconstruction era, at least for this historian, is the idea that something transformative *might* have happened. Following the Civil War, constitutional amendments might have protected the civil liberties of newly freed slaves. Judicial decisions might have built a lattice for racial progress. Economic and land policies might have been enacted to couple legal and political freedoms to practical, day to day equality. But these transformations did not happen. Windows of opportunity closed. Transformative measures became problematic compromises.

The same story of opportunities come and gone makes the history of baseball's segregation during the Reconstruction era a compelling one. Thomas Fitzgerald, the radical baseball leader from Philadelphia, might have been Branch Rickey eighty years earlier. Instead, the white baseball community stripped Fitzgerald of his governing roles. Similarly, Octavius Catto had the makings of a nineteenth-century Jackie Robinson. Articulate, educated, and a fine ballplayer, Catto became a martyr instead of a trailblazer. His death, and the connection of black baseball to violence more broadly, inhibited the growth of black baseball. And then more widely, the white baseball community's obsession with creating a "national game" might have been used to prompt Southerners to reconstruct their ideas about race. Instead, white Southerners won baseball's Reconstruction peace. Civil rights lost out, and then Southerners largely withdrew from the national baseball community anyhow. And so the Reconstruction era became the period of baseball's segregation. Tragically, the norms of segregation in baseball were put in place over the course of one decade. But these quick-planted roots stuck. Not until Jackie Robinson in 1947 would the failings of the post–Civil War generation of ballplayers in terms of racial equality begin to be undone.

ACKNOWLEDGMENTS

This project has taken forever, it seems, to complete. Along the way there have been many people who have helped. My PhD adviser, Michael Kazin, encouraged me to explore baseball as a means of understanding the Reconstruction era. In doing so he gave me the freedom to mix my passion with my field of study. I also must thank my graduate committee at Georgetown (Chandra Manning and Adam Rothman) and my colleagues at George Mason and the University of New Mexico who provided invaluable suggestions as I worked on crafting an argument out of what started as a pile of box scores.

My parents, Lee and Cathy, made countless trips to Washington DC, often arriving just in time to pick up my flagging spirits. They believed in me—almost always more than I believed in myself. They encouraged me to remember what was important versus what was simply pressing. Similarly, my mother-in-law, Jeannie, provided invaluable support. Several times a year she swooped in and spoiled our family with love and kindness. Additionally, my brother, Nate, listened with interest and always provided insightful comments, as we discussed the book on long training runs together. He understood my stresses and supported what I was trying to do.

Finally, when the project started, I was a relative newlywed. When it was finished, I was the proud father of three, and a not-so-newly-wed anymore. The arrival of Carter, Tyler, and Kate made all the difference. Thankfully, Little League games have been the most important baseball events in my life as I have revised and edited this baseball text. I have certainly found my new favorite infielders. None of this would have been possible, or any fun at all, without my wife, Rachael. Her contention that she throws a baseball with better mechanics than I do may just be true. Regardless, she always (always, always) believed that I could complete this baseball project and that it would be something worth finishing. Thanks and I love you.

NOTES

INTRODUCTION

1. Many of the very best sport historians have frequently used the "gentlemen's agreement" to describe baseball's segregation process. This tendency, I believe, has been due mostly to a lack of focus on the beginnings of segregation, rather than a misunderstanding of the topic. For a sampling of the "gentlemen's" explanation, see Gorn, *Sports in Chicago*, 88; Heaphy, *The Negro Leagues*, 4, 11; Lomax, *Black Baseball Entrepreneurs*, 189; and Tygiel, *Baseball's Great Experiment*.
2. *Washington (DC) Daily National Intelligencer*, September 11, 1866.
3. *Sporting Life*, June 29, 1895.
4. Of the many works on Jackie Robinson I have found Tygiel's *Baseball's Great Experiment* to be the most useful.
5. On baseball's patriotic rhetoric, see Butterworth, *Baseball and Rhetorics of Purity*.
6. *Spirit of the Times*, January 31, 1857.
7. Blight, *Race and Reunion*, 198.
8. *New York Clipper*, October 6, 1866.
9. Chadwick, *Chadwick's Base Ball Manual, for 1871*, 11.
10. *Sunday Morning Chronicle*, June 17, 1866.
11. *Memphis Public Ledger*, September 70, 1870.
12. For an excellent synopsis of the teams and leagues of this period, see Ryczek, *When Johnny Came Sliding Home*. My own study is less about the action on the field than the implications and meanings of that baseball activity. Warren Goldstein's *Playing for Keeps* is one exception to this trend. Goldstein addresses how baseball players "worked" to make the game "manly" and to mold it into a pastime that served their needs in a post–Civil War world.
13. On the segregation debate, see Woodward, *Strange Career of Jim Crow*; Litwack, *Been in the Storm So Long*, 262; and Rabinowitz, *Race Relations in the Urban South*.
14. I found the following three works to be particularly pertinent to this study of baseball's dealings with civil rights during Reconstruction: Richardson, *Death of Reconstruction*; Foner, *Reconstruction*; and Hahn, *Nation under Our Feet*.

15. Gorn, *Manly Art*, 13.
16. Quote by Sir John Robert Seely. See Ridder-Symoens and Ruegg, *History of the University in Europe*, 482.
17. I found particularly useful Rotenberg and McDonough's *Cultural Meaning of Urban Space*. Additionally, Elsa Barkley Brown and Gregg D. Kimball's article on urban space in Richmond provided a template for further study. See Brown and Kimball, "Mapping the Terrain of Black Richmond."
18. Riess, *City Games*, 46–47; *New York Clipper*, May 5, 1866.
19. Riess, *City Games*, 46–47; *Washington (DC) Daily National Intelligencer*, September 9, 1866; *Washington (DC) Sunday Herald and Weekly National Intelligencer*, June 20, 1873.
20. *New York Clipper*, April 1, 1871.
21. Charles Douglass to Frederick Douglass, October 16, 1869, Gardiner Collection, American Negro Historical Society (ANHS) Collection, Historical Society of Pennsylvania. The New York Mutuals were among the most prestigious and successful clubs of the 1860s and '70s—the Yankees (without the monstrous payroll) of their day.
22. *Washington (DC) Sunday Herald and Weekly National Intelligencer*, October 12, 1873.
23. Riess, *City Games*, 1; Koppett, *Koppett's Concise History*, 3.
24. *Washington (DC) Sunday Herald and Weekly National Intelligencer*, November 10, 1872.
25. *New York Times*, April 10, 1869; *Wilkes' Spirit of the Times*, May 4, 1867; Sullivan, *Early Innings*, 53–54; Seymour, *Baseball: The Early Years*, 41–42; *Washington (DC) Sunday Herald and Weekly National Intelligencer*, July 24, 1870.
26. Chadwick Scrapbooks, August 1867 (newspaper unidentified), Society for American Baseball Research.
27. Seymour, *Baseball: The Early Years*, 35–45.
28. *Philadelphia Sunday Mercury*, July 20, 1873.
29. *Ball Players' Chronicle*, October 31, 1867.
30. A typical letter from the *New York Clipper*'s correspondence section: "A Card From the Keystone Club to Editor of Clipper—Dear Sir: Learning through the columns of your valuable paper that a number of baseball clubs . . . contemplate visiting our city . . . I would most respectfully state that, from the business and engagements already entered into by many of our players, in conjunction with that long-deferred pleasure, a visit to our NY friends, anticipated during July, it will be impossible for us to contract any additional engagements until after Sept 1st." *New York Clipper*, June 24, 1865.
31. Chadwick, *Game of Baseball*, 15.
32. Schiff, *"Father of Baseball,"* 50–58.
33. *Washington (DC) Daily National Intelligencer*, October 25, 1866. The *New York Clipper* claimed that the first-ever admission-charging female game took place on September 11, 1875. The "Blonds versus the Brunettes" was, according to the *Clipper*, more spectacle than baseball: "As a general thing the attraction is the

novelty of seeing eighteen girls prettily attired in gymnastic dress playing in a game of baseball." *New York Clipper*, September 25, 1875.

34. Chadwick, *Game of Baseball*, 9–10; *New York Clipper*, November 19, 1864; Goldstein, *Playing for Keeps*, 50. Regarding baseball's seemingly endless creation debate, see Block, *Baseball before We Knew It*; and Thorn, *Baseball in the Garden of Eden*.

35. Chadwick, *Chadwick's Baseball Manual*.

36. Ryczek, *Blackguards and Red Stockings*, 15–18.

37. Chadwick, *Game of Baseball*, 15.

38. *Richmond Times*, November 24, 1866.

39. Goldstein, *Playing for Keeps*, 30–31; Scrapbook, 1866–74, Philadelphia Athletics, Baseball Hall of Fame (newspaper unidentified).

40. *New York Anglo-African*, December 10, 1859; *Brooklyn Eagle*, October 17, 1862. Cited in Sullivan, *Early Innings*, 33–35.

41. The designation "mid-Atlantic" does not typically include Virginia. See Marzec, *Mid-Atlantic Region*. I understand this traditional line drawing, but for the purposes of this study I am willing to bend a few geographical rules. The region between Richmond and Philadelphia, as will be demonstrated, had much in common. U.S. Census Bureau, *Compendium of the Ninth Census*, 75.

42. Lane, *William Dorsey's Philadelphia and Ours*, 8; U.S. Census Bureau, *Ninth Census of the United States*, 598. Philadelphia's abolitionist lineage is long and impressive. The Pennsylvania Society for the Promotion of the Abolition of Slavery organized in Philadelphia in 1775, followed by the Pennsylvania Anti-Slavery Society in 1837. See DuBois, *The Philadelphia Negro*, 17–27; and Scharf, *History of Philadelphia*, 734.

43. Countryman, *Up South*; Nash, *First City*, 228; Weigley, *Philadelphia*, 385.

44. *Richmond Times*, August 6, 1866.

45. U.S. Census Bureau, *Ninth Census of the United States*, 598.

46. U.S. Census Bureau, *Ninth Census of the United States*, 18. Includes totals from the cities of Washington and Georgetown.

47. Green, *Washington*, 273–75, 296–301, 311.

48. Simpson, *The Reconstruction Presidents*, 111; Masur, "Reconstructing the Nation's Capital," 182–83; Whyte, *Uncivil War*, 222–34.

1. WASHINGTON DC: A GAME TO BE GOVERNED

1. Melville's *Early Baseball* provides a useful guide to baseball's early history and specifically Young's place in it. More generally, see Allen, *National League Story*, 49–50; and Dickey, *History of National League Baseball*.

2. Stoddart and Sandiford, *Imperial Game*.

3. Nicholas E. Young, "Copy of Record of Various Incidents Especially Concerning Baseball," Player File—Nicholas E. Young, Baseball Hall of Fame.

4. Harry Wright became professional baseball's first manager in 1869 with the Cincinnati Red Stockings. George Wright was a Hall of Fame shortstop who, among other things, claimed to have invented the tradition of batting practice

before ball games. For more information on the Wrights, see Seymour, *Baseball: The Early Years*, 14, 48; and Voigt, *American Baseball*.

5. Kirsch, *Baseball in Blue and Gray*, 43–45.
6. Seymour states of the Civil War and baseball: "There are two commonly accepted beliefs about the effect of the Civil War on baseball's history, both of which are incorrect, or at least only partly true. One is that baseball's growth was halted by the Civil War. The other is that Southern troops learned the game from Northern prisoners, took it home in their knapsacks, and introduced it to the South." Seymour, *Baseball: The Early Years*, 40–41.
7. Young, "Copy of Record of Various Incidents Especially Concerning Baseball."
8. Young, "Copy of Record of Various Incidents Especially Concerning Baseball."
9. *Ball Players' Chronicle*, August 20, 1867; *Washington (DC) Sunday Herald and Weekly Intelligencer*, June 20, 1873; Benson, *Ballparks of North America*, 406; Chadwick Scrapbooks, May 1860, Society for American Baseball Research.
10. *Washington (DC) Daily National Intelligencer*, September 11, 1866.
11. *City Item*, September 2, 1865; Scrapbook, 1866–74, Philadelphia Athletics, Baseball Hall of Fame.
12. John B. Foster, "Washington Challenged the West," *New York Sun*, October 8, 1924.
13. The April 19, 1865, *New York Times* edition read: "Every class, race and condition of society was represented in the throng of mourners, and the sad tears and farewells of whites and blacks were mingled by the coffin to him to whom humanity was everywhere the same." Even the battle-calloused General Ulysses S. Grant wept openly as he paid his final respects. Lincoln's body traveled by a slow train procession back to Springfield, Illinois, seven million mourners lining the tracks to pay their respects. On the impact of Lincoln's death, see McPherson, *Ordeal by Fire*, 521; and McPherson, *Battle Cry of Freedom*, 853–58.
14. Johnson included fourteen categories of exemption to his blanket amnesty, the largest of which was for those Southerners with property valued at more than twenty thousand dollars. See Carter, *When the War Was Over*, 24–25.
15. Whyte, *Uncivil War*, 49.
16. Green, *Secret City*, 76. On race relations immediately after the Civil War, see also the Smithsonian Anacostia Museum and Center for African American History and Culture, *Black Washingtonians*.
17. Young, "Copy of Record of Various Incidents Especially Concerning Baseball."
18. *New York Clipper*, May 20, 1865.
19. Goldstein, *Playing for Keeps*, 34–40.
20. Chadwick Scrapbooks, February 24, 1868 (newspaper unidentified), Society for American Baseball Research.
21. *Washington (DC) Daily National Intelligencer*, September 29, 1866; *Washington (DC) Evening Star*, October 22, 1869.
22. *New York Clipper*, September 5. 1868.
23. U.S. Office of Personnel Management, *Biography of an Ideal*; Van Riper, *History of the Civil Service*.

24. *American Chronicle of Sports and Pastimes*, dated only 1868, Clippings File, Baseball Hall of Fame, 729.
25. *Washington Chronicle*, May 10, 1872.
26. Green, *Secret City*, 33; Whyte, *Uncivil War*, 31; U.S. Census Bureau, *Ninth Census of the United States*, 75–280.
27. L. Brown, *Free Negroes in the District of Columbia*, 14.
28. Whyte, *Uncivil War*, 28; Green, *Secret City*, 54.
29. Petition of Colored Citizens of the District of Columbia, December 1865, in Masur, "Reconstructing the Nation's Capital," 170–71; Green, *Washington*, 335–38.
30. McFeely, *Frederick Douglass*, 224–39, 119–45.
31. B. Quarles, *Frederick Douglass*, 99–110.
32. Masur, "Reconstructing the Nation's Capital," 11.
33. McFeely, *Frederick Douglass*, 104.
34. Williams, *History of the Negro Troops*, 197–200; McFeely, *Frederick Douglass*, 224–30. To obtain the discharge Frederick Douglass wrote to Abraham Lincoln: "I have a very great favor to ask. It is . . . that you will cause my son Charles R. Douglass . . . to be discharged." Lincoln responded: "Let this boy be discharged, A. Lincoln." And it was done.
35. Masur, "Reconstructing the Nation's Capital," 68–69.
36. Charles Douglass to Frederick Douglass, October 16, 1869, Douglass Papers, Library of Congress; McFeely, *Frederick Douglass*, 257–58.
37. Bednar, *L'Enfant's Legacy*, 11–21, 41–56.
38. Bednar, *L'Enfant's Legacy*, 95–120.
39. Newspaper clipping, April 25, 1866, French Papers, Historical Society of Washington DC, 83.
40. *New York Clipper*, May 5, 1866.
41. On the former point, consider the dual-MLB cities of New York, Chicago, and (to a lesser extent) Los Angeles. Even in difficult economic times, few suggestions have been made that clubs share facilities. So entrenched is the idea of each club controlling its own facility that New York City supported the construction of near-billion-dollar new stadiums for both the Yankees and the Mets, both of which opened in 2009.
42. Schweninger, *Black Property Owners in the South*, 200–204.
43. Player File—Arthur P. Gorman, Baseball Hall of Fame; Michael Morgan, "Baseball Is Big League Thanks to the County's Arthur P. Gorman," *Howard Living*, 11–12.
44. Brian McKenna, "Arthur Gorman," Biography Database, Society for American Baseball Research; Lambert, *Arthur Pue Gorman*, 6–7.
45. Ryczek, *When Johnny Came Sliding Home*, 71.
46. *The Constitution and By-Laws of the National Base-Ball Club of Washington DC*, French Papers, Historical Society of Washington DC.
47. *New York Clipper*, October 21, 1865.
48. *New York Clipper*, September 9, 1865.

49. Lambert, *Arthur Pue Gorman*, 10–15.

50. Peverly, *Book of American Pastimes*, 501–7.

51. Peverly, *Book of American Pastimes*, 501.

52. Ellard, *Base Ball in Cincinnati*, 16.

53. Heaphy, *Negro Leagues*, 10–12.

54. *New York Clipper*, December 1, 1866, October 7, 1865. Continuing the geographical fallacy, the *Clipper* also considered Baltimore to be a part of the race for the southern championship at times. See *New York Clipper*, October 10, 1868.

55. Chadwick Scrapbooks (emphasis in the original), Society for American Baseball Research.

56. Chadwick Scrapbooks, Society for American Baseball Research.

57. *Ball Players' Chronicle*, July 25, 1867.

58. *New York Clipper*, October 6, 1866.

59. *Base Ball Player's Book of Reference*, viii.

60. *New York Clipper*, June 24, 1865.

61. The reconciliation on Southern terms is precisely the opposite of what Andrew Doyle argues happened in the 1920s with college football. Doyle, "Turning the Tide."

62. *Ball Players' Chronicle*, July 11, 1867.

2. RICHMOND: MAKE IT A SOUTHERN GAME

1. *Richmond Daily Dispatch*, October 2, 1866.

2. *Richmond Times*, August 6, 1866.

3. *Richmond Times*, October 2, 1866.

4. On the topic of sports in the South more broadly, see Miller, *Sporting World of the Modern South*. Grace Hale's study of the development of whiteness in the South is useful in understanding the customs that governed recreational pursuits. See Hale, *Making Whiteness*.

5. *Richmond Daily Dispatch*, July 2, 4, 1871; *Philadelphia Sunday Mercury*, October 3, 1869.

6. Carlton, *Diary, 1864–1869*, Carlton Papers, Library of Virginia.

7. Chesson, *Richmond after the War*, 57–61.

8. Andrews, *South since the War*.

9. Fleming, *Documentary History of Reconstruction*, 9.

10. *Richmond Times*, November 2, 1866.

11. *Richmond Times*, November 2, 1866.

12. *Richmond Daily Dispatch*, September 8, 1874.

13. The challenge of balancing Reconstruction's many significant political achievements while focusing on its societal shortcomings was a paramount one in conducting this study. I found the following texts among the most helpful in considering both the successes and the failures of Reconstruction: Anderson and Moss, *Facts of Reconstruction*; Blair, *Cities of the Dead*; Foner, *Reconstruction*; Litwack, *Been in the Storm So Long*; Kennedy, *After Appomattox*; and Stampp, *Era of Reconstruction*.

14. *Richmond Times*, July 7, 1866.

15. Berman, *Richmond's Jewry*, 11–20, 228–40.
16. Boyd, *Boyd's Directory of Richmond City, 1870*; *Richmond City Directory, 1873–74*.
17. Pollard, *Lost Cause*, 752.
18. *Richmond Daily Dispatch*, July 3, 1866. On Hollywood Cemetery, see Mitchell, *Hollywood Cemetery*, 63–72.
19. *Richmond Times*, July 11, August 4, 1866.
20. *New York Clipper*, April 3, 1869; *Philadelphia Sunday Mercury*, April 4, 1869; *Wilkes' Spirit of the Times*, April 10, 1869; Hewett, *Roster of Union Soldiers*, 61.
21. "Babcock, Alexander G.," Compiled Service Records of Confederate Soldiers Who Served in Organizations from the State of Virginia, National Archives and Records Administration, M324, 1–15; Scott, *Partisan Life with Mosby*, 258–62, 417–25.
22. *Richmond Daily Dispatch*, April 16, 1866.
23. Richmond City Council Records, "Meeting Minutes," July 7, 1867, October 10, 1870, September 9, October 14, December 10, 1867, Library of Virginia; Boyd, *Boyd's Directory of Richmond City, and a Business Directory of about Fifty Counties of Virginia*; Office of the Assistant Superintendent of the Third District, November 29, 1866, Records of the Bureau of Refugees, Freedmen, and Abandoned Lands, National Archives and Record Administration; O'Brien, *From Bondage to Citizenship*, 17; Rachleff, *Black Labor in the South*, 5.
24. Divine, *Richmond City Directory*; Boyd, *Boyd's Directory of Richmond City, and a Business Directory of about Fifty Counties of Virginia*; Boyd, *Boyd's Directory of Richmond City, 1870*; *Richmond City Directory, 1871–1872*.
25. *Richmond Daily Dispatch*, October 1, 1866; *Richmond Times*, October 9, 1866.
26. *Savannah (GA) Daily News and Herald*, October 10, 1867.
27. *Charleston (SC) Courier, Tri-Weekly*, September 10, 1868.
28. *Richmond Times*, November 8, October 29, 1866. Cholera had added to Richmond's misery. As the humid summer lingered, the *Philadelphia Inquirer* (September 13, 1866) commented on Richmond's cholera pandemic, but clarified that probably only three Richmonders per day were being treated for the epidemic and the victims were "mostly negroes." See also *Richmond Daily Dispatch*, May 2, 1866.
29. For "an estimate of the match games of baseball played during the year 1866," see *Richmond Times*, December 19, 1866.
30. Henry Chadwick married Jane Botts of Richmond, Virginia, on August 9, 1848. Botts was the daughter of Alexander L. Botts, the onetime president of the Virginia State Council and a longtime friend of John C. Calhoun. On the other side of the spectrum, Jane Botts was also related to Richmond's most famous Unionist, John Minor Botts. See Schiff, *"Father of Baseball"*; and Harrison, "Good Playing and Gentlemanly Bearing"; and *New York Clipper*, October 6, 1866.
31. *Richmond Daily Dispatch*, November 12, 1866; *Richmond Times*, November 9, 1866. "It will be seen that the Confederate uniform will not be permitted to be worn in public in this city, after the fifteenth day of this month, and that any person violating this order will be liable to arrest." *Richmond Times*, June 12, 1865; *Atlanta Daily Intelligencer*, October 20, 1866; *Richmond Times*, October 10, 1866.

32. Litwack, *Been in the Storm So Long*, 262.

33. *Richmond Times*, October 3, 1866.

34. The Union Club joined 201 other baseball clubs at baseball's largest national convention. The South effectively boycotted the event, still planning to organize as Southerners rather than as members of the national baseball community. For more on Richmond Clubs' reactions to the National Association of Base Ball Players conventions, see Daniel and Mayer, *Baseball and Richmond*, 5.

35. *Richmond Times*, December 22, 1866.

36. *Georgia Weekly Telegraph and Georgia Journal and Messenger*, September 2, 1870.

37. Lomax, *Black Baseball Entrepreneurs*, 1–13, 32–34; Ribowsky, *Complete History of the Negro Leagues*, 10–17.

38. U.S. Congress, *An Act to Protect All Persons in the United States in Their Civil Rights, and Furnish the Means of Their Vindication* (April 9, 1866), Statutes at Large, 39th Cong., 1st sess., 27–30; *Richmond Daily Dispatch*, April 9, 1866.

39. *Richmond Times*, October 10, 1866; *Richmond Daily Dispatch*, August 24, October 12, 1866; Daniel, "Good Playing and Gentlemanly Bearing."

40. *Richmond Daily Dispatch*, April 28, 1866.

41. *Richmond Times*, August 14, 1866.

42. Boyd, *Boyd's Directory of Richmond City, 1870*; *Richmond Times*, August 10, September 29, 1866; *Richmond Daily Dispatch*, October 6, 1866.

43. *Richmond Times*, October 23, 1866.

44. *Richmond Times*, October 3, 1866. The clerk occupation, of course, was a common one among baseball men. William H. Finn (Pastime) and M. M. French (Spotswood), among others, identified themselves as clerks in the 1866 Richmond city directory.

45. *Richmond Daily Dispatch*, October 2, 1866.

46. Carlton, *Diary, 1864–1869*, Carlton Papers, Library of Virginia.

47. *Richmond Daily Dispatch*, October 2, 1866.

48. *Richmond Daily Dispatch*, October 2, 1866.

49. *New York Clipper*, October 6, 1866.

50. *New York Clipper*, October 13, 1866.

51. On the fear of miscegenation, see Smith, *Racial Determinism*; and Robinson, *Dangerous Liaisons*, 21–56. On the relationship between race and gender, see Gilmore, *Gender and Jim Crow*.

52. *Richmond Times*, July 21, 1866.

53. *New York Clipper*, October 6, 1866.

54. *New York Clipper*, October 25, 1866.

55. *Philadelphia Inquirer*, October 2, 1866.

56. *Richmond Daily Dispatch*, October 2, 1866.

57. *Richmond Daily Dispatch*, October 2, 1866.

58. *Richmond Daily Dispatch*, October 23, 1866; *Richmond Times*, October 10, November 19, October 18, 1866.

59. Championships were decided, before the establishment of the National Association of Professional Base Ball Players in 1871, by popular opinion, on a city-

by-city basis. During the 1866 season, the *Times* and *Daily Dispatch* referred to "championship" matches nearly two dozen times, with the *Times* even calling the Union Club "champions." *Richmond Times*, October 18, 1866.

60. *Richmond Times*, October 19, 1866. The *Times* had earlier referred to the Union Club as a championship club, a mistake it amended in its October 19 edition. "A mistake—By some inadvertence it was stated yesterday morning that the Union Baseball Club was the champion club of the city. The statement was incorrect, as the union boys were fairly defeated in a match game a few days since with the Pastime Club."

61. *Richmond Times*, November 24, 1866.

3. PHILADELPHIA: BASEBALL'S BOOMTOWN

1. *New York Clipper*, March 5, 1870.
2. *North American*, May 19, 1907.
3. *North American*, May 19, 1907.
4. Jules Tygiel used the term *milieu* to discuss the cultural context in which baseball games were and are played; I use it here and will occasionally use it throughout the text similarly. See Tygiel, *Extra Bases*, x–xi.
5. Alexander, *Our Game*, 22.
6. *New York Clipper*, June 24, 1865.
7. *Philadelphia Sunday Mercury*, April 29, 1866.
8. *Philadelphia Sunday Mercury*, June 3, 1866.
9. Called at various times *Fitzgerald's City Item*, the *City Item*, and the *City Item and Visitor*. For the sake of clarity, I will refer to Thomas Fitzgerald's paper simply as the *City Item*.
10. C. Morris, *Makers of Philadelphia*, 122; Scrapbook, 1879–1903, Philadelphia Athletics, Baseball Hall of Fame.
11. *New York Clipper*, July 7, 1867.
12. *Philadelphia Sunday Mercury*, April 29, 1866.
13. McElroy, *McElroy's Philadelphia City Directory for 1865* (entered, according to an act of Congress, in the year 1865, by A. McElroy, in the Clerk's Office of the District Court of the United States, in and for the Eastern District of Pennsylvania).
14. Gopsill, *Gopsill's Philadelphia City Directory for 1869*.
15. *City Item*, April 22, 1865.
16. Vincent, *Rise and Fall of American Sport*, 106–7.
17. *City Item*, March 31, 1866; Scrapbook, 1879–1903, Philadelphia Athletics, Baseball Hall of Fame.
18. Scrapbook, 1866–74, Philadelphia Athletics, Baseball Hall of Fame.
19. The Brooklyn Atlantic-Athletic rivalry had heated up during the war when the Atlantics lured Tom Pratt, the Athletics' ace pitcher, away midseason in 1863. Hailed as "Champions" by the *New York Clipper*, the Atlantics defeated the ascendant Athletics every time the two clubs met in the 1864–66 seasons. The 1866 game in Philadelphia drew forty thousand spectators. See Scrapbooks, 1879–1903 and 1866–74, Philadelphia Athletics, Baseball Hall of Fame; *New*

York Clipper, September 21, 1867; *Philadelphia Inquirer*, June 30, 1866; Seymour, *Baseball: The Early Years*, 21–33; Kirsch, *Baseball in Blue and Gray*, 55; and Shiffert, *Base Ball in Philadelphia*, 47.

20. *Douglass' Monthly*, February 1862, quoted in Weigley, *Philadelphia*, 386.
21. Weigley, *Philadelphia*, 386.
22. Lomax, *Black Baseball Entrepreneurs*, 9; DuBois, *The Philadelphia Negro*, 221.
23. Pennsylvania State Equal Rights' League, *A Synopsis of the Proceedings of the Second Annual Meeting of the Pennsylvania State Equal Rights' League at Pittsburgh*, August 8–10 (Philadelphia: G. T. Stockdale, 1866), 44, ANHS Collection, Historical Society of Pennsylvania.
24. *Philadelphia Press*, June 16, 1866. Before the Pythians organized, the Excelsiors had played the Monitor Club of Jamaica, based in Long Island, and the Bachelor Club of Albany.
25. The location of a club often revealed the makeup of its membership. The Buffalo Base Ball Club hailed from the Seventh Ward, home of the Pythians and Octavius Catto.
26. DuBois, *The Philadelphia Negro*, 46–48.
27. U.S. Census Bureau, *Ninth Census of the United States*, 75–280.
28. Banneker Institution, "Preamble to the Constitution," October 1, 1857, ANHS Collection, Historical Society of Pennsylvania.
29. The Knights of Pythias, as a national organization, embraced a "gentlemen's agreement" on racial segregation. Several members of the Pythian Base Ball Club, Joshua Kelley among them, applied for recognition from the Knights of Pythias organization only to be rejected in 1870. See Martin, "Banneker Literary Institute of Philadelphia"; Casway, "Philadelphia's Pythians," 121; Carnahan, *Pythian Knighthood*, 120; and Tow, "Secrecy and Segregation."
30. *Philadelphia Sunday Mercury*, June 23, 1867.
31. Discrepancies in score were common. In this instance the original scorecard kept by the Pythians read 39–16, while the *Philadelphia Sunday Mercury* tallied the score as 35–16.
32. *Philadelphia Sunday Mercury*, June 30, 1867; Gopsill, *Gopsill's Philadelphia City and Business Directory for 1867–1868*.
33. Baseball reporters often referred to a scoreless game as a "whitewashing." *Philadelphia Sunday Mercury*, September 20, 1868.
34. Powers, *Black Charlestonians*, 17–22; Hamilton, *Black Preacher in America*, 13–23, 37–49; DuBois, *The Philadelphia Negro*, 199.
35. Powers, *Black Charlestonians*, 36–61; Lane, *Roots of Violence*, 16–44; Lane, *William Dorsey's Philadelphia and Ours*, 135–40.
36. Griffin, *Trial of Frank Kelly*; Gregg Kimball, "Richmond's Place in the African American Diaspora," in *Afro-Virginian History and Culture*, edited by Saillant.
37. Waskie, "Biography of Octavius V. Catto"; Lane, *Roots of Violence*, 34.
38. *Men of Color to Arms! Now or Never!*, ANHS Collection, Historical Society of Pennsylvania.
39. Casway, "Philadelphia's Pythians," 120–21.

40. *New National Era*, October 26, 1871.

41. Casway, "Philadelphia's Pythians," 121–22.

42. Waskie, "Biography of Octavius V. Catto."

43. Pennsylvania State Equal Rights' League, *Synopsis of the Proceedings of the Second Annual Meeting*, ANHS Collection, Historical Society of Pennsylvania; Lomax, *Black Baseball Entrepreneur*, 16; *New National Era*, October 26, 1871.

44. Bill Wormley to Octavius Catto, September 11, 1860, ANHS Collection, Historical Society of Pennsylvania.

45. Contract, Octavius Catto and Elisha Weaver, May 12, 1870, ANHS Collection, Historical Society of Pennsylvania.

46. *Philadelphia Sunday Mercury*, July 21, 1867.

47. Octavius Catto to Alert BBC, June 30, 1867, Pythian Base Ball Club Records, ANHS Collection, Historical Society of Pennsylvania. For more on the interactions between the Alert and Pythian Clubs, see chapter 5.

48. Lanctot, *Negro League Baseball*, 19–23.

49. Casway, "Philadelphia's Pythians," 121; *Philadelphia Press*, August 26, 1866.

50. Pythian Base Ball Club to Alert Base Ball Club, June 22, 1867, Pythian Base Ball Club Records, ANHS Collection, Historical Society of Pennsylvania.

51. *Philadelphia Sunday Mercury*, June 9, 1867.

52. Baseball teams usually consisted of only nine players, thus called "nines." Substitutes were rarely used. For a large organization such as the Pythians, multiple "nines" (or squads) represented the club, allowing more men to participate on the field.

53. Philadelphia Recorder of Deeds, "The Liberty Hall Association," June 10, 1867, Philadelphia City Archives.

54. *Philadelphia Sunday Mercury*, December 8, 1867; "Report of the Pythian Scorer," November 26, 1868, Pythian Base Ball Club Records, ANHS Collection, Historical Society of Pennsylvania.

55. *New York Clipper*, November 3, 1866; Goldstein, *Playing for Keeps*, 17–20.

56. Cancelled checks, "Payable to Com. on Reception of Alerts" (July 11, 1867), "Banneker Inst." (September 4, 1867), "The Directors—Balls and Bats" (July 3, 1868), Pythian Base Ball Club Records, ANHS Collection, Historical Society of Pennsylvania.

57. Committee on Reception, "Report, July 1867," Pythian Base Ball Club Records, ANHS Collection, Historical Society of Pennsylvania.

58. Goldstein, *Playing for Keeps*, 20–37.

59. *Philadelphia Sunday Mercury*, July 7, 1867; *New York Clipper*, July 6, 1867.

60. *Philadelphia Sunday Mercury*, July 7, 1867.

61. *New York Times*, December 25, 1882; Vincent, *Rise and Fall of American Sport*, 106; Shiffert, *Base Ball in Philadelphia*, 211–15.

62. *Philadelphia Sunday Mercury*, July 7, 1867.

63. *Philadelphia Sunday Mercury*, October 15, 1871.

64. *Philadelphia Sunday Mercury*, October 6, 1867.

65. *Philadelphia Sunday Mercury*, October 6, 1867.

66. Pythian BBC to Athletic BBC, July 1867, Pythian Base Ball Club Records, ANHS Collection, Historical Society of Pennsylvania.

67. DuBois, *The Philadelphia Negro*, 323.

68. *New York Clipper*, May 20, 1865.

69. *Brooklyn Eagle*, December 10, 1863, June 28, 1864.

70. *North American and United States Gazette*, October 15, 1863; Thomas Fitzgerald, "Light at Last: or, The Shadow on the Casement" and "Who Shall Win?," in *Plays, 1868*, Historical Society of Pennsylvania; Philadelphia School District, Board of Education, *Report of the Special Committee*; *North American and United States Gazette*, January 11, 1868.

71. *North American and United States Gazette*, December 2, 1867, May 3, 1871.

72. *City Item*, May 5, 1866; *Philadelphia Sunday Mercury*, September 18, 1864.

73. *City Item*, May 5, 1866.

74. Ryczek, *When Johnny Came Sliding Home*, 107; Seymour, *Baseball: The Early Years*, 42; Voigt, *American Baseball*, 17; *Wilkes' Spirit of the Times*, September 8, 1866.

75. *Philadelphia Sunday Mercury*, August 26, 1866.

76. *Philadelphia Sunday Mercury*, August 26, 1866. See also *Philadelphia Sunday Mercury*, May 27, 1866.

77. *New York Clipper*, November 4, 1865.

78. *City Item*, February 7, March 7, April 7, 14, 1865.

79. *City Item*, January 14, 1865.

80. "I no longer address you as gentlemen. . . . There is danger in pursuing the policy you have lately adopted. I sincerely and honestly believe that, would you take me back, and give me my former position, I would be enabled to place the club in the proud position it occupies in the estimation of every one save your humble service. . . . I have my weaknesses. Who has not? It is notorious that I was never addicted to telling the truth . . . I overestimated my abilities, and found, when too late, that I did not possess sufficient brains. Keep this quiet, I beg of you, gen-members. . . . You, perhaps, noticed *our* egotism in *our* last epistle in addressing you. *We* will, therefore, be pardoned, and on the ground that *we* know no better. . . . Repent of your folly, and return to the arms of the one who has ever considered you in the light of a loving parent, and who weeps as he signs himself, Fitzitem." *Philadelphia Sunday Mercury*, October 21, 1866.

81. *City Item*, May 27, 1865.

82. Jacqueline Steck, "Thomas Fitzgerald," in *American Newspaper Journalists, 1873–1900*, edited by Perry J. Ashley, vol. 23 of *Dictionary of Literary Biography* (Detroit: Gale Research, 1983).

83. *City Item*, December 9, 1865.

84. *Philadelphia Sunday Mercury*, July 26, 1874.

85. *Philadelphia Sunday Mercury*, January 28, 1866.

86. *Philadelphia Sunday Mercury*, September 9, 1866.

87. *Philadelphia Sunday Mercury*, August 8, 1866.

88. Ryczek, *When Johnny Came Sliding Home*, 101; Ryan Feeney, "The Power of One: Thomas Fitzgerald and the Origins of Interracial Baseball" (unpublished, Baseball Hall of Fame, 2001).

89. Shiffert, *Base Ball in Philadelphia*, 25.

4. PHILADELPHIA: SETTING PRECEDENT

1. "Report of the Delegate to the Convention of Baseball Players—Harrisburg," December 18, 1867, ANHS Collection, Historical Society of Pennsylvania.

2. For a discussion of the development of baseball's rules, see Neft, Cohen, and Neft, *Sports Encyclopedia of Baseball*. For a broader discussion of baseball's evolution, see Kirsch, *Creation of American Team Sports*.

3. George D. Johnson (Mutual BBC) to Pythian BBC, April 23, 1867, Pythian Base Ball Club Records, ANHS Collection, Historical Society of Pennsylvania.

4. *Philadelphia Sunday Mercury*, July 21, 1867.

5. *New York Clipper*, July 27, 1867.

6. *Philadelphia Inquirer*, July 18, 1867.

7. The Alert-Pythian result remained contested, thus was not considered an official loss. *Philadelphia Sunday Mercury*, July 21, 1867.

8. Pythian BBC to C. C. Berry, August 14, 1867, Pythian Base Ball Club Records, ANHS Collection, Historical Society of Pennsylvania.

9. Head Quarters, 1st Battalion, City Guard of Washington DC, to Pythian BBC, Pythian Base Ball Club Records, ANHS Collection, Historical Society of Pennsylvania.

10. *Philadelphia Sunday Mercury*, September 1, 1867.

11. *Philadelphia Sunday Mercury*, September 8, 1867.

12. See also chapter 5.

13. *Philadelphia Sunday Mercury*, December 8, 1867, reported a tally of 30–15; the Pythians' records claimed a victory by the score of 30–9. Because newspapers often relied on secondhand reporting, such discrepancies can be found throughout baseball's early history. The papers, however, rarely misidentified the victor of a particular game.

14. Dorwart, *Camden County*, 74. For the history of Camden and its relationship with Philadelphia, see also Cammarota, *Pavements in the Garden*.

15. Scorecard, October 10, 1867, Pythian Base Ball Club Records, ANHS Collection, Historical Society of Pennsylvania.

16. Check ledger, Pythian Base Ball Club Records, ANHS Collection, Historical Society of Pennsylvania.

17. *Ball Players' Chronicle*, October 3, 1867.

18. *City Item*, March 31, 1866.

19. The *Philadelphia Press* occasionally referred to a rough plot of land in South Camden, New Jersey, as the "Pythians' Grounds," but no record exists to demonstrate that the club had either purchased or leased the property. *Philadelphia Press*, August 26, 1866.

20. *19th Century Scrapbook, 1864–1868*, Baseball Hall of Fame Research Library.

21. *Wilkes' Spirit of the Times*, March 18, 1871.

22. "Last week, by way of a dashing contest for 1870, they [the Athletics] played their last match on their grounds on Columbia Avenue and 17th street, a locality they have occupied since 1865. The increased value of this property, consequent upon the growth of the city, has obliged the club to vacate their old field and return to their former grounds, on 25th and Jefferson streets, which they will occupy in 1871 conjointly with the old Olympic Club." See *New York Clipper*, December 17, 1870; and Scrapbook, 1866–74, Philadelphia Athletics, Baseball Hall of Fame.

23. *Philadelphia Sunday Mercury*, October 27, 1867.

24. *19th Century Scrapbook, 1857–1866*, Baseball Hall of Fame Research Library (emphasis added).

25. Kirsch, *Creation of American Team Sports*, 62–63; Voigt, *American Baseball*, 6–7, 20–23.

26. *Wilkes' Spirit of the Times*, October 19, 1867.

27. Lane, *William Dorsey's Philadelphia and Ours*, 101–2; check ledger, Pythian Base Ball Club Records, ANHS Collection, Historical Society of Pennsylvania.

28. "Report of the Delegate to the Convention of Baseball Players," ANHS Collection, Historical Society of Pennsylvania.

29. "Report of the Delegate to the Convention of Baseball Players," ANHS Collection, Historical Society of Pennsylvania.

30. "Report of the Delegate to the Convention of Baseball Players," ANHS Collection, Historical Society of Pennsylvania.

31. "Report of the Delegate to the Convention of Baseball Players," ANHS Collection, Historical Society of Pennsylvania.

32. "Report of the Delegate to the Convention of Baseball Players," ANHS Collection, Historical Society of Pennsylvania.

33. "Report of the Delegate to the Convention of Baseball Players," ANHS Collection, Historical Society of Pennsylvania.

34. "Report of the Delegate to the Convention of Baseball Players," ANHS Collection, Historical Society of Pennsylvania.

35. "Report of the Delegate to the Convention of Baseball Players," ANHS Collection, Historical Society of Pennsylvania.

36. "Report of the Delegate to the Convention of Baseball Players," ANHS Collection, Historical Society of Pennsylvania.

37. *Ball Players' Chronicle*, August 22, 1867.

38. "Report of the Delegate to the Convention of Baseball Players," ANHS Collection, Historical Society of Pennsylvania.

39. *New York Sunday Mercury* in Chadwick Scrapbooks, 19, Society for American Baseball Research.

40. Shiffert, *Base Ball in Philadelphia*, 213–14. William Ryczek similarly gives Hayhurst too much credit for his flaccid support of the Pythians. See Ryczek, *Baseball's First Inning*, 119.

41. *New York Clipper*, August 4, 1866.

42. Octavius Catto to Charles McCullough, August 12, 1869, ANHS Collection, Historical Society of Pennsylvania.
43. Feldberg, *Philadelphia Riots of 1844*, 23, 34; Clark, *Irish Relations*, 120–21, 144–
   45; DuBois, *The Philadelphia Negro*, 38–39.
44. *Philadelphia Sunday Mercury*, October 11, 1868.
45. *Philadelphia Sunday Mercury*, October 11, 1868; Davis and Haller, *Peoples of
   Philadelphia*, 140–43.
46. *City Item*, May 12, 1866.
47. Just to avoid confusion, there was a "Athletic Base Ball Club" in Washington DC
   composed of African American players that played against other black clubs.
   These Athletics should not be confused with Philadelphia's Athletic Base Ball
   Club. For an account of the former, see *National Republican* (Washington DC),
   August 21, 1867.
48. *City Item*, July 24, 1869. In the same issue Fitzgerald printed the satirical "Athletic Rules," which professed to be the new organizing statutes of the Athletic
   Club. The rules included: "Each member will rise at 5," "Ground nuts forbidden," and "No more social games, except with the Pythians and Atlantics." Confusing, to be sure.
49. *City Item*, July 31, 1869. The same *City Item* edition carried a similarly provoca-
   tive and relatively anonymous letter to the editor, "Can you tell me, sir, why the
   Keystone, or Olympic, or Athletic, or some other first-class organizations—
   refuses to play the colored Pythian Club? . . . [M]y belief is that the Athletics of
   Keystones would, unless they played remarkably well, be beaten by the Pythians."
50. *City Item*, June 26, 1869.
51. Loosely translated, "Go to hell, my dear."
52. *City Item*, July 31, 1869.
53. *City Item*, August 7, 1869.
54. *City Item*, August 14, 1869.
55. Presumably, "Meyrle" refers to Levi Meyerle, despite the slight difference in
   spelling. Meyerle played in the Athletics' infield through the 1860s and 1870s.
   See Player File—Levi Meyerle, A. Bartlett Giamatti Research Center, Baseball
   Hall of Fame.
56. *City Item*, August 21, 1869.
57. *Wilkes' Spirit of the Times*, September 11, 1869.
58. *Wilkes' Spirit of the Times*, September 11, 1869.
59. *New York Clipper*, September 25, 1869.
60. *New York Times*, September 5, 1869; *Wilkes' Spirit of the Times*, September 11,
   1869; *City Item*, September 11, 1869.
61. *City Item*, September 11, 1869.
62. *City Item*, September 11, 1869 (emphasis added).
63. *New York Clipper*, September 25, 1869.
64. *Washington (DC) Daily National Intelligencer and Weekly Express*, October 4, 1869.
65. *City Item*, October 16, 1869.

66. *City Item*, September 11, 1869.
67. *Morning Post* in *City Item*, September 25, 1869.
68. Foner, *Reconstruction*, 371.

5. WASHINGTON DC: NATIONALIZING SEPARATION

1. Curran, *Bicentennial History of Georgetown University*, 269. The notion of one year being particularly "critical," especially during the Reconstruction era, goes back to Beale's *Critical Year*. For Washington DC baseball, the collision of significant on- and off-the-field activities makes 1867, not 1866, the most critical year of all.
2. National Base Ball Club, *Constitution, By-Laws, Rules, and Regulations of the National Base Ball Club of Washington DC, 1867*, French Papers, Historical Society of Washington DC.
3. National Base Ball Club, *Constitution, By-Laws, Rules, and Regulations*, French Papers, Historical Society of Washington DC.
4. French, *Baseball Scrapbook and Memorabilia*, 100, French Papers, Historical Society of Washington DC.
5. French, *Baseball Scrapbook and Memorabilia*, 94, French Papers, Historical Society of Washington DC.
6. Spalding, *America's National Game*, 103.
7. *Ball Players' Chronicle*, June 25, 27, 1867.
8. French, *Baseball Scrapbook and Memorabilia*, 106, French Papers, Historical Society of Washington DC.
9. *New York Clipper*, July 20, 1867; *Ball Players' Chronicle*, July 18, 1867.
10. French, *Baseball Scrapbook and Memorabilia*, 118, French Papers, Historical Society of Washington DC; Ryczek, *When Johnny Came Sliding Home*, 123. Chicago hosted a weeklong baseball convention during the Nationals' visit. Representatives from more than sixty clubs from throughout the Midwest came to witness first-class baseball.
11. *Wilkes' Spirit of the Times*, July 27, 1867.
12. Kirsch, *Baseball in Blue and Gray*, 120.
13. Spalding, *America's National Game*, 109.
14. French, *Baseball Scrapbook and Memorabilia*, 119, French Papers, Historical Society of Washington DC.
15. Ryczek, *When Johnny Came Sliding Home*, 125.
16. *Chicago Republican*, July 28, 1867.
17. *Chicago Republican*, July 28, 1867.
18. French, *Baseball Scrapbook and Memorabilia*, 202, French Papers, Historical Society of Washington DC.
19. French, *Baseball Scrapbook and Memorabilia*, 202, French Papers, Historical Society of Washington DC.
20. Charles Douglass to J. C. White, September 10, 1869, ANHS Collection, Historical Society of Pennsylvania.
21. Alert Base Ball Club to Pythian Base Ball Club, June 6, 1867, ANHS Collection, Historical Society of Pennsylvania.

22. *New York Clipper*, July 6, 1867.

23. *New York Clipper*, October 10, 1868.

24. Charles Douglass to Frederick Douglass, August 22, 1867, Douglass Papers, Library of Congress; Bentley, *History of the Freedmen's Bureau*, 121–27.

25. George D. Johnson (Mutual BBC) to Octavius V. Catto (Pythian BBC), April 23, 1867, ANHS Collection, Historical Society of Pennsylvania.

26. *New York Clipper*, July 27, 1867; *Philadelphia Sunday Mercury*, July 21, 1867, January 28, 1866.

27. Pythian Base Ball Club to Alert Base Ball Club, July 29, 1867, ANHS Collection, Historical Society of Pennsylvania.

28. Charles Douglass to J. C. White, August 3, 1867, ANHS Collection, Historical Society of Pennsylvania.

29. J. C. White to Charles Douglass, August 8, 1867, ANHS Collection, Historical Society of Pennsylvania.

30. Louis A. Bell (Alert BBC) to Pythian BBC, 1867, Pythian Base Ball Club Records, ANHS Collection, Historical Society of Pennsylvania.

31. Kirsch, *Baseball in Blue and Gray*, 119.

32. Charles Douglass to Frederick Douglass, August 10, 1867, Douglass Papers, Library of Congress.

33. Aron, *Ladies and Gentlemen of the Civil Service*, 68–70.

34. Charles Douglass to Frederick Douglass, August 16, 1867, Douglass Papers, Library of Congress.

35. *Philadelphia Sunday Mercury*, September 1, 1867.

36. Charles Douglass to Frederick Douglass, September 2, 1867, Douglass Papers, Library of Congress.

37. Formal invitation, August 31, 1867, at rooms of the Mutual BBC, "Welcome Pythians," Woodward's Hall, D Street, between Tenth and Eleventh, Pythian Base Ball Club Records, ANHS Collection, Historical Society of Pennsylvania.

38. *New York Clipper*, December 21, 1867.

39. *Ball Players' Chronicle*, December 19, 1867; *New York Clipper*, December 21, 1867.

40. The assertion that this declaration by the nominating committee was a constitutional change and that "this era from 1867–1871 represented the only time when the written rules of a national baseball organization prevented blacks from playing on the same diamond alongside white athletes" is, I believe, imprecise. Although a precedent-setting decision occurred, the NABBP did not insert a segregationist clause into its constitution. So, technically, there was a decision to cite, but not a constitutional clause denoting racial segregation. See Heaphy, *Negro Leagues*, 10–11.

41. *New York Clipper*, December 21, 1867.

42. *New York Tribune*, December 12, 1867.

43. *Cleveland Herald*, December 20, 1867.

44. *Milwaukee Daily Sentinel*, December 19, 1867.

45. *City Item*, December 21, 1867.

46. Seymour and Seymour, *Baseball: The People's Game*, 42.
47. Peterson, *Only the Ball Was White*, 16.
48. Sullivan, *Early Innings*, 32.
49. *Ball Players' Chronicle*, December 19, 1867.
50. *New York Times*, November 14, 1870 (emphasis added).
51. Octavius Catto has become the leader of record for the Pythians and thus is ascribed to most everything related to the Pythians. As was discussed in a previous chapter, Raymond Burr, not Octavius Catto, submitted the Pythians' application to the Pennsylvania Association. See Threston, *Integration of Baseball in Philadelphia*, 9.
52. Ribowsky, *Complete History of the Negro Leagues*, 13–14.
53. Shiffert, *Base Ball in Philadelphia*, 56.
54. Seymour and Seymour, *Baseball: The People's Game*, 534–38.
55. Thorn, *Baseball in the Garden of Eden*, 130.
56. Biddle and Dubin, *Testing Freedom*, 367.
57. Thorn and Palmer, *Total Baseball*, 486.
58. Shiffert, *Base Ball in Philadelphia*, 60.
59. Undoubtedly, errors and omissions will be found in this study by other baseball historians. These errors will be duly pointed out and then, hopefully, corrected in future works.
60. Wang, *Trial of Democracy*, 236.
61. Essary, *Maryland in National Politics*, 245.
62. Essary, *Maryland in National Politics*, 257.
63. *Washington (DC) Evening Star*, September 17, 1869; *Washington (DC) Sunday Herald and Weekly National Intelligencer*, September 4, 1870, June 25, 1871, August 3, 1873; *Philadelphia Sunday Mercury*, September 1, 1867.
64. *Washington (DC) Evening Star*, July 7, 1870.
65. *New York Clipper*, May 15, 1869.
66. *New York Clipper*, May 22, 1869.
67. Washington's *Evening Star* took the lead in local reporting on baseball and had a mixed record on political issues. The *Star* had supported Lincoln's reelection in 1864, but distanced itself from the policies of the Radical Republicans. See also White, *Uncivil War*, 23–25.
68. McFeely, *Frederick Douglass*, 272; Bentley, *History of the Freedmen's Bureau*, 199–202.
69. *Ball Players' Chronicle*, February 9, 1871.
70. *Daily Intelligencer*, September 29, 1866; *Chicago Republican*, July 28, 1867.
71. Part of the reason for the openness of the Treasury Department was that the department grew from eleven hundred employees in 1865 to more than nineteen hundred in 1870. See Aron, *Ladies and Gentlemen of the Civil Service*, 57; U.S. Congress, "Clerks Employed in the Treasury Department," 43rd Cong., 1st sess., House of Representatives, Misc. Doc. No. 253, April 20, 1874.
72. *Washington (DC) Evening Star*, August 16, 1869.
73. *Washington (DC) Evening Star*, September 17, 1869.

74. *Washington (DC) Evening Star*, September 18, 1869.

75. *Washington (DC) Evening Star*, September 20, 1869.

76. The Olympics of Philadelphia met the Pythians of the same city on September 3, 1869, in the first mixed-race game on record. Thus, by a few days, Philadelphia beat Washington DC to interracial baseball. The Olympics of Philadelphia, however, had declined in prestige rapidly since their pre–Civil War heyday. See Ryczek's *When Johnny Came Sliding Home* (101), as well as the late-August 1869 editions of the *New York Times* and *New York Clipper*.

77. *Washington (DC) Evening Star*, September 21, 1869.

78. *New York Clipper*, October 2, 1869.

79. *Washington (DC) Evening Star*, September 17, 20, 1869.

80. *New York Clipper*, October 2, 1869.

81. *Baltimore Sun*, September 23, 1869. The *Sun* followed up on the rejection two days later (*Baltimore Sun*, September 25, 1869), clarifying: "The directors of the Maryland Base Ball Club of this city correct the statement that they have refused to play the Olympics of Washington because the latter had engaged a colored club which was not a convention organization. The subject, it is stated, has never been discussed by the Maryland club." The clarification did not deny the intent to punish the Olympics for crossing the race line, only that the issue had been openly discussed.

82. *Washington (DC) Evening Star*, October 13, 1869.

83. Charles Douglass to Frederick Douglass, October 16, 1870, Douglass Papers, Library of Congress.

84. *New York Clipper*, October 23, 1869. Baseball presses often used the term *muffin* to describe novice or poor players.

85. *Brooklyn Eagle*, September 20, 1869.

86. See P. Morris, *Baseball Fever*, 198–99; *Chicago Tribune*, August 24, 1870; and *Weekly Louisianan*, January 29, 1871.

87. *Philadelphia Sunday Mercury*, October 3, 1869.

88. Voigt, *American Baseball*, 36.

89. On the significance of and reasons for barnstorming, see Lanctot, *Negro League Baseball*, 111–16; and White, *Creating the National Pastime*, 128–46.

6. RICHMOND: CALIBRATING A RESPONSE

1. *New York Clipper*, December 18, 1867.

2. *Daily News and Herald*, October 19, 1867.

3. *Daily Phoenix*, October 19, 1867.

4. *Georgia Weekly Opinion*, October 22, 1867.

5. *Wilkes' Spirit of the Times*, October 19, 1867.

6. Chadwick, *Game of Base Ball*, 162.

7. *Atlanta Daily Intelligencer*, December 17, 1867.

8. *Atlanta Daily Intelligencer*, December 17, 1867.

9. *Richmond Daily Dispatch*, October 24, 1866.

10. *Richmond Times*, October 17, 1866.

11. *Washington (DC) Daily National Intelligencer*, October 26, 1866.
12. French, *Baseball Scrapbook and Memorabilia*, untitled newspaper clipping, French Papers, Historical Society of Washington DC.
13. French, *Baseball Scrapbook and Memorabilia*, untitled newspaper clipping, French Papers, Historical Society of Washington DC.
14. See, for example, *Philadelphia Sunday Mercury*, October 3, 1869; *New York Clipper*, June 21, 1873; and newspaper clipping, April 7, 1893, McHarg Family Papers, Georgetown University Special Collections. See also Riess, *Touching Base*, 29.
15. French, *Baseball Scrapbook and Memorabilia*, untitled newspaper clipping, French Papers, Historical Society of Washington DC.
16. *Richmond Times*, October 27, 1866.
17. French, *Baseball Scrapbook and Memorabilia*, untitled newspaper clipping, French Papers, Historical Society of Washington DC.
18. *Richmond Daily Dispatch*, October 27, 1866.
19. *New York Clipper*, October 27, 1866.
20. French, *Baseball Scrapbook and Memorabilia*, untitled newspaper clipping, French Papers, Historical Society of Washington DC.
21. French, *Baseball Scrapbook and Memorabilia*, untitled newspaper clipping, French Papers, Historical Society of Washington DC; *Richmond Times*, October 29, 1866.
22. French, *Baseball Scrapbook and Memorabilia*, untitled newspaper clipping, French Papers, Historical Society of Washington DC.
23. *Richmond Times*, October 29, 1866; *Richmond Daily Dispatch*, October 29, 1866.
24. *Richmond Times*, October 29, 1866; *Richmond Daily Dispatch*, October 29, 1866.
25. French, *Baseball Scrapbook and Memorabilia*, untitled newspaper clipping, French Papers, Historical Society of Washington DC.
26. *Richmond Times*, October 29, 1866.
27. French, *Baseball Scrapbook and Memorabilia*, untitled newspaper clipping, French Papers, Historical Society of Washington DC.
28. *Richmond Daily Dispatch*, November 6, 1866.
29. *Richmond Times*, November 7, 1866.
30. *Richmond Times*, November 10, 1866.
31. *New York Clipper*, April 13, 1867.
32. *Ball Players' Chronicle*, June 27, 1867.
33. *Ball Players' Chronicle*, July 11, 1867.
34. *Richmond Daily Dispatch*, February 25, 1867.
35. *Richmond Times*, August 6, 1866.
36. *Richmond Times*, September 15, November 12, 19, 1866.
37. *Richmond Times*, May 7, 10, 1867, October 10, 1866; *Richmond Daily Dispatch*, November 22, 1866.
38. *Richmond Daily Dispatch*, November 12, 1866.
39. *Richmond Times*, May 10, 1867.
40. *Richmond Daily Dispatch*, April 17, June 14, August 14, 1867.
41. *Richmond Daily Dispatch*, August 28, 1867.

42. *Ball Players' Chronicle*, July 25, 1867; *Daily Intelligencer* (Atlanta GA), May 26, 1867; *Daily Gazette* (Little Rock AR), September 27, 1867; *Daily News and Herald* (Savannah GA), April 22, 1867; *New Orleans Commercial Bulletin*, June 1, 1868.

43. *Daily Intelligencer*, April 23, 1867.

44. *Daily Intelligencer*, June 16, 1867.

45. *National Republican* (Washington DC), April 8, 1868.

46. *Cincinnati Daily Gazette*, November 23, 1869.

47. *New York Times*, October 1, 1867.

48. *Charleston Courier, Tri-Weekly*, September 10, 1868.

49. *Morning Republican* (Little Rock AR), September 8, 1868.

50. *New York Clipper*, June 20, 1868.

51. *Daily News and Herald* (Savannah GA), April 22, 1868; *Daily Phoenix* (Columbia SC), July 23, 1867.

52. *New York Clipper*, June 20, 1868.

53. Somers, *Rise of Sports in New Orleans*, 121.

54. Somers, *Rise of Sports in New Orleans*, 119–20.

55. Schiff, *"Father of Baseball,"* 97–98.

56. Chadwick Scrapbooks, Society for American Baseball Research.

57. Greenberg, *Honor and Slavery*, 124. Greenberg's study focuses on the culture that developed during slavery.

58. Perez, "Between Baseball and Bullfighting," 494.

59. *Daily News and Herald* (Savannah GA), April 22, 1868.

60. *New Orleans Commercial Bulletin*, January 7, 1868; *Ball Players' Chronicle*, July 4, 1867.

61. *Ball Players' Chronicle*, July 4, 1867.

62. *Daily Phoenix* (Columbia SC), September 29, 1867.

63. *The Pickwick Club Historical Summary: Act of Incorporation, By-Laws, Roster of Membership*, 1–5.

64. *Charleston Courier, Tri-Weekly*, July 14, 1868.

65. *National Republican* (Washington DC), April 8, 1868.

66. Kirsch, *Creation of American Team Sports*, 202–3; *Atlanta Daily Sun*, November 8, 1872; *Morning Republican* (Little Rock AR), September 8, 1868.

67. *Cleveland Morning Herald*, May 16, 1871; *Bangor (ME) Daily Whig and Courier*, June 8, 1868; *Daily Patriot* (Concord NH), September 5, 1871; *St. Louis Globe-Democrat*, July 22, 1875.

68. *Bangor (ME) Daily White and Courier*, June 8, 1868.

69. *Richmond Daily Dispatch*, October 7, 1867.

70. *Richmond Daily Dispatch*, June 10, 1867.

71. *Richmond Times*, October 2, 9, 1866.

72. Captain Peter S. Michie, United States Army Corps of Engineers, *Map: Richmond, Virginia, 1865*, Library of Virginia.

73. Richmond City Council Records, August 21, September 9, 1867.

74. *Richmond Daily Dispatch*, May 27, 1867; *Richmond Times*, May 14, 1867; *Philadelphia Sunday Mercury*, November 24, 1867.

75. *Richmond Daily Dispatch*, October 16, 1867.

76. *Philadelphia Sunday Mercury*, October 3, 1869.

77. *Wilkes' Spirit of the Times*, April 10, 1869; *Philadelphia Sunday Mercury*, April 4, 1869.

78. *Charleston Courier, Tri-Weekly*, July 29, 1869.

79. *Charleston Courier, Tri-Weekly*, July 29, 1869; *Daily Phoenix* (Columbia SC), July 28, 1869; *Wilkes' Spirit of the Times*, August 7, 1869.

80. *New York Times*, July 28, 1869.

81. *Charleston Courier, Tri-Weekly*, July 29, 1869.

82. *Charleston Courier, Tri-Weekly*, July 29, 1869.

83. *Charleston Courier, Tri-Weekly*, July 29, 1869.

84. *Charleston Courier, Tri-Weekly*, July 29, 1869.

85. *Charleston Courier, Tri-Weekly*, July 31, 1869.

86. *Daily Phoenix* (Columbia SC), July 28, 1869.

87. *Southern Watchman* (Athens GA), August 4, 1869; *Atlanta Constitution*, July 28, 1869.

88. *New York Times*, July 28, 30, 1869.

89. *Wilkes' Spirit of the Times*, August 7, 1869.

90. *Newark (NJ) Advocate*, July 30, 1869.

91. *New York Times*, October 1, 1867.

92. Godkin, "Philosophy of 'the National Game,'" 168.

93. *New York Times*, August 16, 1869.

94. *New York Times*, August 16, 1869.

95. *Chicago Tribune*, August 16, 1869.

7. PHILADELPHIA: PERMANENT SOLUTIONS

1. Just how fast Jim Crow segregation set in, of course, has long been a historical debate. See Woodward's *Strange Career of Jim Crow*, Rabinowitz's *Race Relations in the Urban South*, and Litwack's *Been in the Storm So Long*.

2. For a broad and insightful analysis of the role of violence during and after Reconstruction, see Shapiro, *White Violence and the Black Response*.

3. Contract, Octavius Catto and Elisha Weaver, "Philadelphia, May 12, 1870: Articles of agreement made this the 12th day of May, 1870 between and by Elisha Weaver of the one part and Octavius Catto of the other part witnessed that the said Elisha Weaver of the one part agrees to sell unto Octavius V. Catto of the second part all his right title and interest in the Liberty Hall Association in Lombard St for the sum of $950.00: said interest represents the one tenth part of the stock in said association subject to the debts and liabilities of said Elisha Weaver now having accrued up to the present date in the above Liberty Hall Association . . ." ANHS Collection, Historical Society of Pennsylvania.

4. Biddle and Dubin, *Tasting Freedom*, 402–3.

5. Octavius Catto to Jacob C. White Jr., October 2, 1870, ANHS Collection, Historical Society of Pennsylvania.

6. Whyte, *Uncivil War*, 99.

7. John Johnson to Octavius Catto, August 14, 1870, ANHS Collection, Historical Society of Pennsylvania; Biddle and Durbin, *Tasting Freedom*, 413.

8. *New National Era*, October 19, 1871.

9. *New National Era*, October 27, 1870.

10. Seymour, *Baseball: The Early Years*, 104–11.

11. *Philadelphia Sunday Mercury*, June 25, 1871.

12. *New York Clipper*, July 8, 1871.

13. *Philadelphia Sunday Mercury*, August 13, 1871.

14. *New York Clipper*, August 19, 1871.

15. *Philadelphia Sunday Mercury*, August 13, 1871.

16. *Philadelphia Sunday Mercury*, August 27, 1871.

17. *New York Clipper*, September 2, 1871.

18. *Philadelphia Sunday Mercury*, August 27, 1871.

19. *New York Clipper*, April 27, 1872.

20. *Philadelphia Sunday Mercury*, June 4, 1871; *New York Clipper*, October 8, 1870; *Weekly Louisianan* (New Orleans), January 29, 1871; *Cleveland Herald*, August 25, 1874.

21. Heaphy, *Black Baseball and Chicago*, 8–9.

22. *Chicago Tribune*, November 2, 1867.

23. *Chicago Tribune*, August 24, 1870.

24. *Chicago Tribune*, August 24, 1870.

25. Avery, *City of Brotherly Mayhem*, 17–20.

26. *Philadelphia Inquirer*, October 11, 1871.

27. *Philadelphia Inquirer*, October 11, 1871.

28. Biddle and Dubin, *Tasting Freedom*, 422–28.

29. *Philadelphia Inquirer*, October 11, 1871.

30. *Philadelphia Inquirer*, October 11, 1871.

31. *New National Era*, October 19, 1871.

32. The conflicting newspaper reports regarding the Catto murder make ascertaining exactly what occurred impossible. For extensive accounts, see *Philadelphia Inquirer*, October 11–15, 1871; and *New National Era*, October 19, 1871.

33. Griffin, *Trial of Frank Kelly*.

34. *Philadelphia Inquirer*, October 12, 1871.

35. *New National Era*, October 19, 1871; *Philadelphia Inquirer*, October 11, 1871.

36. *Philadelphia Inquirer*, October 11, 1871.

37. *Philadelphia Inquirer*, October 12, 1871.

38. *New National Era*, October 26, 1871.

39. *Washington Chronicle* quoted in *New National Era*, October 26, 1871.

40. *Philadelphia Sunday Mercury*, October 15, 1871.

41. *Philadelphia Sunday Mercury*, October 15, 1871.

42. *Philadelphia Press*, October 14, 1871.

43. *Philadelphia Inquirer*, October 12, 1871.

44. *Philadelphia Press*, October 17, 1871.

45. *Philadelphia Sunday Mercury*, October 15, 1871.

46. *Philadelphia Press*, October 17, 1871.
47. *Philadelphia Inquirer*, October 18, 1871.
48. *New National Era*, October 19, 1871.
49. *New National Era*, November 9, 1871.
50. *New National Era*, November 9, 1871.
51. *New National Era*, November 9, 1871.
52. *New National Era*, October 19, 1871.
53. *New National Era*, October 19, 1871.
54. *Philadelphia Sunday Mercury*, July 26, 1874.
55. *Philadelphia Sunday Mercury*, August 23, 1874.
56. Ryczek, *Blackguards and Red Stockings*, 236; *Philadelphia Sunday Mercury*, April 25, 1875; *New York Clipper*, May 8, 1875; *Philadelphia Sunday Mercury*, December 31, 1876.
57. *Philadelphia Sunday Mercury*, August 23, 1874.
58. *Washington (DC) Sunday Herald and Weekly National Intelligencer*, August 22, 1875.
59. *Philadelphia Sunday Mercury*, February 6, 1876.
60. *Philadelphia Sunday Mercury*, December 10, 1876.
61. *Ball Players' Chronicle*, November 7, 1867.
62. *New York Clipper*, December 5, 1868. The total included one "social game" against a Princeton club that the *Philadelphia Sunday Mercury* (November 8, 1868) did not include in its tally. See also *Philadelphia Sunday Mercury*, November 8, 22, 1868; and *New York Clipper*, September 25, 1869.
63. *Philadelphia Sunday Mercury*, November 28, 1869.
64. *New York Clipper*, April 15, 1871. Regarding game play, a few new rules went on the books in 1871, as happened at the beginning of each new baseball season. The ball size was standardized, new rules mandated that called strikes could be levied against a batter who refused to swing at acceptable pitches, and the convention also made standard the practice of batters being allowed to overrun first base. See Voigt, *American Baseball*, 37–38; and Ryczek, *Blackguards and Red Stockings*.
65. *New York Clipper*, December 23, 1871; Ryczek, *Blackguards and Red Stockings*, 95–96.
66. *Philadelphia Sunday Mercury*, November 16, 1873.
67. Shiffert, *Base Ball in Philadelphia*, 114.
68. *Philadelphia Sunday Mercury*, February 7, 1869, June 11, December 31, 1871, January 14, 1872.
69. *New York Clipper*, March 1, 1873; *Philadelphia Sunday Mercury*, November 16, 1873.
70. *New York Clipper*, January 17, 1874; *Philadelphia Sunday Mercury*, September 6, 1874; Chadwick Scrapbooks, 1874, Society for American Baseball Research.
71. *New York Clipper*, February 12, 1876; Ryczek, *Blackguards and Red Stockings*, 224–26.
72. *New York Clipper*, February 12, 1876.

73. *New York Clipper*, February 19, 1876.
74. *Philadelphia Sunday Mercury*, February 13, 1876.
75. *New York Clipper*, August 26, September 30, December 9, 1876; *Philadelphia Sunday Mercury*, December 3, 1876.
76. *New York Clipper*, December 12, 1876.
77. Griffin, *Trial of Frank Kelly*.
78. Avery, *City of Brotherly Mayhem*, 22.
79. Griffin, *Trial of Frank Kelly*.

8. RICHMOND: THE FINAL TALLY

1. *Wilkes' Spirit of the Times*, April 10, 1869; *New York Clipper*, April 3, 1869.
2. Much has been written on the Lost Cause and the role of the Confederate memory in reshaping the South. I found the following works to be the most helpful: Blair, *Cities of the Dead*; Blight, *Race and Reunion*; Cox, *Dixie's Daughters*; and Wilson, *Baptized in Blood*.
3. *Richmond Daily Dispatch*, July 2, 1871.
4. Janney, *Burying the Dead but Not the Past*; Ayers, Gallagher, and Torget, *Crucible of the Civil War*, 165–82.
5. *Petersburg Index and Appeal*, April 6, 1875; *Richmond Daily Dispatch*, May 9, 1876; *Sheriff & Chataigne's Richmond Directory*.
6. *New National Era*, May 5, 1870; Foner, *Reconstruction*, 512; *Richmond Daily Dispatch*, September 27, 1873; McPherson, *Ordeal by Fire*, 265; *New National Era*, June 9, 1874.
7. *New National Era*, January 13, 1870.
8. Dabney, *Richmond*, 216.
9. *Richmond Daily Dispatch*, September 11, 1871.
10. The South's "a-horse-back mode of living" is tellingly captured in Hundley, *Social Relations in Our Southern States*, 29.
11. Franklin, *Militant South*, 33, 174.
12. *Richmond Daily Dispatch*, May 22, July 12, 1876. Horses also became a way of celebrating the Confederacy, as evidenced by reports on the status of Babcock's trusty steed. "An Old War-Horse-Captain AG Babcock has in his possession a regular veteran war-horse. He is known as 'Old Black' and can be seen any day at Captains Babcock's farm, 'Cedar Lawn.' He has the brand 'US' and 'CS' on his shoulder, which shows that he was captured from the Federals during the late war." *Richmond Daily Dispatch*, July 1, 1882.
13. *Richmond Daily Dispatch*, July 28, 1871.
14. *Richmond Daily Dispatch*, July 7, 1875.
15. *Richmond Daily Dispatch*, January 2, 1873.
16. *Charleston Courier, Tri-Weekly*, April 21, 1870.
17. *Atlanta Daily Sun*, January 6, 1872.
18. *Richmond Daily Dispatch*, July 4, 1871.
19. *Petersburg Daily Index*, September 9, 1872.
20. *Philadelphia Sunday Mercury*, October 13, 1872.

21. *New York Times*, January 16, 1871.
22. Maddex, *Virginia Conservatives*, 49.
23. *New National Era*, May 30, 1872; *Richmond Daily Dispatch*, August 26, 1876, September 4, 18, 1875; Maddex, *Virginia Conservatives*, 134–37; Michael Perman's treatment of Southern politics is especially insightful in understanding the Democrats, North and South, and how they intersected. See Perman, *Road to Redemption*, 6, 57–86, 60–61.
24. *Richmond City Directory*, 1871; *Richmond Daily Dispatch*, May 2, 1872.
25. *Richmond Daily Dispatch*, May 4, 14, 1874.
26. *Weekly Louisianan*, September 4, 1875.
27. *Galveston Daily News*, June 20, 1875; *Morning Republican* (Little Rock AR), June 18, 1871.
28. *New York Times*, September 10, 1870.
29. *Wilkes' Spirit of the Times*, October 5, 1870.
30. *New York Clipper*, October 19, 1867; Ryczek, *When Johnny Came Sliding Home*, 102–3.
31. *National Republican* (Washington DC), May 24, 1869.
32. *Daily Cleveland Herald*, August 6, 1870.
33. *Atlanta Weekly New Era*, May 24, 1871.
34. *Boston Daily Globe*, July 10, 1874.
35. *National Republican* (Washington DC), April 19, 1876.
36. *Shenandoah Herald*, May 28, 1879.
37. *Atlanta Daily Constitution*, July 7, 1877.
38. *Philadelphia Sunday Mercury*, April 23, 1876.
39. *Petersburg Index and Appeal*, September 9, 1872.
40. *Petersburg Index and Appeal*, April 6, 1875.
41. *Petersburg Index and Appeal*, April 17, 1875.
42. Gudmestad, "Baseball, the Last Cause, and the New South," 271.
43. See Gudmestad, "Baseball, the Lost Cause, and the New South," 271 (emphasis added).
44. Gudmestad, "Baseball, the Lost Cause, and the New South," 270.
45. *Sheriff and Co.'s Richmond City Directory, 1875–1876*.
46. Hucles, "Many Voices, Similar Concerns," 563–65.
47. *Richmond Daily Dispatch*, July 6, 1875.
48. *Washington (DC) Sunday Herald and Weekly National Intelligencer*, September 5, 1875; *Richmond Daily Dispatch*, September 8, 1875.
49. Gudmestad, "Baseball, the Lost Cause, and the New South," 271–78.
50. Retrosheet, "1874 Final Standings" and "1875 Final Standings," http://www.retrosheet.org.
51. *Richmond Daily Dispatch*, April 29, 1875.
52. *Richmond Daily Dispatch*, April 28, 1875.
53. *New York Clipper*, May 8, 1875.
54. *New York Clipper*, May 8, 1875.
55. *New York Clipper*, May 8, 1875.

56. *Richmond Daily Dispatch*, July 22, 1876.

57. *Richmond Daily Dispatch*, September 12, 1876.

9. WASHINGTON DC: PROFESSIONAL SEPARATION

1. Quoted in Goldstein, *Playing for Keeps*, 136.

2. The eventual benefits of professionalism have been pointed out, but these mostly came during the 1880s. See Ruck, *Raceball*, 21.

3. Melville, *Early Baseball*, 49.

4. Wiegand, *Politics of an Emerging Profession*, 109.

5. Chadwick seemed to recognize the inevitability of open professionalism: "Professionals—This is the term applied to all ball players who play base ball for money. . . . The Rules prohibit players from receiving compensation for their services in a match, but there is scarcely a club of note that has not infringed the rule." Chadwick, *Game of Base Ball*, 44.

6. *New York Clipper*, December 10, 1870.

7. Jackson, *Professions and Professionalization*, 7.

8. *New National Era*, January 20, 1870.

9. Johnson, "City on a Hill," 129–36. A few daring white doctors then rebelled and formed the National Medical Society with the intention of allowing black membership. The integrated group collapsed in a matter of weeks. The white doctors scurried back under the umbrella of the DC Medical Association.

10. Moreno, *Black Americans and Organized Labor*, 29–32. For the difficulty of overcoming race in attempting to unite the working class, see also Gertis, *Class and the Color Line*.

11. Vollmer and Mills, *Professionalization*, 52. In some scholarship optimism about the healing faculties of professionalism and sports sounds relatively similar. Consider the work of Vollmer and Mills, for example, in concert with Richard Thompson's *Race and Sport*: "Modern sport undermines any system of social stratification based on colour" (11).

12. *Chicago Tribune*, September 17, 4, 1870; Heaphy, *Black Baseball and Chicago*, 8–9.

13. *New York Times*, November 14, 1870.

14. *New York Times*, November 14, 1870.

15. *New York Times*, November 14, 1870.

16. *New York Times*, November 14, 1870.

17. *New York Times*, November 14, 1870.

18. There has been a significant amount of scholarship on "virtual representation" and the rise of American nationalism. For a useful sampling of this research, see Reid, *Concept of Representation*; and *New York Times*, November 14, 1870.

19. *New York Times*, November 14, 1870 (emphasis added).

20. Ryczek, *When Johnny Came Sliding Home*, 100, 139, 242; *New York Clipper*, November 26, 1870.

21. *Brooklyn Eagle*, November 14, 1870.

22. *Brooklyn Eagle*, November 17, 1870.

23. *New York Clipper*, December 10, 1870.

24. *New York Clipper*, December 10, 1870.

25. *New York Clipper*, December 10, 1870 (emphasis added).

26. Ryczek, *Blackguards and Red Stockings*, 9–10.

27. Roberts, *Hardball on the Hill*, 18; Ryczek, *Blackguards and Red Stockings*, 12; *New York Clipper*, March 1, 1871; Rader, *Baseball*, 37. Determining when professional baseball began in the United States is a controversial task. For a sampling of this debate, see Melville, *Early Baseball*, 26–34.

28. Seymour, *Baseball: The Early Years*, 59.

29. *New York Clipper*, January 15, April 30, 1870.

30. *Philadelphia Sunday Mercury*, September 29, 1872.

31. "Nicholas Young Clippings File," Baseball Hall of Fame.

32. "Nicholas Young Clippings File," Baseball Hall of Fame.

33. *New York Clipper*, February 19, September 10, 1870; *Philadelphia Sunday Mercury*, January 29, 1871.

34. *New York Clipper*, December 17, 1870; Baseball Scrapbooks, newspaper clipping, Notre Dame Sports Collection.

35. *National Republican*, December 2, 1870.

36. On the issue of financial backing for black baseball, I found Lomax's *Black Baseball Entrepreneurs* to be most helpful. Lomax makes a thorough examination of the economic side of black baseball that explains how black clubs functioned. See also Ruck, *Sandlot Seasons*.

37. *Daily Patriot*, March 20, 1871.

38. *New York Clipper*, April 15, 1871.

39. *Philadelphia Sunday Mercury*, January 29, September 10, 1871.

40. *Sunday Herald*, June 12, 1871; *National Republican*, June 11, 1871.

41. *Washington Chronicle*, June 13, 1871.

42. For more on the effects of professionalization, see Seymour, *Baseball: The Early Years*, 58–62. Seymour concluded, among other things, that professionalism made baseball a less noble and less honest game: "Its premium on winning changed the entire ethic of baseball from one of sport to one of victory by any possible method. It sanctioned if not outright violations of the rules at least taking all one could get within them."

43. *Washington (DC) Sunday Herald and Weekly National Intelligencer*, August 14, 1870.

44. *Washington (DC) Evening Star*, August 10, 1870.

45. *Washington (DC) Sunday Herald and Weekly National Intelligencer*, August 4, 1870; *Washington (DC) Evening Star*, August 10, 1870.

46. *Washington (DC) Evening Star*, July 7, 1870; *Washington (DC) Sunday Herald and Weekly National Intelligencer*, August 14, 1870.

47. *Washington (DC) Sunday Herald and Weekly National Intelligencer*, August 21, 1870.

48. *New York Clipper*, September 3, 1870.

49. Charles Douglass to Frederick Douglass, August 9, 1870, Douglass Papers, Library of Congress.

50. *Washington (DC) Sunday Herald and Weekly National Intelligencer*, September 18, 1870.

51. *Washington (DC) Sunday Herald and Weekly National Intelligencer*, September 18, 1870.

52. U.S. Congress, *Governance of the Nation's Capital*, 42–43.

53. *Washington (DC) Sunday Herald and Weekly National Intelligencer*, August 13, 1871. The connection between Washington's baseball community and the Treasury Department was a close one. It was so tight, in fact, that a mild protest arose in the District in the 1870s regarding the perceived preference given to ballplayers within the department. As an example of these sentiments, see *Washington Chronicle*, February 9, 1871: "Promotions in Departments—to the editor of the Chronicle: The recent promotions in one of the bureaus of the Treasury Department have caused many speculations regarding the basis upon which they were made, from the fact that "base-ballers" were given preference over those who hold out no only more responsible positions, but were entitled to some consideration upon the ground of seniority alone. . . . The feeling of the clerks burns with indignation to contemplate with what force base ball matters are encroaching upon their rights and the best interests for the public service."

54. *New York Clipper*, July 29, 1871.

55. *New National Era*, July 25, 1872.

56. *Washington (DC) Sunday Herald and Weekly National Intelligencer*, June 25, 1871.

57. *Washington (DC) Sunday Herald and Weekly National Intelligencer*, June 30, 1872.

58. *Washington (DC) Sunday Herald and Weekly National Intelligencer*, September 14, 1873; *Wilkes' Spirit of the Times*, August 24, 1867.

59. *New National Era*, April 17, 1873. When the publication officially incorporated in April 1873, Lewis Douglass, Frederick Douglass Jr., and Charles Douglass were all named trustees.

60. *New National Era*, July 24, 31, October 2, 1873.

61. *Washington (DC) Sunday Herald and Weekly National Intelligencer*, September 21, 1873.

62. *Washington (DC) Sunday Herald and Weekly National Intelligencer*, September 28, 1873.

63. *Washington (DC) Sunday Herald and Weekly National Intelligencer*, October 5, 1873.

64. *New National Era*, October 23, 1873.

65. Green, *Secret City*, 96; Johnson, "City on a Hill," 220.

66. *New York Clipper*, May 15, 1869; *Philadelphia Sunday Mercury*, April 25, 1869. The phenomenon of geographically based social remembrance has moved, in the twentieth and twenty-first centuries, from the front yard of the White House to the steps of the Lincoln Memorial. The value of this public space has been validated repeatedly by public demonstrations, not the least of which was the "I Have a Dream" speech by Martin Luther King Jr. See Sandage, "Marble House Divided."

67. *New National Era*, September 28, 1871.

68. *New National Era*, May 23, 1872.

69. *Washington (DC) Sunday Herald and Weekly National Intelligencer*, June 30, 1872, September 6, 1874.

70. *Washington (DC) Sunday Herald and Weekly National Intelligencer*, September 6, 1874.

71. Neither the origins of the Creighton Club nor the caliber of its men is known. The club's name probably paid homage to one of baseball's first great pitchers, James Creighton. Creighton played for the Excelsiors of Brooklyn. He perfected the fast-paced delivery, but died tragically, so the legend goes, when his bladder ruptured while hitting a home run, at the age of twenty-one. See Ryczek, *Blackguards and Red Stockings*, 5–6.

72. *Washington (DC) Sunday Herald and Weekly National Intelligencer*, September 6, 1874.

73. *New National Era*, October 9, 1873.

74. *New York Clipper*, March 18, 1876.

75. *New York Times*, November 1, 1916.

76. *New York Clipper*, March 18, 1876.

77. The Washington Mutual Club was not designated by the *New York Clipper*, the paper that provided the most extensive coverage for the National Association of Amateur Base Ball Players convention, as "colored." Thus, integration happened stealthily. Confirming that the club mentioned was indeed a black club (given the popularity of the "Mutual" name) requires careful cross-referencing, paying particular attention to the Mutual players with the last names Barlow, Bell, Brooks, and Smith. See *New York Clipper*, March 18, 1876, and March 24, 1877, for coverage of the conventions. Then see the following to confirm that the Mutual Club mentioned was indeed Washington's long-standing black organization: *New York Clipper*, September 3, 1870, March 11, 1876; *Philadelphia Sunday Mercury*, August 23, 1874; *New National Era*, August 7, 1873; and *Peoples' Advocate* (Washington DC), September 27, 1879.

78. *New York Clipper*, March 11, 1876, March 24, 1877.

79. *New York Clipper*, March 24, 1877.

80. Melville, *Early Baseball*, 102.

81. William Edward White, an African American, played in one National League game in 1879, "passing" as a white man. See Peter Morris and Stefan Fatsis, "Baseball's Secret Pioneer," www.slate.com/articles/sports/sports_nut/2014/02/william_edward_white_baseball_s_first_black_player_lived_his_life_as_a_white.html. Accessed February 6, 2014.

EPILOGUE

1. That is not to say that baseball is dominated by "white" Caucasian players. Major League Baseball has significant diversity. American-born players share big league base paths with Latin players, many in particular from the Dominican Republic, and hurlers and position players from Asia, among other places. See Ruck, *Raceball*.

2. *USA Today*, April 16, 2012.

3. *New York Times*, October 10, 1999.
4. Peterson, *Only the Ball Was White*, 33–39.
5. Seymour, *Baseball: The Early Years*, 334–35.
6. Quoted in Peterson, *Only the Ball Was White*, 40.
7. Zang, *Fleet Walker's Divided Heart*, 57–64.
8. *New York Age*, February 23, 1889.
9. Walker, *Our Home Colony*.
10. *Sporting Life*, April 11, 1891.
11. Malloy, *Sol White's History of Colored Base Ball*, xv.
12. Lomax, *Operating by Any Means Necessary*, 17278.
13. Posnanski, *Soul of Baseball*, 191.
14. "Report of the Delegate to the Convention of Baseball Players," ANHS Collection, Historical Society of Pennsylvania.
15. *New York Clipper*, December 21, 1867.
16. *New York Clipper*, November 26, 1870; see also November 19, 1870.
17. *New York Clipper*, May 7, 1870.
18. Malloy, *Sol White's Official Base Ball Guide*, 5.
19. For more on Sol White, see Jerry Malloy, "The Strange Career of Sol White: Black Baseball's First Historian," in *Out of the Shadows*, edited by Kirwin, 61–78.
20. Benson, *Ballparks of North America*, 419.
21. Peterson, *Only the Ball Was White*, 123.
22. Lanctot, *Negro League Baseball*, 3–7.
23. Kirwin, *Out of the Shadows*, 147–52.
24. Snyder, *Beyond the Shadow of the Senators*, 33–37.
25. Clark and Lester, *Negro Leagues Book*.
26. Benson, *Ballparks of North America*, 407–9; Snyder, *Beyond the Shadow of the Senators*, 2–11.
27. Thorn and Palmer, *Total Baseball*, 84–86.
28. Snyder, *Beyond the Shadow of the Senators*, 57–59.
29. "Roster Book," Swales Baseball Collection, 1871–1930, New York Public Library; Thorn and Palmer, *Total Baseball*, 1898.
30. Daniel and Mayer, *Baseball and Richmond*, 20–23.
31. Gudmestad, "Baseball, the Lost Cause, and the New South," 298–300.
32. Daniel and Mayer, *Baseball and Richmond*, 113–17, 133–36.

BIBLIOGRAPHY

PRIMARY SOURCES

Baseball Hall of Fame (Cooperstown NY)
    Mills Commission Papers
    Player Files
    Scrapbook, 1866–74, Philadelphia Athletics
    Scrapbook, 1879–1903, Philadelphia Athletics
Georgetown University Special Collections (Washington DC)
    McHarg Family Papers
Historical Society of Pennsylvania (Philadelphia)
    American Negro Historical Society Collection
    Thomas Fitzgerald Plays
    Leon Gardiner Collection
Historical Society of Washington DC
    Edmund F. French Baseball Scrapbook and Memorabilia, 1859–71
Library of Congress (Washington DC)
    Beadle's Dime Base Ball Player
    Frederick Douglass Papers
Library of Virginia (Richmond)
    Cornelius Carlton Papers
    Richmond City Council Records
National Archives and Records Administration (Washington DC)
    Compiled Service Records of Confederate Soldiers
    Records of the Bureau of Refugees, Freedmen, and Abandoned Lands
    Records of the United States House of Representatives
    United States Manuscript Census, 1860, 1870
New York Public Library
    Swales Baseball Collection, 1871–1930
Notre Dame Sports Collection (South Bend IN)
    Baseball Scrapbooks
Philadelphia City Archives
    Philadelphia Bureau of Water Papers
    Philadelphia Recorder of Deeds, Miscellaneous Collections

Society for American Baseball Research (Phoenix AZ)
Biography Database
Henry Chadwick Scrapbooks (Microfilm)

SECONDARY SOURCES

Adelman, Melvin L. *A Sporting Time: New York City and the Rise of Modern Athletics, 1820–1870.* Urbana: University of Illinois Press, 1986.

Alexander, Charles C. *Our Game: An American Baseball History.* New York: Henry Holt, 1991.

Allen, Lee. *The National League Story: The Official History.* New York: Hill & Wang, 1961.

Anderson, Eric, and Alfred A. Moss, eds. *The Facts of Reconstruction: Essays in Honor of John Hope Franklin.* Baton Rouge: Louisiana State University Press, 1991.

Andrews, Sidney. *The South since the War: As Shown by 14 Weeks of Travel and Observation in Georgia and the Carolinas.* Boston: Ticknor and Fields, 1866.

Aron, Cindy Sondik. *Ladies and Gentlemen of the Civil Service: Middle-Class Workers in Victorian America.* New York: Oxford University Press, 1987.

Ashe, Arthur R. *A Hard Road to Glory: A History of the African-American Athlete, 1619–1918.* New York: Warner Books, 1989.

Avery, Ron. *City of Brotherly Mayhem: Philadelphia Crime & Criminals.* Philadelphia: Otis Books, 1997.

Ayers, Edward L., Gary W. Gallagher, and Andrew J. Torget, eds. *Crucible of the Civil War: Virginia from Secession to Commemoration.* Charlottesville: University Press of Virginia, 2006.

The Base Ball Player's Book of Reference: Containing the Rules of the Game for 1866; with an Explanatory Appendix; Full Instructions for Umpires; Instructions for Scoring; the Three Best Averages of Each Club for 1865, Etc. New York: J. C. Haney, 1866.

Beale, Howard K. *The Critical Year: A Study of Andrew Johnson and Reconstruction.* New York: Harcourt, Brace, 1930.

Bednar, Michael J. *L'Enfant's Legacy: Public Open Spaces in Washington DC.* Baltimore: Johns Hopkins University Press, 2006.

Benson, Michael. *Ballparks of North America: A Comprehensive Historical Reference to Baseball Grounds, Yards, Stadiums, 1845–Present.* Jefferson NC: McFarland, 1989.

Bentley, George R. *A History of the Freedmen's Bureau.* New York: Octagon Books, 1974.

Berman, Myron. *Richmond's Jewry, 1769–1976: Shabbat in Shockoe.* Charlottesville: University Press of Virginia, 1979.

Bevis, Charlie. *The Major Leagues' Struggle to Play Baseball on the Lord's Day, 1876–1934.* Jefferson NC: McFarland, 2003.

Biddle, Daniel R., and Murray Dubin. *Testing Freedom: Octavius Catto and the Battle for Equality in Civil War America.* Philadelphia: Temple University Press, 2010.

Blair, William A. *Cities of the Dead: Contesting the Memory of the Civil War in the South, 1865–1914.* Chapel Hill: University of North Carolina Press, 2004.

Blight, David W. *Beyond the Battlefield: Race, Memory, and the American Civil War.* Amherst: University of Massachusetts Press, 2002.

———. *Race and Reunion: The Civil War in American History.* Cambridge MA: Harvard University Press, 2001.

Block, David. *Baseball before We Knew It: A Search for the Roots of the Game.* Lincoln: University of Nebraska Press, 2005.

Borchert, James. *Ally Life in Washington: Family, Community, Religion, and Folklife in the City, 1850–1970.* Urbana: University of Illinois Press, 1980.

Bowers, Claude G. *The Tragic Era: The Revolution after Lincoln.* Cambridge MA: Houghton Mifflin, 1929.

Boyd, William H. *Boyd's Directory of Richmond City, and a Business Directory of about Fifty Counties of Virginia, Together with a Compendium of the Government, Courts, Sheriffs, Institutions, and Trades, Compiled by Wm. H. Boyd.* Richmond VA: West, Johnson, 1869.

———. *Boyd's Directory of Richmond City and a Business Directory of Norfolk, Lynchburg, Petersburg, and Richmond, Together with a Compendium of the Government, Courts, Institutions, and Trades, 1870.* Richmond VA: State Journal Office, 1870.

Brown, Elsa Barkley, and Gregg D. Kimball. "Mapping the Terrain of Black Richmond." *Journal of Urban History* 21, no. 3 (1995): 296–346.

Brown, Letitia Woods. *Free Negroes in the District of Columbia, 1790–1846.* New York: Oxford University Press, 1972.

Butterworth, Michael. *Baseball and Rhetorics of Purity: The National Pastime and American Identity during the War on Terror.* Tuscaloosa: University of Alabama Press, 2010.

Cammarota, Ann Marie T. *Pavements in the Garden: The Suburbanization of Southern New Jersey, Adjacent to the City of Philadelphia, 1769 to the Present.* London: Associated University Presses, 2001.

Carnahan, James R. *Pythian Knighthood: Its History and Literature.* Cincinnati: Pettibone Manufacturing, 1888.

Carnes, Mark C. *Secret Ritual and Manhood in Victorian America.* New Haven CT: Yale University Press, 1989.

Carter, Dan T. *When the War Was Over: The Failure of Self-Reconstruction in the South, 1865–1867.* Baton Rouge: Louisiana State University Press, 1985.

Casway, Jerry. "Philadelphia's Pythians." *National Pastime,* no. 15 (1995): 120–23.

Chadwick, Henry. *Chadwick's Baseball Manual.* London: George Rougledge & Sons, 1874.

———. *Chadwick's Base Ball Manual, for 1871.* New York: American News, 1871.

———. *The Game of Baseball: How to Learn It, How to Play It, and How to Teach It, with Sketches of Noted Players.* 1868. Reprint, Camden House, 1983.

Charlick, Carl. *The Metropolitan Club of Washington: The Story of Its Men and of Its Place in City and Country.* Washington DC: Judd & Detweiler, 1965.

Chesson, Michael. *Richmond after the War, 1865–1890*. Richmond: Virginia State Library, 1981.

Cimbala, Paul A., and Randall M. Miller, eds. *The Freedmen's Bureau and Reconstruction: Reconsiderations*. New York: Fordham University Press, 1999.

Clark, Dennis. *The Irish in Philadelphia: Ten Generations of Urban Experience*. Philadelphia: Temple University Press, 1973.

——. *The Irish Relations: Trials of an Immigrant Tradition*. Rutherford NJ: Farleigh Dickinson University Press, 1982.

Clark, Dick, and Larry Lester. *The Negro Leagues Book: A Monumental Work from the Negro Leagues Committee of the Society for American Baseball Research*. Cleveland: SABR Press, 1994.

Countryman, Matthew J. *Up South: Civil Rights and Black Power in Philadelphia*. Philadelphia: University of Pennsylvania Press, 2006.

Cox, Karen L. *Dixie's Daughters: The United Daughters of the Confederacy and the Preservation of Confederate Culture*. Gainesville: University Press of Florida, 2003.

Cunningham, Frank. *Knight of the Confederacy: Gen. Turner Ashby*. San Antonio: Naylor, 1960.

Curran, Robert Emmett. *The Bicentennial History of Georgetown University: From Academy to University, 1789–1889*. Washington DC: Georgetown University Press, 1993.

Dabney, Virginius. *Richmond: The Story of a City*. New York: Doubleday, 1976.

Daniel, W. Harrison. "Good Playing and Gentlemanly Bearing: Baseball's Beginnings in Richmond, 1866–1883." *Virginia Cavalcade* 48 (Summer 1999): 118–33.

Daniel, W. Harrison, and Scott P. Mayer. *Baseball and Richmond: A History of the Professional Game, 1884–2000*. Jefferson NC: McFarland, 2005.

Davis, Allen F., and Mark H. Haller, eds. *The Peoples of Philadelphia: A History of Ethnic Groups and Lower-Class Life, 1790–1940*. Philadelphia: University of Pennsylvania Press, 1973.

Dickerson, Donna L. *The Reconstruction Era: Primary Documents on Events from 1865 to 1877*. Westport CT: Greenwood Press, 2003.

Dickey, Glenn. *The History of National League Baseball since 1876*. New York: Stein and Day, 1979.

Divine, William J. *The Richmond City Directory, 1866*. Richmond VA: E. P. Townsend, Booksellers & Stationer, 1866.

Dodd, Donald B., and Wynelle S. Dodd. *Historical Statistics of the United States, 1790–1970*. Tuscaloosa: University of Alabama Press, 1973.

Dorwart, Jeffrey M. *Camden County, New Jersey: The Making of a Metropolitan Community*. New Brunswick NJ: Rutgers University Press, 2001.

Doyle, Andrew. "Turning the Tide: College Football and Southern Progressivism." *Southern Cultures* 3, no. 3 (1997): 28–51.

DuBois, W. E. B. *Black Reconstruction in America: An Essay towards a History of the Part Which Black Folk Played in the Attempt to Reconstruct Democracy in America, 1860–1880*. Reprint, with an introduction by David Levering Lewis. New York: Oxford University Press, 2007.

———. *The Philadelphia Negro*. Philadelphia: University of Pennsylvania Press, 1899.

Duke, Maurice, and Daniel P. Jordan, eds. *A Richmond Reader, 1733–1983*. Chapel Hill: University of North Carolina Press, 1983.

Dunning, William. *Essays on the Civil War and Reconstruction and Related Topics*. New York: Macmillan, 1898.

Ellard, Henry. *Base Ball in Cincinnati: A History*. 1908. Reprint, Jefferson NC: McFarland, 2004.

Essary, J. Frederick. *Maryland in National Politics*. Baltimore: John Murphy, 1915.

Feldberg, Michael. *The Philadelphia Riots of 1844: A Study of Ethnic Conflict*. Westport CT: Greenwood Press, 1975.

Fleming, Walter. *Documentary History of Reconstruction: Political, Military, Social, Religious, Educational, and Industrial, 1865 to the Present Time*. Cleveland: Arthur H. Clark, 1906.

Foner, Eric. *Nothing by Freedom: Emancipation and Its Legacy*. Baton Rouge: Louisiana State University Press, 1983.

———. *Reconstruction: America's Unfinished Revolution, 1863–1877*. New York: Harper and Row, 1989.

Franklin, John Hope. *The Militant South, 1800–1861*. Cambridge MA: Beacon Hill Press, 1956.

Friedman, Murray, ed. *When Philadelphia Was the Capital of Jewish America*. Philadelphia: Balch Institute Press, 1993.

Gertis, Joseph. *Class and the Color Line: Interracial Class Coalition in the Knights of Labor and the Populist Movement*. Durham NC: Duke University Press, 2007.

Gilmore, Glenda E. *Gender and Jim Crow: Women and the Politics of White Supremacy in North Carolina, 1896–1920*. Chapel Hill: University of North Carolina Press, 1996.

Godkin, E. L., ed. "The Philosophy of 'the National Game.'" *Nation* 9, no. 217 (1869).

Goldstein, Warren. *Playing for Keeps: A History of Early Baseball*. Ithaca NY: Cornell University Press, 1989.

Gopsill, James. *Gopsill's Philadelphia City and Business Directory for 1867–1868: Being a Complete and Accurate Index to the Residents of the Entire City, Their Names, Businesses, and Location*. Philadelphia: James Gopsill, 1867.

———. *Gopsill's Philadelphia City Directory for 1869: Being a Complete and Accurate Index to the Residents of the Entire City, Their Names, Business, and Location*. Philadelphia: James Gopsill, 1869.

Gorn, Elliott J. *The Manly Art: Bare-Knuckle Fighting in America*. Ithaca NY: Cornell University Press, 1986.

———. *Sports in Chicago*. Chicago: Chicago History Museum, 2008.

Gorn, Elliott J., and Warren Goldstein. *A Brief History of American Sports*. Paperback ed. Urbana: University of Illinois Press, 2004.

Green, Constance McLaughlin. *The Secret City: A History of Race Relations in the Nation's Capital*. Princeton NJ: Princeton University Press, 1967.

———. *Washington: Village and Capital, 1800–1878*. Princeton NJ: Princeton University Press, 1962.

Greenberg, Kenneth S. *Honor and Slavery: Lies, Duels, Noses, Masks, Dressing as a Woman, Gifts, Strangers, Death, Humanitarianism, Slave Rebellions, the Pro-slavery Argument, Baseball, Hunting, and the Old South.* Princeton NJ: Princeton University Press, 1996.

Griffin, Henry H. *The Trial of Frank Kelly, for the Assassination and Murder of Octavius V. Catto, on October 10, 1871.* Philadelphia: Daily Tribune, 1877.

Gudmestad, Robert H. "Baseball, the Last Cause, and the New South in Richmond, Virginia, 1883–1890." *Virginia Magazine* 106, no. 3 (1998): 267–300.

Hahn, Stephen. *A Nation under Our Feet: Black Political Struggles in the Rural South from Slavery to the Great Migration.* Cambridge MA: Belknap Press of Harvard University Press, 2003.

Hale, Grace E. *Making Whiteness: The Culture of Segregation in the South, 1890–1940.* New York: Pantheon Books, 1998.

Hamilton, Charles V. *The Black Preacher in America.* New York: William Morrow, 1972.

Harrison, Daniel W. "Good Playing and Gentlemanly Bearing: Baseball's Beginnings in Richmond, 1866–1883." *Virginia Cavalcade* 48, no. 3 (1999): 118–33.

Heaphy, Leslie A., ed. *Black Baseball and Chicago: Essays on the Players, Teams, and Games of the Negro Leagues' Most Important City.* Jefferson NC: McFarland, 2006.

———. *The Negro Leagues, 1869–1960.* Jefferson NC: McFarland, 2003.

Hershberg, Theodore. *Philadelphia: Work, Space, Family, and Group Experience in the Nineteenth Century, Essays toward an Interdisciplinary History of the City.* New York: Oxford University Press, 1981.

Hewett, Janet B. *The Roster of Union Soldiers, 1861–1865.* Vol. 1. Wilmington NC: Broadfoot, 1997.

Hoffman, Steven J. *Race, Class, and Power in the Building of Richmond, 1870–1920.* Jefferson NC: McFarland, 2004.

Holland, Barbara. *Gentlemen's Blood: A History of Dueling from Swords at Dawn to Pistols at Dusk.* New York: Bloomsbury, 2003.

Hucles, Michael. "Many Voices, Similar Concerns: Traditional Methods of African-American Political Activity in Norfolk, Virginia, 1865–1875." *Virginia Magazine of History and Biography* 100, no. 4 (1992).

Hundley, D. R. *Social Relations in Our Southern States.* 1860. Reprint, New York: H. B. Price, 1974.

Jackson, J. A., ed. *Professions and Professionalization.* Cambridge: Cambridge University Press, 1970.

Janney, Caroline E. *Burying the Dead but Not the Past: Ladies' Memorial Associations and the Lost Cause.* Chapel Hill: University of North Carolina Press, 2007.

Johnson, Thomas R. "The City on a Hill: Race Relations in Washington DC, 1865–1885." PhD diss., University of Maryland, 1975.

Kennedy, Stetson. *After Appomattox: How the South Won the War.* Gainesville: University Press of Florida, 1995.

King, Leroy O., Jr. *100 Years of Capital Traction: The Story of Streetcars in the Nation's Capital.* College Park MD: Taylor, 1972.

Kirsch, George B. *Baseball in Blue and Gray: The National Pastime during the Civil War*. Princeton NJ: Princeton University Press, 2003.

——. *The Creation of American Team Sports: Baseball and Cricket, 1838–1872*. Urbana: University of Illinois Press, 1989.

Kirwin, Bill, ed. *Out of the Shadows: African American Baseball from the Cuban Giants to Jackie Robinson*. Lincoln: University of Nebraska Press, 2005.

Klarman, Michael J. *From Jim Crow to Civil Rights: The Supreme Court and the Struggle for Racial Equality*. New York: Oxford University Press, 2004.

Koppett, Leonard. *Koppett's Concise History of Major League Baseball*. New York: Carroll & Graf, 1998.

Lambert, John R. *Arthur Pue Gorman*. Baton Rouge: Louisiana State University Press, 1953.

Lanctot, Neil. *Negro League Baseball: The Rise and Ruin of a Black Institution*. Philadelphia: University of Pennsylvania Press, 2004.

Lane, Roger. *Roots of Violence in Black Philadelphia, 1860–1900*. Cambridge MA: Harvard University Press, 1986.

——. *William Dorsey's Philadelphia and Ours: On the Past and Future of the Black City in America*. New York: Oxford University Press, 1991.

Leifer, Eric M. *Making the Majors: The Transformation of Team Sports in America*. Cambridge MA: Harvard University Press, 1995.

Lesko, Kathleen M., Valerie Babb, and Carroll R. Gibbs. *Black Georgetown Remembered: A History of Its Black Community from the Founding of "the Town of George" in 1751 to the Present Day*. Washington DC: Georgetown University Press, 1991.

Litwack, Leon. *Been in the Storm So Long: The Aftermath of Slavery*. New York: Vintage Books, 1980.

Lomax, Michael. *Black Baseball Entrepreneurs, 18601901: Operating by Any Means Necessary*. Syracuse NY: Syracuse University Press, 1996.

Maddex, Jack P., Jr. *The Virginia Conservatives, 1867–1879*. Chapel Hill: University of North Carolina Press, 1970.

Malloy, Jerry, ed. *Sol White's History of Colored Base Ball, with Other Documents on the Early Black Game, 1886–1936*. Lincoln: University of Nebraska Press, 1995.

Martin, Tony. "The Banneker Literary Institute of Philadelphia: African American Intellectual Activism before the War of the Slaveholders' Rebellion." *Journal of African American History* 87 (Summer 2002): 303–22.

Marzec, Robert P., ed. *The Mid-Atlantic Region: The Greenwood Encyclopedia of American Regional Cultures*. Westport CT: Greenwood Press, 2004.

Masur, Katherine. "Reconstructing the Nation's Capital: The Politics of Race and Citizenship in the District of Columbia, 1862–1878." PhD diss., University of Michigan, 2001.

Mayo, James M. *The American Country Club: Its Origins and Development*. New Brunswick NJ: Rutgers University Press, 1998.

McCaffery, Peter. *When Bosses Ruled Philadelphia: The Emergence of the Republican Machine, 1867–1933*. University Park: Pennsylvania State University Press, 1993.

McElroy, A. *McElroy's Philadelphia City Directory for 1865: Containing the Names of the Inhabitants of the Consolidated City, Their Occupations, Places of Business, and Dwelling Houses; a Business Directory; a List of Streets, Lanes, Alleys, City Offices, Public Institutions, Banks, Etc.* Philadelphia, 1865.

McFeely, William S. *Frederick Douglass.* New York: W. W. Norton, 1991.

McKitrick, Eric L. *Andrew Johnson and Reconstruction.* New York: Oxford University Press, 1960.

McPherson, James. *Battle Cry of Freedom: The Civil War Era.* New York: Ballantine Books, 1988.

──────. *Ordeal by Fire: The Civil War and Reconstruction.* 3rd ed. Boston: McGraw-Hill, 2001.

Melville, Tom. *Early Baseball and the Rise of the National League.* Jefferson NC: McFarland, 2001.

Miller, Patrick, ed. *The Sporting World of the Modern South.* Urbana: University of Illinois Press, 2002.

Mitchell, Mary H. *Hollywood Cemetery: The History of a Southern Shrine.* Richmond: Virginia State Library, 1985.

Mjagkij, Nina, ed. *Organizing Black America: An Encyclopedia of African American Associations.* New York: Garland, 2001.

Moreno, Paul D. *Black Americans and Organized Labor: A New History.* Baton Rouge: Louisiana State University Press, 2006.

Morris, Charles. *Makers of Philadelphia: An Historical Work.* Philadelphia: L. R. Hamersly, 1894.

Morris, Peter. *Baseball Fever: Early Baseball in Michigan.* Ann Arbor: University of Michigan Press, 2003.

Moss, Richard J. *Golf and the American Country Club.* Urbana: University of Illinois Press, 2001.

Nash, Gary B. *First City: Philadelphia and the Forging of Historical Memory.* Philadelphia: University of Pennsylvania Press, 2002.

Neft, David S., Richard M. Cohen, and Michael L. Neft. *The Sports Encyclopedia of Baseball.* New York: St. Martin's Press, 2002.

O'Brien, John Thomas, Jr. *From Bondage to Citizenship: The Richmond Black Community, 1865–1867.* New York: Garland, 1990.

Orfield, Gary. *The Reconstruction of Southern Education: The Schools and the 1964 Civil Rights Act.* New York: Wiley-Interscience, 1969.

Perez, Louis A., Jr. "Between Baseball and Bullfighting: The Quest for Nationality in Cuba, 1868–1898." *Journal of American History* 81, no. 2 (1994).

Perman, Michael. *The Road to Redemption: Southern Politics, 1869–1879.* Chapel Hill: University of North Carolina Press, 1983.

Peters, William. *A Class Divided: Then and Now.* New Haven CT: Yale University Press, 1987.

Peterson, Robert. *Only the Ball Was White: A History of Legendary Black Players and All-Black Professional Teams.* New York: McGraw-Hill, 1970.

Peverly, Charles. *The Book of American Pastimes.* New York, 1866.

Philadelphia School District, Board of Education. *Report of the Special Committee Appointed by the Board of Controllers, on the Subject of Introducing Vocal Music into the Public Schools of Philadelphia: Thomas Fitzgerald, Chairman*. Philadelphia, 1860.

The Pickwick Club Historical Summary: Act of Incorporation, By-Laws, Roster of Membership. New Orleans: Pickwick Club, 1929.

Pierce, Truman Mitchell. *White and Negro Schools in the South: An Analysis of Biracial Education*. Englewood Cliffs NJ: Prentice Hall, 1955.

Pollard, Edward A. *The Lost Cause: A New Southern History of the War of the Confederates*. New York: E. B. Treat and Col., 1866.

Porter, David L, ed. *Biographical Dictionary of American Sports, Baseball*. New York: Greenwood Press, 1987.

Posnanski, Joe. *The Soul of Baseball: A Road Trip through Buck O'Neil's America*. New York: HarperCollins, 2008.

Powers, Bernard E., Jr. *Black Charlestonians: A Social History, 1822–1885*. Fayetteville: University of Arkansas Press, 1994.

Quarles, Benjamin. *Frederick Douglass*. New York: Atheneum, 1969.

Quarles, Chester L. *The Ku Klux Klan and Related American Racialist and Antisemitic Organizations: A History and Analysis*. Jefferson NC: McFarland, 1999.

Rabinowitz, Howard N. *Race, Ethnicity, and Urbanization: Selected Essays*. Columbia: University of Missouri Press, 1994.

———. *Race Relations in the Urban South, 1865–1890*. Urbana: University of Illinois Press, 1980.

Rachleff, Peter J. *Black Labor in the South: Richmond, Virginia, 1865–1890*. Philadelphia: Temple University Press, 1984.

Rader, Benjamin. *Baseball: A History of America's Game*. Urbana: University of Illinois Press, 1992.

Reach, Alfred J., and Company. *Catalogue: A. J. Reach and Co., Importers, Manufacturers, and Dealers in Baseball, Lawn Tennis, Cricket, Football, Fishing Tackle, and General Sporting Goods*. Philadelphia: Reach, 1882.

Reichler, Joseph L., ed. *The Baseball Encyclopedia*. New York: Macmillan, 1982.

Reid, Phillip. *The Concept of Representation in the Age of the American Revolution*. Chicago: University of Chicago Press, 1989.

Ribowsky, Mark. *A Complete History of the Negro Leagues, 1884–1955*. New York: Carol, 1995.

Richardson, Heather Cox. *The Death of Reconstruction: Race, Labor, and Politics in the Post–Civil War North, 1865–1901*. Cambridge MA: Harvard University Press, 2001.

Richmond City Directory, Containing a General Directory of the Citizens of Richmond and Manchester, and Also a Business Directory, of the Cities of Richmond, Petersburg, Norfolk, Portsmouth, Dansville, Farmville, Lynchburg, Lexington, Staunton, Harrisonburg, Fredericksburg, Alexandria, and Charlottesville, Etc, Etc., 1873–74. Richmond VA: BW Gillis, 1873.

Richmond City Directory, Containing a General Directory of the Citizens of Richmond and Manchester and Also a Business Directory, 1871–1872. Richmond VA: BW Gillis, 1871.

Ridder-Symoens, Hilde de, and Walter Ruegg, eds. *A History of the University in Europe.* Vol. 3, *University in the Nineteenth and Early Twentieth Centuries (1800–1945).* Cambridge: Cambridge University Press, 1991.

Riess, Steven. *City Games: The Evolution of American Urban Society and the Rise of Sports.* Urbana: University of Illinois Press, 1989.

———. *Touching Base: Professional Baseball and American Culture in the Progressive Era.* Westport CT: Greenwood Press, 1980.

Roberts, James C. *Hardball on the Hill: Baseball Stories from Our Nation's Capital.* Chicago: Triumph Books, 2001.

Robinson, Charles Frank, II. *Dangerous Liaisons: Sex and Love in the Segregated South.* Fayetteville: University of Arkansas Press, 2003.

Rotenberg, Robert, and Gary McDonough, eds. *The Cultural Meaning of Urban Space.* Westport CT: Greenwood Press, 1993.

Rothrock, Carol K. *The Promised Land: The History of the South Carolina Land Commission, 1869–1890.* Columbia: University of South Carolina Press, 1969.

Ruck, Rob. *Raceball: How the Major Leagues Colonized the Black and Latin Game.* Boston: Beacon Press, 2011.

———. *Sandlot Seasons: Sport in Black Pittsburgh.* Urbana: University of Illinois Press, 1987.

Ryczek, William J. *Baseball's First Inning: A History of the National Pastime through the Civil War.* Jefferson NC: McFarland, 2009.

———. *Blackguards and Red Stockings: A History of Baseball's National Association, 1871–1875.* Jefferson NC: McFarland, 1992.

———. *When Johnny Came Sliding Home: The Post–Civil War Baseball Boom, 1865–1870.* Jefferson NC: McFarland, 1998.

Saillant, John, ed. *Afro-Virginian History and Culture.* New York: Garland, 1999.

Sandage, Scott. "A Marble House Divided: The Lincoln Memorial, the Civil Rights Movement, and the Politics of the Memory, 1939–1963." *Journal of American History* 80, no. 1 (1993): 135–87.

Scharf, John Thomas. *History of Philadelphia, 1609–1884.* Philadelphia: L. H. Events, 1884.

Schiff, Andrew J. *"The Father of Baseball": A Biography of Henry Chadwick.* Jefferson NC: McFarland, 2008.

Schwenigner, Loren. *Black Property Owners in the South, 1790–1915.* Urbana: University of Illinois Press, 1990.

Scott, John. *Partisan Life with Col. John S. Mosby.* New York: Harper & Brothers, 1867.

Sentence, David P. *Cricket in America, 1710–2000.* Jefferson NC: McFarland, 2006.

Seymour, Harold. *Baseball: The Early Years.* New York: Oxford University Press, 1960.

Seymour, Harold, and Dorothy Seymour. *Baseball: The People's Game.* New York: Oxford University Press, 1991.

Shapiro, Herbert. *White Violence and the Black Response: From Reconstruction to Montgomery.* Amherst: University of Massachusetts Press, 1988.

Sheriff & Chataigne's Richmond Directory, Containing a General Directory of the Citizens of Richmond and Manchester, Also a New Map of Richmond and Complete Business Directory; Also a List of Post Offices of the States of Virginia, West Virginia, and North Carolina, Compiled by Sheriff & Chataigne, 1874–1875. Richmond VA, n.d.

Sheriff & Co.'s Richmond City Directory, 1875–1876: General Directory of the Citizens of Richmond and Manchester. Richmond VA: West, Johnson, 1876.

Shiffert, John. *Base Ball in Philadelphia: A History of the Early Game, 1831–1900.* Jefferson NC: McFarland, 2006.

Simpson, Brooks D. *The Reconstruction Presidents.* Lawrence: University Press of Kansas, 1998.

Skocpol, Theda, Ariane Liazos, and Marshall Ganz. *What a Mighty Power We Can Be: African American Fraternal Groups and the Struggle for Equality.* Princeton NJ: Princeton University Press, 2006.

Smith, John David, ed. *Racial Determinism and the Fear of Miscegenation, Pre-1900.* New York: Garland, 1993.

———. *When Did Southern Segregation Begin? Readings Selected and Introduced by John David Smith.* Boston: Bedford / St. Martin's, 2002.

Smithsonian Anacostia Museum and Center for African American History and Culture. *The Black Washingtonians: The Anacostia Museum Illustrated Chronology.* Hoboken NJ: John Wiley and Sons, 2005.

Snyder, Brad. *Beyond the Shadow of the Senators: The Untold Story of the Homestead Grays and the Integration of Baseball.* Chicago: Contemporary Books, 2003.

Somers, Dale A. *The Rise of Sports in New Orleans, 1850–1900.* Baton Rouge: Louisiana State University Press, 1972.

Spalding, Albert G. *America's National Game: Historic Facts Concerning the Beginning, Evolution, Development, and Popularity of Base Ball.* 1911. Reprint, Lincoln: University of Nebraska, 1992.

Stampp, Kenneth. *The Era of Reconstruction, 1865–1877.* New York: Alfred A. Knopf, 1965.

Stoddart, Brian, and Keith A. P. Sandiford. *The Imperial Game: Cricket, Culture, and Society.* New York: St. Martin's Press, 1998.

Sullivan, Dean A., ed. *Early Innings: A Documentary History of Baseball, 1825–1908.* Lincoln: University of Nebraska Press, 1995.

Takagi, Midori. *"Rearing the Wolves to Our Own Destruction": Slavery in Richmond, Virginia, 1782–1865.* Charlottesville: University Press of Virginia, 1999.

Thompson, Richard. *Race and Sport.* London: Oxford University Press, 1964.

Thorn, John. *Baseball in the Garden of Eden: The Secret History of the Early Game.* New York: Simon & Schuster, 2011.

Thorn, John, and Pete Palmer, eds. *Total Baseball: The Ultimate Encyclopedia of Baseball.* New York: HarperPerennial, 1993.

Threston, Christopher. *The Integration of Baseball in Philadelphia.* Jefferson NC: McFarland, 2003.

Tow, Michael. "Secrecy and Segregation: Murphysboro's Black Social Organizations, 1865–1925." *Journal for Illinois State Historical Society* 97, no. 1 (2004): 2740.

Trelease, Allen W. *White Terror: The Ku Klux Klan Conspiracy and Southern Reconstruction.* New York: Harper and Row, 1971.

Trotter, Joe William, Jr., and Eric Ledell Smith, eds. *African Americans in Pennsylvania: Shifting Historical Perspectives.* University Park: Pennsylvania State University Press, 1997.

Tygiel, Jules. *Baseball's Great Experiment: Jackie Robinson and His Legacy.* New York: Oxford University Press, 1983.

———. *Extra Bases: Reflections on Jackie Robinson, Race, and Baseball History.* Lincoln: University of Nebraska Press, 2002.

———. *Past Time: Baseball as History.* New York: Oxford University Press, 2000.

U.S. Census Bureau. *Compendium of the Ninth Census.* 1872. Reprint, New York: Arno Press, 1976.

———. *Ninth Census of the United States, 1870.* Vol. 1, *Population and Social Statistics.* Washington DC: U.S. Government Printing Office, 1872.

U.S. Congress. *Governance of the Nation's Capital: A Summary History of the Forms and Powers of Local Government for the District of Columbia, 1790 to 1973.* 101st Cong. Washington DC: U.S. Government Printing Office, 1990.

U.S. Office of Personnel Management. *Biography of an Ideal: A History of the Federal Civil Service.* Washington DC: U.S. Government Printing Office, 2003.

Van Riper, Paul P. *History of the United States Civil Service.* Evanston IL: Row, Peterson, 1958.

Vincent, Ted. *The Rise and Fall of American Sport: Mudville's Revenge.* Lincoln: University of Nebraska Press, 1994.

Voigt, David Q. *American Baseball.* Vol. 1, *From Gentleman's Sport to the Commissioner System.* University Park: Pennsylvania State University Park, 1983.

Vollmer, Howard M., and Donald L. Mills, eds. *Professionalization.* Englewood Cliffs NJ: Prentice Hall, 1966.

Walker, Clarence E. *A Rock in a Weary Land: The African Methodist Episcopal Church during the Civil War and Reconstruction.* Baton Rouge: Louisiana State University Press, 1982.

Walker, Moses Fleetwood. *Our Home Colony: A Treatise on the Past, Present, and Future of the Negro Race in America.* Steubenville OH: Herald, 1908.

Wang, Xi. *The Trial of Democracy: Black Suffrage and Northern Republicans, 1860–1910.* Athens: University of George Press, 1997.

Waskie, Andy. "Biography of Octavius V. Catto: Forgotten Black Hero of Philadelphia." Afrolumensproject, Philadelphia Department of Records.

Weigley, Russell F., ed. *Philadelphia: A 300 Year History.* New York: W. W. Norton, 1982.

Welke, Barbara. *Recasting American Liberty: Gender, Race, Law, and the Railroad Revolution, 1865–1920.* Cambridge: Cambridge University Press, 2001.

White, Edward. *Creating the National Pastime: Baseball Transforms Itself, 1903–1953.* Princeton NJ: Princeton University Press, 1996.

Whyte, James H. *The Uncivil War: Washington during the Reconstruction, 1865–1878.* New York: Twayne, 1958.

Wiegand, Wayne A. *The Politics of an Emerging Profession: The American Library Association, 1876–1917.* New York: Greenwood Press, 1986.

Will, George F. *Men at Work: The Craft of Baseball.* New York: Macmillan, 1990.

Williams, George W. *A History of the Negro Troops in the War of the Rebellion, 1861–1865.* New York: Harper & Brothers, 1888.

Williamson, James J. *Mosby's Rangers: A Record of the Operations of the Forty-Third Battalion Virginia Calvary.* New York: Ralph B. Kenyon, 1896.

Wilson, Charles R. *Baptized in Blood: The Religion of the Lost Cause.* Athens: University of Georgia Press, 1980.

Woodward, C. Vann. *The Strange Career of Jim Crow.* New York: Oxford University Press, 1955.

Zang, David W. *Fleet Walker's Divided Heart: The Life of Baseball's First Black Major Leaguer.* Lincoln: University of Nebraska Press, 1995.

INDEX

CPSIA information can be obtained
at www.ICGtesting.com
Printed in the USA
LVHW032100120220
646728LV00003B/255

9 781496 219534